The man no one knew . . .

"For his enemies, the Communists, he was the hated and feared 'gray hand' or the 'gray general,' the master spy behind every act of sabotage or espionage from the Russian Urals to the German Elbe. For his one-time employers, the CIA, he was the 'Kraut General'—that is, for those who dared admit he even existed. For the rest, there was no such person."

—from the foreword

GEHLEN:
Master Spy
of the Century

Charles Whiting

BALLANTINE BOOKS • NEW YORK
An Intext Publisher

BALLANTINE BOOKS, INC.
101 Fifth Avenue, New York, N.Y. 10003

THE GEHLEN-SKORZENY "APPARAT" IN SOVIET OCCUPIED TERRITORIES (MARCH 1945)

North Sea

Baltic Sea

Leningrad

THE FRONT

Budapest

Warsaw

Minsk

Kiev

Orel

Moscow

Vologda

Odessa

Scherhorn's "Lost Regiment" disappeared here

✠ = SS/Army Groups over 2,000 men

TYPICAL GEHLEN OPERATING METHOD IN THE EARLY SIXTIES: TRANSMISSION OF INFORMATION

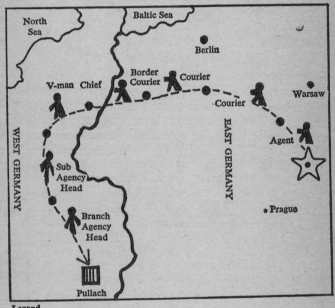

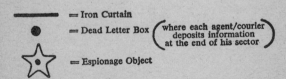

Legend

— = Iron Curtain

● = Dead Letter Box (where each agent/courier deposits information at the end of his sector)

☆ = Espionage Object

FOREWORD

A rival once called him bitterly: "The product of a moment of mental lovemaking between Mata Hari and General Ludendorff." *Newsweek* magazine described him as the "man in the shadows," and the reputable Swiss *Weltwoche* characterized him harshly as "the man without a face."

For his enemies, the Communists, he was the hated and feared "gray hand" or the "gray general," the master spy behind every act of sabotage or espionage from the Russian Urals to the German Elbe. For his one-time employers, the CIA, he was the "Kraut General"—that is, for those who dared admit he even existed. For the rest, there was no such person.

Even his long-time employees and associates dared not call him by his real name. For them he was *"der Herr Präsident"* or *"der Herr Doktor,"* and when he appeared among them so suddenly in those silent crepe-soled shoes he affected, his piercing eyes hidden behind the dark glasses, even the most hardened ex-SS man tended to grow silent, as if he felt the cold finger of fear trace its way down his spine. They knew what happened to those who failed or crossed the good Herr Doktor Schneider!

For a while his very signature was a state secret in Bonn, and as late as 1955, after he had been running his huge spy service in the East for nearly twelve years, *Time* magazine with all its tremendous resources, could still call him the "anonymous Prussian" and maintain that the mere mention of his name was enough to "make U.S. intelligence chiefs in Germany clam up and try to look blank."

The man they were mystified or horrified by was Lieutenant General Ghelen, the master spy who served Hindenburg, Hitler, the CIA, and finally the West German Federal Republic for twenty-six long years as chief of anti-Soviet intelligence. He worked for his various masters with brilliant, cold, almost clinical precision, ignoring Hitler's furious demand that he "should be locked away in a lunatic asylum," just as he ignored American generals' scornful refusal to work with "that Kraut," or German Socialist demands that he be removed as head of what they called "Adenauer's FBI."[1]

Week after week, year after year, decade after decade he labored lovingly, putting together the myriad pieces of the massive intelligence jigsaw puzzle which had been forwarded to him by the thousand agents of a score of European nationalities who were in his employ on three continents; and then passing on the result to his various masters, seemingly unconcerned by what use to which they put it.

Reinhard Gehlen was a new kind of spy. He disdained—as far as it was possible in the underworld of intelligence—the traditional "cloak and dagger" approach to espionage with its seductive blondes, seedy backstreet bars and sudden death. He was the World's first "technocrat of espionage,"[2] the like of which had

---

[1] Chancelor Konrad Adenauer, first post-war head of the West German government.

[2] Though, to a somewhat more modest extent, the honor of being the first "technocrat of intelligence" might go to General Sir Kenneth Strong, Eisenhower's chief intelligence officer during the war, and British postwar military intelligence chief who likewise disdained the traditional approach to gathering material about the enemy.

never been seen before in thirty-three centuries of intelligence. Under his guidance, the whole business of "information gathering" was transformed. Naturally, he still had use for the individual agent; indeed, he made wide use of long-range penetration groups in wartime Russia and aggressive espionage of the old school. But essentially the success of his operations depended upon the assiduous bespectacled collector of economic statistics, the scholarly political analyst, the trained professional general staff officer—the "backroom boys," as the British call them (without too much regard to the true age of these men, who are usually in their mid-forties).

During the first three years of his career as a master spy, Reinhard Gehlen, the shy regular colonel in his early forties, set up a massive organization employing hundreds of agents and analysts who knew everything about the Russian enemy, from the type of cigarette smoked by base supply troops in Moscow to the name of the current mistress of a divisional commander on the Crimean front. A welter of statistics descended hourly upon Gehlen's headquarters (located at first in a Russian forest and later in East Prussia) in a manner which caused the old-school agent to laugh at so much effort expended for seemingly no effective purpose.

But Gehlen's methods did pay off, and if they added considerably to the expense of espionage, they also set a trend and have since become part and parcel of every postwar espionage organization from the CIA to the KGB. With the advent of Gehlen, espionage entered a new and "respectable" phase. The days of the beautiful countess of yore, the false whiskers and the thrilling chase were over. In their place was the clean-cut, middle-class graduate, officially recruited from great universities,[3] whose greatest adventure was the daily

---

[3] Russia is reliably reported, indeed, to have a "college of espionage."

drive on the freeway to his office, where he would do nothing more dangerous than check his computer figures or the latest "monitor satellite" report. This was Gehlen's unique contribution to the centurys-old art of espionage: *he turned it into a cold, calculable science.*

Although his approach to his job was unemotional, Gehlen's activities throughout his twenty-six year career as a spymaster were motivated by one great passion: his hatred of the Soviet system of government. It started innocently enough when he was still a schoolboy in Breslau, his hometown, which now belongs to Poland. While he was attending a political meeting at a Breslau theater, the place was attacked by a communist mob, and he and his terrified mother were only rescued by the efforts of a middle-aged man whom the young Gehlen called a "nice man"—the Communist deputy Gruschwitz. But in spite of the fact that he and his mother were saved by a communist, from God-knows-what-kind of fate at the hands of the red mob, the pattern of his hatred had been programmed. As he told a fellow officer a few years later, "In that time of political chaos, it became clear to me to what degree the Communist idea was a threat to 'all our ideals.' "

It was a belief that was to be the motivating force for the rest of his life, for even after he had finally retired—at least, *officially*—from the business of espionage, he wrote in his memoirs:

"Has the Soviet Union lost its menace? I must answer that question with a decided negative. . . . The Soviet Union is not a 'static power,' content to protect its possessions. On the contrary it is politically a highly active and aggressive world power, which is prepared to use all means in the future to achieve the desired solution."

And the seventy year old General warns us on the

very last page of his memoirs, after a long life devoted to an activity with which "only a gentleman may dirty his hands" (as he has often remarked in the past) that "TIME IS RUNNING OUT."

For decades the motto of British intelligence has been, "All news is bad news—*if it's about us!*" It was a maxim that Reinhard Gehlen, the cold-eyed spymaster with his pale, expressionless face and overlarge ears followed all his long career in intelligence. For decades he refused to be photographed (It was rumored that certain large American weeklies were prepared to pay a four figure sum for a recent photo of *"der General."*) He lived sealed off from the world in his HQ at Pullach near Munich, or in his guarded private residence in a small town a few miles away. He changed his cars and identity frequently, and carried a loaded gun (after all the Communists had a million marks reward on his head). A packed suitcase, standing ready for a quick getaway, was always by the door of his office. Even his family were drawn into the conspiracy of silence, his eldest son used to introduce his reserved, somewhat word-shy father to school friends as a person who "worked in the patents department of a government office—or something like that," while his daughter took her school-leaving examination in nearby Munich under a false name.

But Reinhard Gehlen was only successful in hiding his true identity in this Garbo-like manner while he was at the height of his power, fighting the hottest of "cold wars" by supplying the United States and NATO with most of their information on what was happening on the other side of the Iron Curtain. When, after two decades of brilliant intelligence work in Eastern Europe he started to encounter his first real failures, and scandals rocked his organization, tongues began to wag. There were enough people in both East and West who hated and feared him, and as his reputation commenced to slip, they were only too eager to add their knowledge to a picture which was beginning to emerge. A malicious snippet here about agents abandoned in East Germany, an evil rumor of political blackmail in West Germany there, a few whispered words about use of prostitutes in special "spy" brothels . . . The German magazine *Stern* estimated the cost in "human life" of his operations was "tremendous" and that "200 of his spies who were recruited like insurance salesmen found themselves in East German jails in short order." It's companion weekly *Spiegel,* "the gadfly of the German establishment," wrote a series of disclosures pointing up the "gross failures" of the Gehlen spy organization, showing that his agents were not even safe in their own homeland.[4]

The bits and pieces of information about the nefarious activities of this long-term man of mystery commenced to accumulate. And slowly but surely a true picture of Reinhard Gehlen, who had dominated the European intelligence scene for so many long years, started to come to light. For the writer interested in this most tantalizing figure, it was at last possible to write an honest, relatively objective and realistic account of his life. This, then, is what this book sets out to do: to present for the first time the full human portrait of the most powerful and most fascinating spymaster of our age, the first technocrat of espionage

---

[4] For instance Karl Zinnecker, a Gehlen courier, "fell" out of a train on his way to Frankfurt. Gehlen's people removed the files of the case from the local police station and "investigated" it themselves. Their findings remain secret to this day. Ex-policeman Albert, who warned Gehlen in vain of a top spy in his organization, was promptly accused of high treason and put in jail. The next day he hanged himself. A Dr. Schlömel testified he had committed suicide. It just happened that the good doctor was Gehlen's half-brother.

(albeit at great cost in human life and suffering) who changed the entire character of intelligence. It is the story of the "gray general," Gehlen: Germany's master spy.

BOOK ONE

These documents are completely idiotic . . .
he should be committed to a lunatic asylum!

Adolf Hitler about General Gehlen
January, 1945

1

The Generaloberst's train rattled crazily through the night. Outside it was snowing hard, great heavy flakes falling solidly and steadily, as if some god were determined to blot out the war-ravaged German countryside.

It was midnight and the coldest night in Europe within living memory. At the front, the machine guns froze up and refused to fire. Soldiers crouching in the snow because the ground was too iron-hard for them to dig foxholes froze to death within two hours, and when their numbed comrades found them, their bodies were covered from head to toe in brilliant white hoarfrost. Icicles hung from their nostrils. They would breathe no more.

But Generaloberst Heinz Guderian, whose train this was, did not hear the noise, nor see the snow, nor feel the cold. His mind was too occupied with other things. Earlier he had taken off his uniform with the broad wine-red stripe of the general staff officer running down the trousers, and slipped between the sheets of his bunk bed and tried to sleep, but without success. On this night of January 8/9, 1945, the medium-sized, energetic commander of all Germany's armies in the East was too worried by what he had seen in the last forty-eight hours to be able to sleep.

Guderian turned once again in the narrow bed and the blue light from the blacked-out bulb above caught his face and made it look even paler than it already was with the heart disease that one day would kill him. He was in a damnable position. While the Führer gambled everything on the great attack against the Anglo-American lines in the Ardennes, taking from him the bulk of his armored troops to do so, the Russians were massing for an all-out offensive on his front in the East. His years of military experience, poised him for an enemy attack, and now the reports from his chief of intelligence told him that he had only a matter of days before the Russian hordes swamped his thinly-held positions. His only hope was to be able to convince the Führer to withdraw the two tank armies employed in the West in the Ardennes, and hurry them to the Eastern Front. *But could he convince Adolf Hitler, completely absorbed in his great offensive in the West?*

Since the battles of the fall of 1944, the Eastern Front had stabilized along the line of the River Vistula in the north, down to Hungary in the south. But Heinz Guderian knew that the uneasy peace on his front wouldn't last for long. The Russians, taking advantage of Hitler's "last gamble" in the West, were massing for their last great winter offensive. And if this time they managed to break through (which he thought likely after what he had seen during his tour of his defenses in these last two days), nothing would be able to stop them till they got to Berlin.

Heinz Guderian was basically a leader of men. Throughout his military career, although he had graduated finally to the general staff, he had been a fighting soldier, hot-blooded and effervescent, never happier than when he was engaged in active military operations.

It had been Guderian who picked up the idea spread by the British military thinkers, Captain B. H. Liddell Hart and General J. F. C. Fuller, that the tank was going to be the major weapon of any future war, and he had put it into practice. His *blitzkrieg* tactics had taken Nazi Germany from victory to victory in the early years of the war. The armored dashes across Poland, Belgium, France and Russia had all been thanks to his dramatic, driving leadership.

But Guderian was no diplomat; he did not have the ability to talk anyone around to his way of looking at things. He said his piece in his blunt, uncompromising military manner—and that was that. In 1941 he had implored Hitler to let him drive hell-for-leather to Moscow. The Leader had ordered him instead to encircle, and take, the city of Kiev. Guderian successfully carried out the operation, but because he had lost valuable time doing so, he asked Hitler to postpone the drive for Moscow till the spring of 1942. Hitler had refused, and the disastrous attack of that winter was launched on the Russian capital. It failed miserably and Guderian was relieved of his command. It had taken two years and the Stalingrad debacle before Hitler summoned him back to take command of the armies in the East.

Despite the fact that Hitler had even promoted him to Chief of the Army High Command, the rupture between Adolf Hitler and his outspoken, undiplomatic general was only superficially healed. Each time they met, Guderian's temper would get the better of him despite the fact that his doctors had told him he must not excite himself because of his heart, and he would not hesitate to tell the Führer the hard truths of the situation in the East.

But now, tossing and turning in the narrow confines of his bed while the train raced through central Germany toward Hitler's headquarters in the medieval castle at Ziegenberg, near Giessen, Guderian told himself he must not lose his temper with Hitler. The issue was far too important. If the Russians broke through this time, his beloved homeland, East Prussia, would be lost forever; he had not the least doubt about that. As he was to write much later about that fateful night: "For us Prussians it was our immediate homeland that was at stake, that homeland which had been won at such cost and which had remained attached to the ideals of Christian, Western culture through so many centuries of effort, land where lay the bones of our ancestors, land that we loved." This time he must not fail!

Heinz Guderian woke up as the special train finally came to a stop at the little Hessian town of Lich. Raising himself from the bed, he rubbed a circle free of condensation on the window. It had stopped snowing. He stared out dully at the winter landscape. Long icicles hung down from the station roof, and farther on, the little half-timbered farmhouses were half buried in snow. The skinny pines that surrounded them were heavy with plump, brilliant white caps. He told himself that the scene looked so peaceful, even beautiful; yet there was neither peace nor beauty in the world on this winter's morning. Far away on the horizon the morning sky was still tinged pink with fires left behind by the raiding bombers of the Allied air forces.

He could hear the first throaty sounds of the NCOs rapping out orders. They would be unloading his staff car from the rear of the train. Yes, there was the flat, frustrating noise of someone trying to turn over the motor. It seemed to go on for ever, as if the big vehicle would never start. Then with a thick ugly roar, the eight cylinders began to fire, the noise shattering the morning peace.

At the door of his compartment there came a polite, hesitant little tap. That would be his adjutant, Major Baron Freytag von Loringhoven. The vital day had begun.

There were twenty high-ranking officers and party officials present in General Jodl's large study at Ziegenberg, "Goat Mountain," waiting with Guderian for the Führer to appear. There was Keitel, head and shoulders above everyone else, Himmler, as pale and meek-looking as ever despite his reputation of being the most feared man in Europe; Goering, resplendent in yet another of his fantastic, self-designed, bemedaled uniforms. The two latter men were engaged in conversation with their liaison officers at Hitler's HQ while Guderian stood a little apart, deep in thought, his eyes on the door through which the Führer would come.

Once again he ran through the measures that he knew he must take on the basis of his own observations these last few days and what his chief of intelligence had told him: withdrawal of the score of German divisions locked up uselessly in Courland in the north; transfer of Sepp Dietrich's Sixth Panzer Army from the Ardennes front to the East; and the withdrawal of a large number of troops farther east to the Vistula, so that he could create a reserve to meet the impending Russian attack. If he could get Hitler to accept these measures, then he knew he had a chance of saving the Eastern Front from an overwhelming catastrophe.

Suddenly there was a stir in the room. The idle chatter ceased. Even Goering, with his booming voice, and speech full of racy, air force slang, stopped in midsentence. One of Hitler's six-foot-tall SS adjutants had opened the door to the inner room and sprung to attention. The Leader was about to enter.

Adolf Hitler came slowly and carefully into the conference room. He was bent, his double-breasted gray-uniformed jacket hanging loosely from him, his face pale yellow and aged. Guderian noted that ever since the bomb attempt on his life the previous July, the Leader dragged his left foot behind him. He greeted each of the men present individually with a warm, almost clammy hand and then fell into the chair that an adjutant shoved under him. With the aid of his right hand he placed his useless left hand on the table in front of him. Heinz Guderian noted the move and assumed that the hand had also been injured in the bomb attempt. Like most of those present who thought the same, he was wrong. It had been Hitler's right hand that had been injured. The partially paralyzed left hand was the result of a long series of injections that Hitler's shady personal doctor, Dr. Theodor Morell, had been giving him ever since 1942. Recently, Hitler had told his personal SS chauffeur and sometimes confidant, Erich Kempka, that his left hand was just a nuisance and all that he could do with it was to tuck it away in his pocket. But the gesture of placing the useless limb on the table sufficed—at least for the Leader's intimates. The conference could begin.

Guderian started his presentation eagerly. "My Leader," he began in his somewhat harsh voice, the product of years of bellowing on barracks squares, "I have come here to report again today because our information makes us confident that the Russian winter offensive will commence in three days—on the twelfth of January. Its aim will be Berlin!"

He paused for a moment to let the impact of the last sentence sink in. Hitler's yellow face showed no expression. The only sound in the room was that of his trembling left hand on the map in front of him.

"I should like to report on the situation in the East with the same complete openness that I used on December 24 and 31.[1] On January 6, I visited Army Group A in Cracow myself, and informed myself of the situation there." He swallowed for a moment and took a large breath. "My Leader, it is five minutes to twelve," he said, using the German phrase for the eleventh hour.

---

[1] On these two days Guderian had also tried to persuade Hitler to withdraw troops from the Ardennes to fight on the Eastern Front.

Swiftly the medium-sized officer who had over three decades of military service behind him sketched in the situation on the Eastern Front. As he, with the aid of his chief of intelligence, saw it, the Russians could be expected to launch an all-out attack from the Baltic to the Balkans, with a massive force totaling some 22 army corps and 225 divisions. Barely glancing down at his notes, he lectured Hitler on the Russian strengths. They outnumbered the German defenders of the Eastern Front in infantry by a ratio of 11:1; in armor by 7:1; in artillery and aircraft by at least 20:1.

It was an amazing performance. Guderian seemed to know *everything* about the Russians apparently massing on his front: positions of individual divisions, their strengths, the names of their commanders—everything. It was almost as if he had a spy in virtually every Russian formation down to the smallest rear echelon company. The other officers and officials present in the room, many of whom had spent night after night for years at such conferences, listened to him openmouthed. They had never heard anything like it before. The report bordered on military genius.

Finally, Heinz Guderian finished his exposé. Breathing hard and licking his suddenly dry lips under the clipped iron-gray military mustache, he passed the relevant maps and diagrams over to the Leader, and positioned himself at Hitler's good ear, the left one. (The eardrum of the right ear had been shattered by the July bomb attempt on his life.) Then he waited for the Führer's reaction.

For a while, Hitler did not seem to react at all. His face was still yellow, and his sick eyes apathetic. But then his intimates began to notice the tiny red flush that was starting to spread from the lower part of his face. They stiffened, prepared for the explosion. They knew what that flush heralded: one of the Führer's sudden blind, terrifying rages that could frighten even the most battle-hardened general or the most hard-boiled politician, for during such rages Hitler was near to madness. Towering above the others, Keitel squared his shoulders (almost as if he expected a physical assault) and clenched his big square jaw so that he looked more wooden than ever. Then it came.

"These documents are completely idiotic!" Hitler roared. He brought his good fist down hard on the table in front of him, so that it shook. Guderian flushed angrily and felt his heart begin to pound frighteningly.

"Who prepared this rubbish?" Hitler yelled, and without waiting for an answer, cried, "Whoever he is, he should be committed to a lunatic asylum!"

Guderian stared at the furious face and felt the blood pound at his own temples.

Abruptly he too, lost his temper. "The man who prepared these," he shouted back so loudly that his adjutant, Baron von Loringhoven, at the back of the room, bit his lip with fear, (Guderian could go too far and forfeit his life in the process), is General Gehlen, one of my best general staff officers. And I should not have shown them to you if I disagreed with them." He swallowed hard and felt himself growing short of breath. But his rage got the better of him. *"If you want General Gehlen sent to a lunatic asylum,"* he roared, his face only a matter of inches from the Führer's, *"then you had better have me certified as well."*

Three days after that unruly conference at Ziegenberg Castle, the Russians launched their great offensive, as the mysterious General Gehlen had predicted. They started by attacking Guderian's beloved homeland, East Prussia, and swiftly built up their forces so that by the end of the first forty-eight hours of the Soviet offensive, the exact number of divisions, armored and infantry, predicted at that stormy confrontation between the Führer and General Guderian was observed in action. The man whom Hitler had threatened to send to a lunatic asylum was proved one hundred percent right about the Russian intentions; as he had been, time and time again, in the past two years.

2

Who was this man?

Reinhard Gehlen, General Guderian's chief of Intelligence, was born the son of an Imperial German officer and a Flemish noblewoman, in 1902, in Eastern Germany. Six years later, when his father quit the Army and went into business as a publisher, they moved to the Silesian town of Breslau, where Reinhard grew up. He was a quiet, pale, undersized boy, whose outstanding characteristics were large ears and a petulant, almost sensuous lower lip that contrasted oddly with his pallid, ascetic face.

Breslau, in Lower Silesia, which a thousand years before had been wrested from the Poles, and today is again Polish, left a lasting impression on the young schoolboy. Here, close to Germany's "ethnic frontier" with the Slavic peoples, and living as part of a population that called itself German (often referred to contemptuously by Germans living farther inland as *Wasserpolacken,* "water Poles"), the German upper class to which the Gehlens belonged were very much aware of their "mission"; to colonize and control the non-German population on the other side of the border and "germanize" the Slavic elements within their own ranks.

Gehlen's father, Walther, was no exception. In the circles which he frequented, there was much talk of

Germany being a "Nation without Space"; a problem which could only be solved by the traditional *Drang nach Osten,* the "drive toward the East," which the Germans had been conducting since the days of the black "Teutonic Knights." Years before Hitler took over power and actually began to put into practice the theories and policies talked about so lengthily by Breslau's German middle class, Gehlen's father was able to publish a book in which he wrote: "The Germans are the only people in Europe where a large percentage of the population lives on foreign territory. They are a people without room. Seventy-six million Germans live in Central Europe, but Germany itself only contains sixty-two million of them." Walther then went on to show how the remaining fourteen million were spread all over Europe, and wrote that they really should somehow be incorporated into Germany proper. Six years later, Adolf Hitler was going to make that attempt at the expense of his neighbors to the east.

It was against this background that young Reinhard, one day to be called "the spy of the century," grew up. He was intensely patriotic and very conscious of Germany's role in the world. Yet he revealed little of the thoughts that went on in his tall, domed, thinker's brow. Exceedingly courteous and polite, he was at the same time very cagey, his only demonstrable passions being horses and mathematics. Only when he discussed these two subjects did his cold, calculating eyes light up and did he seem able to find the words, lacking at other times, with which to express himself. As one of his schoolmates, Herbert Urban, remembers: "He was a cool calculator, his youthful passions were figures and formulas." It was an ideal approach for a man whose adult life would be spent planning and analyzing everything down to the smallest, and apparently most insignificant detail, and locking the results away in a mind that was constructed like a steel filing cabinet.

In 1914, Walther Gehlen went to war as a captain in the Imperial German Army, and returned four years later a defeated man. The fact that his beloved father belonged to a defeated army did not deter the teen-age Reinhard from following his parent's footsteps: he wanted to become an Army officer too.

In 1920, two weeks after his eighteenth birthday, and being the proud possessor of the high school diploma which was the necessary prerequisite for a commission, the pale-faced, skinny-shouldered high school graduate volunteered for the German Army. He was posted as a cadet officer to the 1st Battery of the 6th Artillery Regiment, the start of a forty-eight-year-long military career which took him up to the rank of lieutenant general.

But in that year of 1920, the German Army did not seem a very promising career to most young men of Reinhard Gehlen's age group. The Treaty of Versailles, after World War I, had limited the German Army to exactly 100,000 men who were forced to serve twelve years, and were not allowed heavy weapons such as tanks or heavy guns. Nor were they able to purchase military aircraft. The Reichswehr, as the postwar German Army was called, commanded by corseted, monocled General von Seeckt, with his immaculate uniforms and exquisite manners, was little more than a glorified police force, it's main function being to keep control within Germany's own frontiers if the occasion arose, which it did, mainly because of extreme left- and right-wing groups.

Yet the dog days of the German Army, with its greatest triumphs seemingly behind it, had its consolations for the energetic, hardworking cadet officer Gehlen. The Reichswehr was, or soon would be, an all-professional army, where every man was trained to step in and take over the responsibility of the rank above him, with the enlisted man, for example, able to carry out the tasks of an NCO., and the NCO. those of an officer, and so on up the ladder. In addition, the Reichswehr was staffed by officers who had been beaten in the field and were now attempting to analyze the causes of that defeat. Unlike the armies of the victors (the United States, France, and the United Kingdom), the Reichswehr was not preparing to refight World War I. They would be applying the lessons of that lost war to a new strategy, and a new set of tactics, to ensure that they would not lose the next war.

In the nineteen-twenties, the aims of the youthful Reinhard Gehlen were set modestly on being promoted to second lieutenant and rising slowly up the ladder of promotion. In 1923 he passed his course and was commissioned as an officer in the 3rd Artillery Regiment. For three years he served with this regiment before he was posted to the famous German cavalry school at Hanover, where he spent a further two years, leaving with the rank of first lieutenant.

The long interwar years passed slowly, with Gehlen perfecting his knowledge of the inner workings of this highly professional army in a score of outwardly dreary and routine military jobs. But the officer who had enthusiastically told a fellow schoolboy in the year of Germany's defeat, 1918, "The Army will come again, don't worry; that's why I want to become an officer," was not deterred.

Gehlen has said recently that "the period between 1926 and 1928 was the most pleasant of my whole military career. I could devote myself completely to the horses and tournaments."[1]

It was also the period in which he thought he had met his wife. Riding out one day from the Hanover Cavalry School, "I met two very attractive ladies. Sisters I thought, one being a little older than the other." He managed to engage them in a short conversation

---

[1] In a statement to *Quick* magazine, October 20, 1971.

and parted with the hope that "we might meet again soon."

The opportunity came sooner than he thought. On the following Sunday, he was invited out to a party at the house of his riding teacher and there he met the "two sisters" again. One of them turned out to be the wife of his teacher, the other his daughter. Forty-odd years later, Gehlen remembers that "I wished the ground would open and swallow me up when he asked me where I'd met the two ladies."

But the well-bred young officer soon overcame his embarrassment. He began to see more of the wealthy young lady, who like himself was a passionate horse-lover, and before long he decided to ask her to marry him.

The young woman consented—but with a proviso: that he give up his army career. She needed a husband who would help her to manage her financial and business affairs. It was a harsh choice for young Reinhard. He loved the girl, yet ever since his earliest youth he had dreamed of a career as a soldier. As he put it many years later, "after a long battle with myself I finally came to a decision." He decided that he could not sacrifice his profession as a soldier. "In a friendly manner" he decided to break their conditional engagement and not see her again. But "this whole affair affected me greatly and left a great impression on me for years to come. After that I was never as happy again as I had been prior to then."

But having made his decision, Gehlen stuck to it. Although he was officially supposed to serve three years at the Hanover Cavalry School, he requested a transfer a year before his time was up. He hated to be parted from his beloved horses, yet he could not bear being close to the girl. His request was approved and he was posted to Schweidnitz, a small Silesian garrison town not far from the Polish frontier. And there he finally met the woman who would remain with him for the rest of their foreseeable years.

Herta von Seydlitz-Kurzbach, the daughter of a retired officer, was working as a secretary in a military unit when he first met her; despite her aristocratic name, that had been borne by one of Germany's greatest generals two centuries before, the family was now relatively poor. In the days when officers still tried to marry into rich families, young Herta could offer Gehlen nothing but herself.

In 1931, they finally decided to marry; by that time, Reinhard Gehlen had reached the lowest "marriageable age" as prescribed by Army regulations; he was twenty-seven and, in addition, he could prove (as was also required by the military) that he could support a wife.

But even on his honeymoon Reinhard Gehlen could not forget he was a soldier. Back at Schweidnitz a new commander was expected. When Gehlen heard this, he broke off the honeymoon and returned immediately to welcome him as military protocol required.

When Hitler came to power in 1933, Gehlen was thirty-one years of age and not yet a captain; but now a new wind blew through Germany. Hitler was determined to reverse the stipulations of the hated Treaty of Versailles (the "Versailles diktat" as he called it) which had emasculated Germany, and to do that he needed soldiers. In secret, the Reichswehr began to build up its strength, contrary to the terms of Versailles. Conscription was introduced and promotion commenced to speed up.

In 1933, Gehlen was posted to the General Staff School in Berlin, and promoted to captain one year later. In July, 1935, he finally achieved his aim; he was posted to the German War Ministry to work on the General Staff.

At last he was able to embark on his real career, moving into that secret world of the military planner, complete with its classified maps and hidden statistics necessary for the projection of the massive battles and military operations of the future.

Captain Reinhard Gehlen had his foot in the door. Before him lay the fantastic clandestine world of the planner whose decisions could change the lives and futures of millions of his fellow human beings.

There are no contemporary records of the thirty-three-year-old staff captain available. The man who one day was going to be called "the spy without a face," of whom it was claimed that only two single photographs had been made of him within a quarter of a century since 1945, was careful to cover his tracks, removing virtually every trace of his career that might have helped his enemies. Yet one can attempt to form a picture of the young officer in those dangerous years of the late thirties which led to the outbreak of World War II.

He was married by now to the daughter of an ex-Hussar officer who was descended from the famous Prussian military aristocratic family, the Von Seydlitzs. He knew that he did not care for the routine duties of an artillery regiment and that his only chance of the rapid promotion he now sought was through the staff, where he stood a good chance of having his talents recognized by some superior officer who would appreciate his true value. Captain Gehlen was not good at projecting himself. He had no talent for small talk or the slightly off-color story in the mess. On the contrary, he was a poor conversationalist, often fumbling for the words that could express his thoughts.

There was nothing outstanding about his physical appearance either that could distinguish him from a score of other junior staff officers. His deep-set blue eyes in the pale face were often veiled and withdrawn —one might even say "guarded"—as if he were already preparing himself for that role of master spy with a million rubles set on his head by the Russians as a reward for his capture or assassination. His voice was soft and polite, an attribute unusual in a German officer of those days. In fact, one could say of the thirty-three-year-old Captain Gehlen that his outstanding characteristic was that he possessed none.

When Germany launched its blitzkrieg against Poland in September, 1939, Major Gehlen marched to the sound of the guns as operations officer with the 213th Infantry Division. Unfortunately, his division arrived on the scene too late to take part in the three-week battle for the hopelessly outnumbered little country. Nonetheless, he was awarded the Iron Cross, 2nd Class, and ordered to report to the operations department of the General Staff as personal assistant to General Halder.

Halder took to Gehlen at once. At last Gehlen had found the superior officer who could recognize his true talents. In Gehlen's performance report for February, 1941, Halder wrote: "A fine example of a general staff officer. Far above the average in personality, ability and industry. Great operational ability and a great deal of foresight in his way of thinking." One year later the highly impressed general wrote of his subordinate: "Modest, sympathetic personality. Very hardworking. Applies himself to the limit of his endurance in his job."

During the planning for "Operation Barbarossa," Gehlen did outstanding staff work in drawing up plans for the bringing up of reserves, and the continuation of transport. So impressed was Halder that he wrote of Gehlen's suggestions: "Very good work. . . . [it] combines splendid rational ability with unusual energy. . . and soldierly spirit. This man is fitted for a leading position within the general staff."

As the German Army smashed on from victory to victory in Soviet Russia, cropped-headed, broad-shoul-

dered General Halder was becoming increasingly dissatisfied with the work of his military intelligence department. It seemed to him that its chief, Colonel Kinzel,
knew virtually nothing of the enemy's resources and
military potential. While Hitler, back in Berlin, triumphantly roared at screaming, adulatory audiences that
the Russian subhumans were finished, the Russians still
kept fielding ever new divisions, as if they had an in-
exhaustible supply of men and new materiel.

Naturally, Halder understood Kinzel's difficulties. He
knew that since the late 1920s, a suspicious Soviet
Union had virtually sealed itself off hermetically from
the rest of the world. Any non-Russian in that country
was automatically assumed to be a spy and was trailed
and reported upon by the GPU. In addition, stringent
regulations were laid down by the Russians relating
to the places where a foreigner might travel and stay.
Even foreign Communists who had fled to Russia, the
"Mother of the Revolution," by the hundreds in the
troubled thirties, were suspect and limited in their
places of residence. By the time the war had broken
out, Russia was as much isolated from the outside
world as it had ever been in the darkest days of the
hated Czar. As the German military attaché in Moscow, Lieutenant General Kostring commented ruefully:
"An Arab in a white flowing robe could walk through
Berlin unnoticed easier than a foreign agent in Russia."

Nonetheless, Halder thought his middle-aged intelligence chief Kinzel, could do a much better job than he
was doing. After all, the Germans had captured nearly
a million Russian prisoners and their documents by
this time, surely they and their papers could yield
valuable information about the Russian strengths and
resources? Kinzel did not seem to think so, and Halder's
anger at his subordinate grew steadily. In December,
1941, he noted: "Signs of breakdown in the Intelligence
Service." And then, three months later: "Chief of For-

eign Armies East[2] has to be replaced, no longer satisfies my needs."

The moment of decision had come. But who should replace Kinzel?

Small, sharp-featured, quick-talking Colonel Heusinger, Halder's operations officer, suggested his friend Major Gehlen.

For some days Halder hesitated. Gehlen was "too young for such a responsible post," he told Heusinger. Besides, he had no experience in intelligence work. Indeed, a couple of years before, during Gehlen's only contact with Halder's intelligence branch, he had caused some trouble and there had been angry protests from the intelligence men about "Gehlen's meddling" in their affairs.

Heusinger persisted. He told Halder that Gehlen was a skilled organizer, who had proved his ability time and again, and it was an organizer that Foreign Armies East needed most at the moment: someone with general staff training who could rapidly put the intelligence house in order.

In the end, General Halder was convinced. On the last day of March, 1942, Colonel Kinzel was fired from his vital post, and twenty-four hours later Gehlen was transferred to the Foreign Armies East to take over his job.

So it was that on April 1, April Fool's Day, Reinhard Gehlen took over perhaps the most important staff job in the whole Eastern Command. From now on he was to head an outfit to which came the combined mass of information gained by the entire German intelligence services: wily Admiral Canaris's civilian intelligence organization, the *Abwehr;* young, cocky, ambitious SS Colonel Schellenberg's Nazi Secret

---

[2]The strange name given to Germany's military intelligence in the East.

Service of the *Sicherheitsdienst*[3]; and the results of
Goering's Luftwaffe reconnaissance outfits. All this in
addition to the efforts of his own Foreign Armies East.

By virtue of General Halder's signature below his
orders to report to the Foreign Armies East office, the
obscure, retiring Lieutenant Colonel with the pale face
and high-domed forehead of the intellectual and thinker
became one of the most powerful and knowledgeable
men in the whole of Western Europe; and he was to
remain so for the next twenty-six years.

Reinhard Gehlen was exactly forty years old.

---

[3] *Abwehr* means basically counterespionage, though it
naturally was used for active espionage against Germany's
enemies; *Sicherheitsdienst* was the Nazi political police
organization and numbered the infamous Gestapo among
its ranks.

3

A month after Gehlen took over his new command, a young major wearing the peaked cap adorned with the metal *Edelweiss*[1] badge of the mountain troops reported to his office.

"Major Herre posted from the Alpine Corps," he reported, clicking his heels and saluting smartly. Gehlen returned the younger man's salute and told him to sit down.

Heinz Danko Herre did so a little ungraciously. He was a regular Army officer in his early thirties who had been on the staff of a fighting outfit, and did not like the idea of having been posted to this rearline unit. Intelligence did not appeal to him one bit.

But Gehlen did not notice his new recruit's mood, or perhaps he preferred not to. Almost immediately after they had exchanged the usual preliminary courtesies, he began to explain to Herre his dissatisfaction with the present state of Foreign Armies East. Its personnel were too old and too unimaginative. It didn't possess enough Russian experts or men with frontline experience who could correctly evaluate the information obtained from the various sources at their disposal.

The handsome, square-jawed Herre listened attentively, trying to size up the man on the opposite side

---

[1]An alpine flower

23

of the desk. Lieutenant Colonel Gehlen was not a very convincing speaker, often fumbling for words, or hesitating a little too long between phrases, yet Herre could see that Gehlen was enormously intelligent, and enthusiastic about his new post as commander of Foreign Armies East.

Gehlen soon came to his reason for having Herre posted to him, explaining that the time had come to get rid of the dead wood in his new unit. He needed new blood; young men who had both frontline experience and knowledge of Russia and its language. Herre had these qualifications.

Hurriedly the young major, who spoke Russian fluently, protested that he did not want to leave the front for an HQ job, but Gehlen waved away his objections. "I'm sorry, Major," he said. "My general staff officers must be young, have frontline experience and know Russian. The officers I've got here who fulfill these requirements can be ticked off on the fingers of one hand; that's the reason I need you." He leaned forward over his desk, his deep-set blue eyes piercing the other officer. "The department I have just taken over is amateurish and does not work seriously enough. You understand?"

The thirty-two-year-old major pulled a face, but didn't say anything. He realized abruptly, that he was a member of Germany's intelligence service.

Ignoring Herre's obvious dislike of his new job, Gehlen explained quickly how he was going to reorganize Foreign Armies East. He would get rid of most of his present subordinates except young Captain Wessel, a tall, skinny officer with a great talent for analysis, and replace them with younger, battle-experienced men. More important, he wanted to change the role of the military intelligence unit. Up to now it had passively accepted anything and everything it had been given by the various other intelligence agencies, its sole task being that of passive analysis. Now that would have to change.

As Gehlen saw it, Foreign Armies East would have to go deep into Russia to obtain its real intelligence. In Soviet Russia the decisions were not made at the front; they were made far to the rear in Moscow, in the Kremlin, because the Russian dictator Joseph Stalin always had the final say in major military decisions. Consequently, Foreign Armies East must be able to penetrate the Russian front and send its men into the heart of Russia proper; with a bit of luck, to Moscow itself.

Herre pricked up his ears. This sounded interesting and adventurous. Leaning forward a little in his chair now, he listened while Gehlen explained how he wanted a force of paratrooper linguists, perhaps half-German and half-Russian deserters, or anti-Communists, who would be trained to parachute deep into Russian territory. There they would either hide out as best they could and radio reports back to Foreign Armies East on Russian dispositions, troop movements and so on; or they would actually infiltrate into key Russian Army and Party organizations and remain there permanently until either the NKVD, the dreaded Russian secret police caught them, or their services were required elsewhere.

"Up to now," Gehlen concluded, "our sources of information have been worthless, but I intend to change all that."

Yes, Herre told himself, but where would he find the elite linguist paratroopers he needed for his long-range penetration operation? Who would be brave enough to take that kind of hair-raising risk?

But Lieutenant Colonel Gehlen found them. In the summer of 1942, he recruited the fourth pivotal member of his Foreign Armies East team, forty-five-year-old Major Hermann Baun, one of the German Army's leading Russian experts. Baun had actually been born in Russia in the seaport of Odessa, where he had learned to speak not only fluent Russian but also Ukrainian, a very useful language. Many of the intelligence service's potential agents were drawn from Ukrainians, who were intensely nationalistic and anti-Communist to boot.

Gehlen took an instant dislike to the middle-aged, dark-eyed officer who was beginning to put on fat, but he controlled his feelings, knowing that Baun was the only man who could supply him with the personnel he required for his long-range penetration group.

At that time, Major Baun controlled a small intelligence unit of his own, "Walli I," as it was called by its cover name. This outfit consisted of German and Russian renegades, recruited mostly from the German PW camps, and had originally been created to secure Russian documents which might fall into German hands as the victorious armies pushed eastward during the early stages of Operation Barbarossa. But Baun had not been content with just this routine task. The man whom the chief of the German Abwehr, Admiral Canaris, testified "had a particular talent for intelligence work" was more ambitious; he wanted to infiltrate his specialists behind the Russian lines, to create confusion and to sabotage anything they could lay their hands on. When Gehlen first met him in 1942, he had already started doing this in a small way and was beginning to report his first successes to his superiors.

For Gehlen, then, Baun was a man he needed in his organization. During the course of their first meeting that summer, he convinced Baun that the two groups should work together. In the end Baun agreed, and finally moved his headquarters to the little Ukrainian town of Vinnitsa where he started a crash training course for a host of new agents recruited from the teeming German PW camps. Now Gehlen was ready to begin operating. He had his team together: Herre, Wessel and Baun, so the greatest spy operation in all the thirty-three centuries of espionage, could get underway.

In the first memo he dictated to his German WAC secretary, he told his staff "our work must be characterized by responsibility, and must be undertaken cleverly and methodically . . . we must take special care with our files and avoid reporting the same old conclusions time and time again."

The slim, balding spymaster's main injunction was that his men must ensure that "we present a picture of the enemy situation which goes beyond the obvious." And in all the years of spying to come, Reinhard Gehlen would be able to attain high level quantity and quality of information that "goes beyond the obvious."

While Gehlen's experts went to work questioning and cross-questioning the many thousand ragged, beaten, Russian prisoners of war who were pouring daily into the German Army cages, Baun's agents started to slip through the Russian lines by the score. In 1942, for every hundred sent out on their dangerous missions, only fifteen returned, yet there were always more recruits available in the PW cages, attracted to the German cause by genuine hatred of the Communist creed or by the promise of decent treatment after the mud, misery and hunger of the cage.

Some of these agents surrendered themselves to the nearest Red Army post as soon as they had freed themselves from their parachutes, others were captured before they could start to operate, but a goodly number managed to establish themselves safely behind the Russian lines. They joined the supply and transport service of the Red Army, an ideal way to find out about troop movements; they went to work in Soviet factories producing materiel for the front, again an ideal vantage point for discovering the strengths and weaknesses of the Russian war production machinery; they even joined the Communist Party.

One of Baun's most trusted agents actually managed to install himself in Moscow itself. A radio operator who went under the cover name of "Alexander" had the temerity to join a Soviet signals battalion stationed in the capital. Using the cover and the false papers supplied by Gehlen's organization, this daring agent who held the Soviet rank of captain, daily received top secret Red Army directives to be transmitted to the various corps and divisions. Naturally, those same top secret directives also reached his cold-eyed boss Colonel Gehlen, many hundred miles away on the other side of the front.

Gehlen was not satisfied with espionage alone; he also wanted to do active damage to Soviet war potential and military strength. Recruiting the services of "Walli III," made up of Russian and Ukrainian anti-Communists and commanded by a Lieutenant Colonel Schmalschlaeger, he parachuted its members to link up the numerous anti-Russian partisan bands roaming the rear areas of the Soviet front. These bands, which were often not much more than bandit outfits, terrorized the rear areas, attacking lonely Russian convoys, sabotaging railroads, cutting military telegraph lines and communications, and generally causing so much trouble that the Red Army had to divert relatively large forces from the front to deal with them.

They were never able to do this completely and successfully, for, as we shall see, these bands were still operating in the wide open spaces of the western part of the Soviet Union seven and eight years after the shooting war had ended!

Now the information started to pour in about the Russian strength, dispositions and intentions. Gehlen's huge steel filing cabinets began to fill up with myriad details of the enemy forces. From the ration strength of a typical Siberian rifle division, its field post office number, the number of party members within its ranks, right up to the name of the divisional commander's current mistress. At last the cold-eyed German spymaster could start making predictions, confident predictions, about the enemy's intentions.

As early as July, 1942, Gehlen was confident that the Russians would not evacuate the beleaguered fortress of Stalingrad as Hitler predicted. On the strength of information received from one of Baun's spies who reported that the Soviet Military Council had decided on July 13 to withdraw its troops across the River Volga because of German pressure and defend Stalingrad to the last, he passed on his belief that the Germans would be faced with a hard fight in the huge, sprawling, industrial city.

Hitler did not believe his report, and ordered the pressure against the Russians increased.

Two months later, Gehlen warned that the Russians were preparing for a counterattack in the area. One month after that, he cautioned that "there is no evidence to prove that the Russian has given up his idea of thrusting across the River Don." Then on November 12, Gehlen wrote an urgent report, based on the painstaking work of the Foreign Armies East, warning that "We must reckon with an attack on the Rumanian Third Army[2] soon. Its aim will be to cut the rail link with Stalingrad in order to force a withdrawal of German troops in the Stalingrad area."

Again Hitler did not heed his warning.

In despair, Gehlen turned to his old friend and mentor Colonel Heusinger. In a conversation they had together at the latter's HQ at Mauerwald in December, 1942, he told Heusinger, "I'd like to express my doubts about the decision to hold Stalingrad. In the mornings I can hardly get a word in edgeways at the staff conferences. I fear we're underestimating the Russians," he said, shaking his head.

---

[2] The Rumanians, at that time Germany's allies, held part of the long Stalingrad line.

Heusinger nodded. "You confirm what I'm afraid of myself. The chief of staff thinks so too. He's been fighting hard since November 22 to get them to give up Stalingrad."

Gehlen gave the other man a chilly smile. He knew who "them" was—the Leader, Adolf Hitler.

There was a pause in the conversation, then Gehlen asked if General Hoth, who was trying to break through to relieve Stalingrad, would make it.

Heusinger tweaked his somewhat sharp nose and pursed his lips in thought. "Perhaps he'll make it to Stalingrad so that Paulus [the commanding general within the city] can link up with him. . . . Hitler's setting his hopes on the Tiger[3]. The first squadron has already gone up to Hoth, and the Führer has proclaimed that the 'tiger squadron is in a position to destroy a whole Russian tank corps'." Heusinger twisted his face into a contemptuous sneer. "As if you can win a war with slogans!"

Gehlen laughed sympathetically. "Then it would be Goebbel's[4] first victory," he commented.

But despite the fact that the German dictator wanted to hear only good news that fitted in with his own delusions, and regarded everything to the contrary as, "defeatist rumormongering," Gehlen persisted in sending in predictions of Russian intentions which were growing increasingly accurate as the months passed.

Two weeks before the Russian counteroffensive in the Orel area, Gehlen accurately reported the time and place of the Russian attack—July, 1943, Orel. He pulled off the same trick one month later when his agents supplied him with the information which allowed him to warn the German High Command that

---

[3]Heusinger was referring to the new German heavy tanks armed with a powerful 88mm gun which at this time had not yet been used in battle.

[4]The club-footed Nazi propaganda minister.

the Russians would launch their main attack against the German "Hagen" line at Bryansk in the neighborhood of the small town of Sevsk.

Thus it was, that just over one year since he had taken over his new command, a justifiably self-satisfied Colonel Gehlen could write in a memo to his staff: "The developments in the fighting on the Eastern Front in these last few days have shown that our estimates of the enemy situation have been right, down to the last detail. A couple of days ago the Chief of the General Staff showed his appreciation of this fact."

Now Colonel Gehlen felt he was in a position to carry out one of the boldest intelligence schemes of the whole war: *he would get Russian to fight against Russian!*

4

The eighteen men crowded in the ancient old transport plane (called "Auntie Ju" because of its reliability), were pale but noisy, shouting against the roar of the Ju-52's three engines, passing the vodka bottles from mouth to mouth, wiping their lips expressively with the backs of their hands after every slug. But twenty-two-year-old Sergeant Hans Putzer, in charge of the fourteen Russian renegades and three Germans who made up his team, knew that their merriment and noise were only superficial. They knew—just as he did—that there was no turning back now. In a few minutes they would be over their target. As he rolled the cyanide capsule nervously between his thumb and forefinger, he told himself that in five minutes he might well be a dead man.

On that April 28, 1942, Sergeant Putzer, a former carpenter from the mountains of the South Tyrol, was flying his first mission. Its objective was the securing of Height 520, some two hundred miles behind the Russian front line between the towns of Maikop and Tuapse. Here were located the vital oil refineries toward which the German infantry somewhere down below were advancing; and the new chief of German intelligence did not want those refineries destroyed by the fleeing Soviets. In addition, he wanted to prevent the Russian rear guards, reeling back under the weight of the German spring offensive, from blowing up the tactically important pass between Maikop and Tuapse.

Now the eighteen men crowded into the tight fuselage of the ancient transport, dressed in German uniforms but each carrying a captured Russian one in the rucksack strapped to his chest, were on the first major long-distance penetration mission planned by Colonel Gehlen which might well prove the validity of his new concept of "aggressive intelligence."

Over the door of the Ju-52 the green light began to blink off and on. It was the signal for the saboteur-spies to hook up their parachutes. Otto Bloner, one of Putzer's NCOs, who had been yodeling for the Russian volunteers, stopped short, his mouth stupidly open. Putzer, a strapping dark-haired youth, hardened by weeks of training in the Bavarian Alps, got to his feet and hooked up, ready.

"I was first to go," he recalls today, "but as the signal came for me to jump, the jumpmaster struck me in the ribs and shouted 'get out.' I jumped."[1] As the howling wind grabbed him and he felt himself falling at a tremendous rate, pure fear overcame him. "My first thought was—*My God, the parachute won't open!*" But it did, and he felt the brutal but reassuring jerk under his armpits. His rapid descent ceased immediately and he breathed out hard. But his relief was short-lived. As the ground loomed up ever larger and Putzer adjusted the shrouds and peered down, his heart sank. The pilot had dropped them over the wrong dropping zone! This wasn't the DZ that he had examined a dozen times in the map room back at headquarters!

His realization was confirmed a moment later. They had been spotted. To the right of a small straw-roofed village a machine gun opened up. Green-and-white tracer started to zigzag through the air, at first slowly

---

[1] Interview with the German magazine *Quick,* October 27, 1971.

and then with ever-increasing rapidity as it came closer and closer. Moments later a half-dozen rifles joined in. "Tracer hammered away at us from all directions," as Putzer recounts it. "Slugs hissed about our ears. We were floating directly above the Russian machine guns."

Desperately he twisted and turned, fighting with the shroud lines so that his 'chute would take him out of range of the deadly fire that spattered through the air all about him like heavy summer rain. The roofs of the little Russian cottages swept below his feet. Beyond them he glimpsed a thick fir wood. Gritting his teeth and praying as he had never prayed before, he forced the chute to take him toward it. And he succeeded.

Moments later he was directly above it. He carried out the drill automatically: feet rolled up together under the stomach, head tucked in, hands pressed over the face. Not a moment too soon! On all sides the hard twigs plucked at his clothes. Branches clouted him painfully on the body. Half conscious, he was aware of the firs giving as he came down among them, away from the murderous fire that he could still hear coming from the direction of the village. For the moment, at least, he was safe.

For what seemed like hours, the young noncom hid in the wood while the machine gunfire continued almost without pause, finally to peter out and be succeeded by four single shots. Then silence. "Later," he recalled after the war, "I learned that those four shots meant that four of my captured comrades had been slaughtered. Shot in the neck."

Slowly, as the hours went by and there was no more shooting, the German began to take stock of his situation. He was over two hundred miles behind the Russian lines. He did not speak more than a few words of the language and, although he was armed and had Russian money and a limited supply of jewelry (supplied by the German Intelligence Service for bartering with the local populace), he realized that his position was desperate. The Soviet military police would have alerted the whole district and, even if the local peasantry were anti-Communist, they undoubtedly would not risk their lives to help him in those circumstances. What was he to do? As he thought of the mess he had landed himself in, he couldn't help groaning aloud.

Suddenly he forgot his self-commiseration. In the distance he could hear someone making his way cautiously—very cautiously—through the undergrowth! He twisted his head to one side, listening. It was not only one person. It sounded as if there were two or three of them. "I almost stopped breathing," he remembers. "I was scared that my breathing could betray me. Were they Russians or my people?"

In the darkness, gripping his Walther pistol sweatily, the young German could distinguish two figures making their way stealthily in his direction. He bit his lip hard. If this were a Russian patrol out looking for him, wouldn't there be more of them? Were they the survivors of his own group? In the end he decided to take a chance. He raised his head and, still keeping his pistol aimed at them, he gave the agreed signal: the cry of the Caucasian forest owl.

The two dark figures stopped dead.

As Putzer tells it today: "I didn't dare give the signal a third time, but waited till they moved again. Then I gave the cry. This time they stopped and replied with the same call—a couple of times in succession."

Joyfully the young German got to his feet. He wasn't alone! He ran quickly toward the two men, who turned out to be two of his Russian team. They had survived the murderous ground fire, but reported that Otto Bloner, who was the group's radio operator, had been captured in the village.

Putzer knew what that meant. The Russians would not hesitate to apply pressure, at first mental, and then physical. It would be only a matter of hours before poor Otto, who had been so proud of his yodeling, talked. Perhaps he had already. One thing was sure. The Russians knew, or would soon know, the purpose of the group's mission. The bold attempt to capture the vital height between Maikop and Tuapse and hold it until German troops arrived was a failure even before it had gotten underway.[2]

Reinhard Gehlen's first mission had failed miserably.

Shortly after Gehlen had taken over command of the Foreign Armies East, a tall, skinny Soviet soldier, whose uniform was tattered and dirty and bore no badges of rank, surrendered to a group of grinning Dutch SS men. The bony-faced, bespectacled Russian had been betrayed to the Dutch renegades by a group of peasants fearful that his presence might endanger their lives.

The Dutch soldiers took their captive for yet another of the lousy beaten "Ivans" whom they captured by the score every day, but the battalion intelligence officer was not so sure. There was an air of authority about the immensely tall Russian with the sad face. He began to question him. Who was he? What was he doing hiding out in the peasant's house? Where was his unit?

_____

[2]Sergeant Hans Putzer managed to get back to the German lines. Accompanied by the two Russians, he walked for three months and sixteen days. They fed themselves with bread made from Indian corn that the Russians "organized" in the local villages on their route westward. When that ran out, the bold little group shanghaied a Soviet Army truck, forcing the drivers to turn into a lonely valley. There one of the drivers made a grab for his machine pistol. He did not live to make use of it. "In those days," Putzer says, "the hard law ruled: you or me." They took the Russians' uniforms and passes and, after a hearty meal made with the supplies, pushed on, and in the end managed to cross successfully to the German lines. Putzer received the Iron Cross First Class in Berlin a few weeks later; and, in spite of the tremendous strain of that almost unbelievable journey, continued to serve in Gehlen's clandestine service right to the end of the war.

How did he get there? The questions came with brutal rapidity.

In the end the captive gave in. "I'm Andrei Andreevich Vlasov," he said, "last surviving commander of the Second Assault Army." He paused, then added simply, "My rank is that of lieutenant general."

The intelligence man was shocked into silence. He had landed a big fish indeed. The Dutch renegades, unknown to themselves, had captured a man who was one day to be the greatest renegade of them all.

As a teen-ager, Vlasov, who came of peasant stock, had been drafted into the new Red Army to fight against the Whites. He soon proved his military ability in spite of his highly unmilitary appearance, and was promoted to company commander one year later. Then when the fighting was over, his promotions were so rapid that Stalin granted him the privilege of going to China to be military adviser to Generalissimo Chiang-Kai-shek. Recalled in 1939, he was given command of the 99th Infantry Division, composed of men from over forty-four different nationalities, and generally regarded as a tough, disorderly outfit. But Vlasov knocked it into shape, and when the war came, was highly regarded as one of Russia's up-and-coming generals.

In 1941, he fought himself out of the German encirclement at Berdichev, and gained a high reputation for his defense of Kiev. Together with the future Marshal Zhukov, he followed this up with his tough defense of Moscow as commander of the Twentieth Army. Then in the spring of 1942, he was ordered to take command of the Second Assault Army. This unfortunate command had been ordered to relieve the besieged seaport of Leningrad in late 1941, but had itself been surrounded and decimated in the marshes of the Volkhov region. For Vlasov, it was a death sentence. Stalin had ordered him to fight to the last man and he went to take up his new task with the feeling that he had been written off, betrayed by the Soviet dictator. As a result, when he was taken prisoner after hiding from the Germans with a handful of officers who disappeared one by one as they fled from the German patrols for nearly three weeks, the tall general with the horn-rimmed glasses was prepared to collaborate with the enemy almost at once.

Unlike other senior Russian officers who had also been prepared to work with their captors, he was not (as a confidential report said of him) "a mere seeker after political glory and accordingly will never be willing to lead hirelings. His stated objective is to fight as Germany's ally for a socialist Russia and to rid his country of Stalin's system of terror."

Gehlen first became aware of Vlasov some time in December, 1942, when a Baltic-German officer on his staff, Major Strik-Strikfeldt, who had already in 1941 drawn up a plan to form a Russian "National Army" of 200,000 men to fight against the Communists, made a reference to the captive Russian general as the "Russian Charles de Gaulle."

Gehlen liked the idea, and although he regarded himself as completely apolitical, strictly a military technician, he realized that the Nazi treatment of their Russian subjects as "subhuman" and third-class citizens was alienating millions of potential allies. He decided that the ex-Soviet general would make an ideal rallying point for an army of Russian anti-Communists, and ordered Major Strik-Strikfeldt to take over Vlasov while he, Gehlen, tried to get support for his original idea.

In the meantime, Vlasov should try to recruit a staff of other high-ranking officers who thought the same way he did. To do this, he gave out information that Vlasov was recruiting a staff of experts who were prepared to help Gehlen with his long-range penetration groups.

So it was, that under the nose of the racialist Nazi Gauleiter of the Ukraine, Koch, a gross ex-party bully boy who tyrannized his "subjects" and was interested only in how many of their pretty pale-blond women and girls he could sleep with, Vlasov moved freely from PW camp to PW camp, recruiting his "staff."

Vlasov went to work with a will. Swiftly he collected a group of men, including two major generals and a former assistant editor of the Russian Party newspaper *Izvestia,* who thought like himself. These men decided that they would recruit a "Russian National Committee" which would set up its headquarters at Smolensk, in captured Russian territory. Here they would publish their "Smolensk Manifesto," the major points of which were the abolition of collective farms, the reestablishment of private enterprise, freedom of speech and press, and the liberation of all political prisoners.

In addition, the committee decided to set up the "Russian Army of Liberation," the ROA,[3] which would be formed from Russian auxiliaries already working with the German Army on an unarmed basis, fresh deserters brought over by their own propaganda efforts, and the thousands of recruits they anticipated getting from the German PW cages.

Reinhard Gehlen was delighted by the plan; it was exactly what he wanted—a massive Russian force fighting on the German side and taking the pressure off the German Army, which in early 1943 was already beginning to feel the strain of the prolonged fighting in the Soviet Union.

But Vlasov had barely begun forming his "National Committee" when trouble started at the Leader's HQ. Himmler himself wrote to Hitler warning him of the activities of the renegade Russian general; they were clearly contrary to the Führer's own order that no one should attempt to make any form of agreement with Russian nationalists.

---

[3]*Russkaya Osvoboditelnaya Armiya.*

Desperately, Gehlen tried to head off Hitler's anticipated rage by starting a crash campaign to use Vlasov to gain deserters from the enemy. Propagandists from Vlasov's National Committee went into action on the German front on April 20, 1943, talking Russian soldiers on the other side of the line into deserting; the operation was an outstanding success. Within the first month of getting "Operation Silver Strip" started, 2,500 Russian soldiers deserted. A few weeks later it was 6,000; two whole Russian regiments had gone over to the Vlasov propagandists!

But at this point, Hitler took a hand in the game. On June 1, 1943, Gehlen had written a report for Hitler, emphasizing the success of the Vlasov propaganda operation. When the Führer read it, he exploded. "It's crazy!" he roared. "I shall never build up a Russian Army! It is a specter of the first order!"

Eight days later he ordered that Gehlen should not form a Vlasov army. The most he would allow his intelligence chief to do was aid the Russian renegade in his attempts to gain deserters by means of front propaganda.

Four months later, Gehlen was still trying to change the Leader's mind. In a conversation he held at that time with Heusinger who asked him "What's the situation with the Vlasov movement?" he replied, "We've been trying in vain to get permission to build it up. Himmler seems to be having more success.[4] I'm sure he'll get permission. . . . I guarantee we could have set up two to three divisions if we had received permission."

Heusinger nodded understandingly. "Up to six months ago he thought we could manage without these

---

[4]By this time the head of the SS and fanatical racist Heinrich Himmler was interested in this new source of fighting men and in the end it was Himmler who succeeded in getting the Vlasov Army set up. But by that time (November, 1944), it was too late.

people. Now he doesn't want to confess he needs them."

Gehlen knew that the "he" the chief of Operations was referring to was Hitler, but he didn't say anything for the moment.

"Sometimes *he* concerns himself with silly little details," Gehlen said suddenly to the senior officer who had already told him previously that Hitler didn't believe Gehlen's statistics about the Russian fighting strength. "My most reliable agent, who has brought in the best information I have about Russia, I can't use any more because he is half Jewish."

Heusinger nodded once more. It was all he dare let himself comment on the situation, for now he knew that Gehlen no longer believed in Hitler.

The chief of the Army's Eastern Intelligence Service had fooled himself for three long years into believing that Hitler was being led astray by those around him—the Palace hangers-on. If someone could get through them with the real information, then the Leader would react accordingly, he had thought. But now, the two officers sitting in the unheated room on that gray, depressing November day, knew as the Army-issue clock inexorably ticked away the minutes of their life, that this was not the case. Hitler was simply not prepared to believe what he did not want to believe, and he did not want to acknowledge the true situation on the Russian front. As Heusinger had remarked at the beginning of their conversation: "What can we do to make Hitler give up his illusions about the Russian fighting strength? He is convinced that the Russians will bleed to death as long as we force them to fight for every yard of ground, but in doing so we are killing ourselves."

For the first time in his long career as a "military technician," Gehlen realized that he had been forced into the sphere of politics. Hitler's ban on the Vlasov movement, which he had seen as possibly one of the last measures available to Nazi Germany to save itself from defeat, made him realize at long last that Germany was ruled by a man controlled by an obsession. A fatal obsession, which would make him lead his country to its destruction with the blind purposefulness of a sleepwalker.

Was there nothing he could do about the situation, Gehlen asked himself. In his own headquarters there were aristocratic anti-Nazi officers who were prepared to take an active part in getting rid of Hitler, even to the extent of murdering him. But Gehlen, although he tolerated these men, wanted no part in such radical action.[5] He had sworn an oath of loyalty to Hitler and his fate was linked up with that of his commander in chief's. He could not contribute in any way to getting rid of him. His whole background and military training made him shudder at the thought; it was almost like raising one's hand to strike one's own mother.

Was there no other way of convincing Hitler of the true state of affairs on the Russian front before it was too late?

That whole dreadful winter of 1943-1944, while Germany reeled back in defeat after defeat, and the writing grew ever larger on the wall, the man who Hitler was soon going to promote to the rank of general racked his brains for a way to convince his Leader. After the defeat of the last great German counter-attack in 1943, Gehlen knew now that Germany would have to go on the defensive permanently in the East. One day soon, the Russians would launch their great offensive which would fling the German armies out of Russia, and send them reeling back to Germany

---

[5]In the postwar period when General Gehlen actively supported the CIA, attempts were made to prove that he was an active anti-Nazi, but there is no real evidence which supports this contention. Although he protected his anti-Nazi officers from the Gestapo after the failure of the bomb attempt on Hitler's life in July, 1944, Gehlen was never one of them.

itself. If somehow, he told himself, he could get the word back to the Leader's HQ about when and where that offensive would start, perhaps he could convince Hitler to make his dispositions accordingly.

The more he thought about it, the more he became convinced that this was the only way to get through to Adolf Hitler, so far away in the unrealistic atmosphere of his headquarters. What he needed was a long-range penetration of the Soviet homeland. Even more necessary was that it be done by really highly-specialized agents who could bring back the information he needed to draw up his estimate of the Russian intentions. If he could get such a group of agents in and out of Russia in time, he *might* be able to bring about a complete change in the Führer.

In Gehlen's rage at Hitler's ban on the Vlasov Army, he had told Herre in disgust that "Hitler's policy in Russia treats the Russians like a colonial people and alienates the mass of the people against us." Now, however, he relized it was too late to worry about such things. Soon the Germans would be driven out of Russia altogether and whatever value Vlasov might have had would vanish. In this new year of 1944, he would have to forget such dreams and face up to hard reality—*and make the Leader do the same if he could*. "Operation Thrush" and a dozen similar operations was in process of being born.

5

On the morning of August 8, 1944, a hot, sultry day, Lieutenant Colonel Schäfer, who was responsible for personnel at Foreign Armies East, reported to General Gehlen's office. After a brief exchange about the state of the weather, the colonel got down to business. "Sir," he said, "the preparations for Operation Thrush which you approved on July 18 are completed."

Gehlen thought the other man was being a little too pedantic, for he knew quite well when he had approved the plans for "Thrush," but he refrained from comment. He contented himself with a nod.

"We can commence as soon as you like, sir," The Colonel was saying.

"I see," Gehlen said.

Quickly the other officer filled Gehlen in on the objectives of the operation. They were twofold: first, to radio back details of enemy concentrations and intentions in the Vitebsk region; secondly—and this was the more daring part of the operation—obtain details of the Russian industrial situation, especially about those factories producing tanks in Moscow nearly eight hundred miles away from Gehlen's HQ. It was a tall order.

Gehlen smiled approvingly when the colonel had finished his brief exposé. "Good," he commented, dabbing his brow with a brilliant white handkerchief. "And who are the men concerned? Have you already chosen them?"

"Yes, sir. They are Captain Müller, and Lieutenant Skriabine, and they are both trained and ready to go."

"And their cover names?"

"Müller is 'Gregor,' and Skriabine is 'Igor.' "

Vassili Antonovich Skriabine, "Igor," was a twenty-four-year-old Russian, who had been born in Gorki. His parents had been liquidated as "anti-Communist," but somehow or other "Igor" had managed to wangle a place at the Technical University in Moscow. However, he had failed to complete his degree. Instead, he had been called up for the Red Army at the outbreak of the war. After training as an officer, he had fled to the Germans at the first available opportunity. His hatred of the regime which had executed his parents had made him volunteer for the German intelligence service.

The other man, Albert Müller, was a German. He had been born in Leningrad in 1909 and had studied for a year in the Soviet Union before returning to Germany in 1928. Müller, in addition to being fluent in Russian, was a skilled radio and electronics specialist.

These two men, "Gregor" and "Igor," both volunteers for their highly dangerous mission, had been in training for nearly a year. They had been thoroughly instructed in the clandestine routines of the secret agent: the use of codes, radio techniques; enemy formations and their habits; demolitions and explosives, and all the rest. But even with this training, Gehlen had not been satisfied. He had ordered them to his headquarters for a highly specialized crash course on the latest spy techniques. For him, "Operation Thrush" was to be one of the most important missions ever carried out by his long-range reconnaissance teams.

Time and again he had inquired of his subordinates how the two key agents were getting on, and emphasized that Igor and Gregor should have their cover absolutely perfect before they were dispatched. He even insisted that the two young men should know the title of the latest movie running in Moscow's chief theater, and the number of cigarettes allowed a non-industrial worker on his weekly ration. But now, finally, they were ready to go.

On the night of August 10, 1944, the two of them boarded the Luftwaffe plane that was to fly them across the Russian lines. Gregor was wearing the earth-brown blouse and dark breeches of a Soviet soldier, with the broad, stiff epaulettes of a general staff major on his shoulder. Igor wore the lighter uniform of a first lieutenant in the Red Air Force. Both men were relatively calm. Before boarding the plane they downed a stiff schnapps with the airfield's commander. Now it was ten minutes after midnight on a dark moonless night. Time to go.

The plane shook with the vibration of the twin motors as it strained to gain height, and the two agents could feel the metal at their backs get progressively colder by the second. Finally, the pilot achieved the desired altitude and the noise of the plane's motors sank a little so that it was possible to converse. The two agents, however, were not inclined much to conversation; they both knew that they were setting off on a potential suicide mission. Admittedly, Gehlen was prepared to risk a valuable Luftwaffe plane to bring them back if and when they completed their task; yet who knew how long they could survive so far behind the enemy lines? The slightest slip and the NKVD agents who were everywhere in Soviet Russia would have them.

Igor thought of the fate of his parents, and suddenly shuddered compulsively. One slip and they would end up for a couple of days in some grimy, bloodstained secret police cellar, until the NKVD had knocked out all the information they could from their shattered bodies before the dawn encounter with the firing squad against an inner wall of the prison.

Some twenty minutes later, the plane was over their dropping zone. An NCO balanced his way along the shaking fuselage to where the two pale-faced men sat in their flying coveralls. He nodded, not even deigning to speak over the roar of the motors which the pilot was now throttling back preparatory to the drop. Obediently, the two followed him like lambs being led to the slaughter.

The door was already open and waiting for them. A cold wind penetrated the plane. Gregor took up his position gripping each side of the door, his feet poised for the jump. With wide, staring eyes Igor watched as the NCO's hand descended on his comrade's back— *hard*. Then suddenly, he was gone, snatched out into the black void, as if some gigantic hand had reached into the plane and taken him.

Now it was Igor's turn. With feet like lead, he shuffled to the door. The NCO looked at him. In the flickering green light of the plane's interior, the sergeant's face looked as if it had been painted with thick gray paint. Igor took up his position. The hand came down. Automatically, conditioned by so many months of training, he jumped. Moments later he was falling crazily into the darkness, the wind threatening to rip the very clothes from his powerless, paralyzed body. Above him the plane completed a wide, slow circle and then, picking up speed, hurried westward to the safety of German air space.

Three quarters of an hour later, it landed at the field where it had taken off, to report that both agents had jumped successfully. Now began the long wait in the silent wooden barracks with the high, swaying radio masts outside, for the first sign of life from agents Igor and Gregor.

At nine o'clock precisely, on the morning after the drop, Major Gregor Posyuchin reported to Army Headquarters and demanded to be taken to the headquarters of the 11th Guards Rifle Division. The clerks snapped into action. It didn't do to offend a staff major like Posyuchin—you could find yourself transferred to the front very quickly if you did. A little while later, Staff Major Posyuchin was being ushered into the presence of broad-shouldered, bemedaled Major General Koslov, the commander of the 11th Guards. After a brief exchange of pleasantries, the staff major handed the divisional commander a sealed envelope stamped in large letters with the words "STRICTLY CONFIDENTIAL."

Koslov read the letter it contained quickly, and then looked up at the young, much decorated Major. "Yes, I'll do my best to give you every help you need on your tour of the front."

The carefully forged document had worked. The staff major gave a mental sigh of relief. The trick had come off and "Gregor" was now in a position to inspect the whole length of the front held by the Guards Division at his leisure.

For the next two days, Gregor in his disguise as Staff Major Posyuchin not only examined the Guards' positions in detail, he also visited its entire rear echelon transport system, its depots and its map rooms. Even during his "off-duty" time, Gregor was not idle. He befriended several of the officers detailed to him by General Koslov and gained valuable information from them too.

As for the general, he was so impressed by the staff officer that he gave a drunken farewell party for Gregor at which Gregor, who was a man who could handle his liquor, obtained further information about the 11th's front which he knew his boss Gehlen would give his eyeteeth to have. The next morning, as a final gesture, General Koslov placed his own staff car at his guest's disposal to take him back to the nearest large town, Vitebsk.

In Vitebsk, Gregor met Igor as planned, and that same night the two men disappeared into the sprawling woods that fringed the town. At the prescribed time of nine-thirty, Igor began to tap his first coded signal back to Gehlen's HQ, while a nervous, tense Gregor, with his hand clasped around the butt of his pistol, peered into the darkness suspiciously.

Back in the isolated wooden barracks, the signal from Igor was greeted with a shout of triumph. Hurriedly the operator who had been trained to recognize Igor confirmed who it was, and the coded message was rushed for a decoding. Two-and one-half hours later, at midnight, on August 13 General Gehlen was reading Gregor's detailed report of the Russian concentrations and intentions in the Vitebsk region. The first part of Operation Thrush had been carried out successfully.

A little later that same night, with the rumble of heavy guns somewhere far off at the front the only sound, the two men crouched in the undergrowth, and began opening the large envelope that Gregor produced from his blouse. It contained their instructions for the next assignment. Huddled together, the two men read it by the blue light of their blacked-out flashlight.

The large envelope contained another envelope, which in turn contained other, smaller ones; in fact, the original envelope contained five envelopes in all, each containing new papers and new instructions for each separate phase of Operation Thrush.

For the time being, Major Posyuchin was now to disappear, to be replaced by "First Lieutenant Krassin," while Igor was now to become Lieutenant Kruilov. According to their instructions, the two lieutenants had been freed from their frontline duties in order to return to the Moscow Labor Exchange where their valuable technical knowledge could be better used in Moscow war-production factories which were crying out for skilled workers.

Again the excellent cover documents produced for them by Gehlen's expert forgers worked. On August 14, 1944, they boarded a Moscow-bound military train, carrying soldiers demobilized either because of wounds or because their services were needed in the capital. In Moscow the two agents reported immediately for assignment to new duties, and without the slightest trouble received jobs within the area of the capital. Igor was appointed to "Gosplan," the Soviet Russian National Planning Organization, and Gregor to a factory producing electrical parts.

This time it was Igor who had the more important role; because of his job with Gosplan he was even offered a private room, a special privilege in over-crowded Moscow. Naturally it was only a matter of a few days before he acquired a roommate, Gregor. The second phase of Operation Thrush was underway.

For one whole month the two agents did not attempt to get in touch with the barracks far away beyond the Russian lines. Although they knew that General Gehlen would be anxiously awaiting their report, both Gregor and Igor knew they had to be careful. Moscow was full of spies and informers, who would report immediately any suspicious conduct.

But this did not mean that Gregor and Igor were not keeping their eyes and ears open. In their respective positions they were ideally located to find out what Gehlen needed to know about the state of Russia's war production; in particular, the tank production figures for the numerous war plants situated in and around the capital. Finally, in the second week of September, they were ready to contact their HQ.

That night, when they thought that the rest of the inhabitants of the ancient, rambling house in which they lived were asleep, they brought out their concealed radio, hastily fitted together the various pieces of the clandestine apparatus and prepared to send their second report. In the thick, heavy stillness of the sleeping house, Igor bent over the apparatus, earphones clapped over his head, and began giving out his call signal, while Gregor, who was usually tense at such moments, held his breath and waited expectantly for the sudden crash at the door which would herald the fact that they had been discovered.

But no crash came. Nor did any response come in from that faraway wooden barracks. Nothing—just a dead stillness. Igor licked his lips. What had happened? For a moment neither man reacted. Then suddenly Igor pulled off his earphones and, with his hair tousled and standing on end, began to examine the secret radio.

A moment later he glanced up at a waiting Gregor. "That's it," he said in Russian (they both conversed in that language in case anyone hearing the suspicious sound of someone speaking in German would start investigating).

"What?" Gregor asked, perplexed.

"The batteries. They're dead!"

In their desperate need, they had resorted to a dangerous means of making their radio run, by attaching it to the main system. It was the only way that Igor could think of to obtain power. Once more Igor crouched over his key and started tapping out the opening signal.

Suddenly Gregor started. Fear made the hair stand up at the back of his head. *Every time Igor touched the key, the lone bulb hanging in the center of the room flickered!* It flickered in the same rhythm as Igor's application of the morse code.

"Stop!" he cried urgently. "Look at the light!"

Igor's finger flew from the key. He saw immediately what Gregor meant; it was possible that the electric lights throughout the whole house were flickering like their own naked flyblown bulb.

The minutes passed leadenly.

Gregor was about to heave a sigh of relief in the belief that the scare had been for nothing, when there was a gentle tap on their door. Gregor opened it hurriedly.

It was Marfa, a pretty girl in her early twenties who lived across the corridor from them. Smiling hugely, she explained that she was having trouble with her electric cooker for some reason. Usually at this time of night, when most people were turning in dog-tired from the long day in Moscow's war plants, electricity was plentiful; fewer people were cooking then or heating their rooms. Tonight the current seemed to keep coming and going. Could they help her?

Gregor's lips had gone dry with shock. He forced his face into a smile. The girl hadn't realized what was going on after all!

Then the smile flew from his face. Marfa's eyes had fallen on the earphones which lay on the couch where Igor had forgotten to hide them in his panic at the sound of the knock on the door. Paralyzed with fear, Gregor saw the light of understanding begin to dawn on Marfa's face.

6

After the first moment of paralyzing shock, Gregor
reacted. Seizing the girl by the arm, he dragged her
inside roughly and flung the door closed behind her.
His brain was racing. What were they going to do
with the girl? Kill her? Could they do that safely without causing any suspicion in the house? How did they
get the body out? Where did one hide a body in the
teeming capital? A thousand questions sped through
his mind.

He need not have worried. Marfa turned out to be
an anti-Communist, who was relatively easily persuaded to work together with the two good-looking,
sympathetic German agents. In the course of that long
night they persuaded her that she was safe with them
and told her a little of their mission. Surprisingly
enough, Marfa, safe in the heart of her country's capital,
agreed not only to keep silent but also to help them in
their dangerous work.

In the next weeks, Marfa helped them considerably,
taking over a myriad minor duties and tasks which
she could perform more easily than they could, without
arousing suspicion. In the end, Gregor asked headquarters to give its permission to recruit the pretty
Russian girl as an agent, and Gehlen approved. Marfa
became a German spy.

On the night of October 11, Gregor and Igor radioed
their most important message thus far to HQ while

Marfa stood guard at the door. (In the meantime she had obtained batteries for them in Moscow where everything was in terribly short supply and one had to have good connections to get anything that was not on ration.

During the course of his job with Gosplan, Igor had become friendly with a corrupt high official of the Russian National State Railroads. For a long time Igor had played him along, supplying him with vodka and long Russian cigarettes until finally, during the course of one marathon drinking session, he had asked the fateful question: would he, the official, be prepared to reveal the composition of the entire Soviet freight system for the months of November and December?

Slowly the drunken Russian nodded his greasy-haired head and, wiping his vodka-wet lips, said thickly that he would—for a price.

"Forty thousand rubles!"

It was a very large sum of money indeed, but the information that the drunken official was offering was of incalculable importance. Any trained general staff officer could from this information work out Soviet military intentions for the spring of the following year.[1] Igor sensed immediately that he had made one of the greatest intelligence coups of the entire war in the East.

Gehlen did not hesitate upon receiving the news. The only problem was how to get the money to the Russian. He decided to send it by way of a man who was a Russian renegade with the cover name of Piotr. The courier was dropped safely on the outskirts of Moscow and quickly made contact with Gregor and Igor. They handed the money over to the corrupt official who gave them the vital plans—with one stipula-

---

[1]Because of the poor Soviet roadnet, which contained nothing like the German autobahns, the Soviet General Staff, Stavka, was forced to rely almost completely on the Russian railroads.

tion. They could retain them for *one night only!*

The following night the three agents and their assistant, Marfa, photographed document after document, with Gregor making occasional written notes of what appeared to him to be vital information. He knew Gehlen had forbidden them to do this, but in this case he felt he was justified.

When dawn came, the three exhausted agents had completed their task and Igor was able to return the plans to the Russian, who stowed them away in the railroad office safe where he had gotten them. The plan was theirs! Now, how were they going to get it back to Gehlen's HQ!

Gehlen was worried by that problem too. Calling a conference of his senior officers, he gave them full details of the great coup and then asked for their opinions on how they were to get the vital information through the Russian lines. The group decided that a plane should be sent to fetch back not only the microfilm of the plans but also the agents; in Gehlen's opinion this might be the last chance of ever getting their men out of Russia.

Gregor, Igor and Marfa were overjoyed when the news came through that they were going to be taken out. Swiftly they set to work searching the rural area around Moscow for a suitable landing zone for the light Luftwaffe plane that Gehlen had promised to send. Finally they found an acceptable spot in the neighborhood of Dzerzhinsk some sixty or seventy miles west of Moscow[2].

---

[2]Piotr did not accompany them. After his job as courier was finished, he pushed on to Volgoda in the far north of European Russia, where he contacted a large number of German soldiers who had escaped from Russian PW camps or had managed to escape capture during the great retreat. He carried with him a large sum of money for them to help their partisan activities against the Russian

The night of the rescue attempt was cold and wet, and the three agents crouched miserably in the grass, continually checking their watches and cocking their heads to the wind to catch any sound which might indicate the approach of the long-awaited machine. When it was time to ignite the signal fire which would indicate the dropping zone to the rescue plane, Gregor and Igor set to work and soon had, what appeared to them, a gigantic bonfire going.

The flames crackled higher and higher, and the whole area seemed bathed in bright blood-red light. Gregor and Igor looked at each other in horror as the fire surely could be seen miles away. The minutes ticked by, and still there was no plane. Gregor licked his dry, cracked lips, as the flames mounted. The tension was unbearable. Would the damn plane never come? Thirty minutes passed. Slowly the frightened agents began to think that everything had been in vain. The plane was not coming, they would be left to their fates; there was going to be no rescue attempt this night—or any other night.

Then suddenly, Igor let out a half-stifled cry of delight. Even before they could identify it, the plane had landed and a shadowy figure had sprung out and was roaring at them above the hellish noise of the twin motors.

Gregor was the first to react. As he started to run to the plane, came the outraged command to stop. Lead began to beat the grass around them like hot summer rain on a tin roof. They had been spotted! Tracers cut the air. Like myriad red, angry bees, the bullets zigzagged through the night.

---

rear echelon. This group, which had radio contact with Gehlen's HQ, was one of the many which managed to exist and operate behind the Russian lines long after the Germans had left Russia. Indeed, some of them were still probably operating long after the "thousand-year Reich" had lost the war.

Gregor ran as he had never run before. The pilot had spotted the danger, and was racing his engines. Gregor could see the plane's tail as it started to lift, and redoubled his efforts, his breath coming in short, sharp gasps, his lungs threatening to burst at any moment with the effort.

He made it! Eager, clumsy hands grabbed under the armpits and hauled him in. Even as he collapsed on the heaving metal floor of the plane, more dead than alive, the machine started to rise.

In his fear and horror that he might not make the plane, Gregor had not noticed that he had been wounded in the arm. The crew cut away his clothing, bandaged the bleeding arm as best they could, and gave him a shot of morphine. But Gregor did not feel the pain; his thoughts were with poor Igor and Marfa left behind.

God, he groaned to himself, clasping his head with his good hand, what will happen to them? And then his mouth dropped open. The microfilm! He had given it to Igor to hide. *Igor had the vital information!*

A few hours later Gregor, now dressed in the uniform of a captain in the German Army, reported to Lieutenant Colonel Schäfer. In a mood of black despair he confessed that the vital information was still in Igor's possession. Then suddenly he realized that he still had his notes. Quickly calling for the civilian clothes he had just discarded, with the aid of a hastily found razor blade, he undid the lining of the jacket and brought out his penciled notes. With a gesture of triumph he handed them over to his superior officer, who hurried away with them.

In a matter of minutes they were on the desk of General Gehlen himself and the spymaster settled down to trying to make sense of them while Captain Müller, who felt like a man who had come back from the dead, tossed and turned in his bed, completely exhausted yet unable to sleep, haunted by what had happened at that lonely grove near Moscow a few hours before.[3]

----

[3]Surprisingly, Igor and Marfa escaped capture. One week later Gehlen's HQ was surprised to receive Igor's code signal and moments later the news that they were going to break out on their own. Accordingly, Gehlen's men confirmed that Marfa and Igor should try to reach the German lines in East Prussia. The troops in the area where they would cross would be warned to look out for them.

Unfortunately, on that very night the two fugitives were caught up in the gigantic Soviet offensive which they had done so much to warn the Germans about. It is not known, therefore, whether they ever got through; and naturally, Gehlen's people are not telling. Perhaps an elderly Igor and Marfa are still operating in Moscow—who knows?

7

With the vital information that Gregor and half a dozen similar agents had collected that fall, Gehlen set about preparing his estimate of the Russian intentions.

Six hundred kilometers from him, another general was equally at work on a related job. Brigadier General Edwin Sibert, who in six months's time was to play such a decisive role in Gehlen's life, was trying to figure out from his position in the Hotel Alpha in the tiny capital of Luxembourg what the German intentions were in the West. He failed miserably. General Omar Bradley's chief of intelligence completely rejected the idea that the Germans would ever again be in a position to launch a counterattack in the West. The result was the Battle of the Bulge.[1]

Gehlen, however, did not fail. Although as December, 1944, approached the weather worsened locking Central Europe in its coldest winter for over a quarter of a century, he knew that Stalin would undoubtedly take advantage of Hitler's planned offensive in the West as soon as it got underway. It was an opportunity he would not miss, even if the senior generals of the Stavka, Russia's High Command, would protest the weather was too bad to launch an attack. Feverishly,

[1]It must be stated that he was in good company. Virtually every other major intelligence man in the Anglo-American armies failed to predict "Hitler's last gamble."

as November gave way to December Gehlen worked out his detailed analysis of the Russian intention.

Finally it was ready, and he was able to pass it on to General Heinz Guderian, the commander of the Eastern Front. Guderian accepted Gehlen's analysis in its entirety. As the small, tough panzer general wrote later of Gehlen: "The work of the Foreign Armies East was absolutely reliable. I had known its commander General Gehlen long enough to be able to judge his staff, his methods, and his conclusions."

Armed with Gehlen's conclusions, Guderian set off on the long journey from his East Prussian HQ to Hitler's, located in the Ziegenburg Castle in the West, where the Leader had set up camp for the course of the Ardennes counterattack. On the afternoon of Christmas Eve he arrived at Supreme Headquarters and explained Gehlen's analysis to the Leader.

Hitler had little time for Guderian. The Eastern Front was quiet at present; that was all he was interested in. His attention was directed exclusively to the Ardennes front, where, in his opinion, the "decisive battle of the war" was being fought.

When Guderian had finished his analysis, Hitler declared that the reports prepared by Foreign Armies East were based on a Russian bluff. In his opinion, the huge number of enemy rifle divisions which Gehlen had declared were massing in the East were explained by the fact that their average rifle division had a strength of only 7,000 men, compared to 12,000 in a German division. As for the Russian armored divisions—they hadn't a tank to their name!

Working himself up into one of his frightening artificial rages which had made many a battle-hardened general tremble, he cried, "It's the greatest imposture since Ghengis Kahn! Who's responsible for producing all this rubbish?"

Guderian got the same reception when he appealed to Himmler.

The bespectacled head of the SS commented, "You know, my dear Generaloberst, I don't really believe the Russians will attack at all. It's all an enormous bluff. The figures given by your department Foreign Armies East are grossly exaggerated. They're far too worried. I'm convinced there's nothing going on in the East."

As Guderian told himself in resignation, "There was no arguing against such naiveté."

All the same, urged on by Gehlen's one hundred percent conviction in the reliability of his forecast, Guderian tried again on New Year's Eve. He failed once more to convince Hitler, while, as we have already seen, his visit to the Leader nine days later was an absolute fiasco, its only result being a further worsening of the already bad relations between Hitler and his general.

For Gehlen, Guderian's lack of success was the last straw. He realized now that Hitler simply closed his ears to anything he did not want to hear. Yet Gehlen was too much of a loyal soldier to give up completely. He involved himself in a dozen desperate little schemes to stave off the final inevitable defeat which he knew must come soon.

Together with SS Secret Service chief, smooth-talking, young, clever General Schellenberg, and six-foot-four hulking Colonel Skorzeny (the man who had rescued Mussolini, and had created so much havoc and chaos behind the U.S. lines with his jeep team sabotage groups disguised in GI uniforms), he helped to launch parateam after parateam behind the Russian lines.

At that time the advancing Russians had occupied only the main cities in their lines of march. Behind them they left large areas where individual groups of Germans and their Russian, Ukrainian and Polish collaborators could operate with relative freedom. As Skorzeny records in his autobiography, many of the German telephone lines were intact weeks after the Russians had taken over, and his headquarters was still able to contact its men way behind the Russian lines in this manner. In fact, he relates the story of a German firm in Lodz, in central Poland, far behind the Russian lines, telephoning its Berlin head office and asking whether it should take up war production again as the Russians had simply passed through the city and failed to set up any form of Russian administration! We do not know the Berlin head office's reply.

Together with Skorzeny, Gehlen planned many a raid behind the Russian lines. Some of these raids were aimed at sabotaging and cutting Russian communications; others, to make contact with and, if possible, rescue large numbers of German soldiers cut off deep in the heart of the Soviet Union.

One such operation was launched after the gigantic Austrian commando and Gehlen, who contrasted so strongly with the swashbuckling SS colonel, met for the first time in the winter of 1944. General Jodl, Hitler's chief of Operations, introduced the two men and explained that the High Command was faced with a nasty problem: "One which it is specially important for the High Command to wash its hands of" (as Skorzeny's adjutant Radl commented cynically later).

During the summer debacle in the East, nearly twenty-five German divisions had collapsed, leaving thousands of men in Russian hands. Some of these units had refused to surrender even though their divisional commanders had ordered them to do so. Thus it was that, owing to the stubborness of a regimental commander, Lieutenant Colonel Scherhorn, who had collected together the remnants of a dozen regiments, two thousand German soldiers now found themselves at liberty deep in the heart of Russia.

Skorzeny asked where they were located.

Gehlen answered that radio reports of their presence were coming in from the Minsk region.

Skorzeny did a quick calculation. Minsk was in the

White Russian area, a devil of a long way from the nearest German positions.

Jodl took up the conversation again. The High Command had been aware of Scherhorn's group for nearly three months now, but their latest radio messages were becoming desperate appeals for help; they could not hold out much longer. Could he, Skorzeny, help?

Otto Skorzeny, his face slashed with the scars of his student dueling days in Vienna when his motto had been "Forget the danger, go for the head," could. He had always had a soft spot for a brave man; and Scherhorn was undoubtedly a brave man. He agreed to try. Briefed by Gehlen, who warned him that the radio messages from Scherhorn might be a trap, Skorzeny flew back immediately to his Friedenthal HQ near Berlin and set about preparing a parachute team to aid Scherhorn—*that is* (as a small inner voice warned), *if Scherhorn really exists.*

A few days later a very unlikely crew lined up before Skorzeny. There were nearly thirty of them. The leaders were Baltic Germans, who spoke Russian fluently; the rest were Russian renegades who had gone to work for their former enemies. But there was no noticeable difference between the two ethnic groups. All had had their heads cropped down to bare stubble in the Russian fashion. For the last few days none of them had shaved and Skorzeny had ordered them to wash as little as possible so that even at a distance their smell alone would identify them as Soviet soldiers of that time. Carrying round-barreled Soviet grease guns, they were clad in sacklike, earth-colored Russian infantry uniforms, smoked black Russian *marhokha* cigarettes and had, as their means of identification, worn, greasy ID cards. A grinning Skorzeny, looking at the unsavory bunch who a few days before had been trim, well-disciplined, clean SS troopers, was pleased. They looked the part in every detail save that one or two fumbled a little awkwardly with their cigarettes which were rolled in ordinary coarse newspaper. He hoped it was *Pravda*. But he need not have feared. Gehlen had thought of everything, even down to that detail.

Group A of the team took off in the special plane provided by his own Squadron 200, which always worked with him on these missions. Five hours later, after covering hundreds of miles of Russian territory, the team's first message was received: "Poor landing. Enemy have spotted us. We're under machinegun fire." That was the last heard of Group A.

"Undeterred, Skorzeny dispatched his Group B. For five nights nothing was heard of the volunteers and the Austrian commando began to believe that perhaps Gehlen was right after all. The whole operation was a Soviet trick. Then on the fifth night, an excited decoding clerk cried, "Obersturmbannführer—Obersturmbannführer, we've got them!" Group B had not only landed safely, but had managed to link up with Lieutenant Colonel Scherhorn, and the brave officer was on the radio himself, ready to express his thanks.

Skorzeny followed up this success with the dispatch of Group C. It vanished without trace. Group D followed. It landed without incident, but failed to find Scherhorn. Under the command of SS Sergeant R., the group decided to attempt the impossible—to walk back to the German lines! And the group succeeded. R. even had the nerve to enter a Soviet officers' mess where as a supposed Russian officer he was feasted by his "fellow officers." A few weeks later he reached the German lines near the Lithuanian border and reported to his commander by telephone. "Sergeant R. reporting for duty. No casualties."

Now that Skorzeny had made contact with Scherhorn, he decided to try to get him and his men out by airlift. But the two thousand German soldiers trapped hundreds of miles away in the heart of Russia were too weak to clear runways in the thick forests where they were hiding. Skorzeny ordered a doctor to parachute in to them. He broke both legs on landing and died of exposure. Another doctor made it safely. He started to tend the weakened, undernourished men, some of whom were also suffering from wounds. A runway was started, and Skorzeny began to fly in food and supplies. Swiftly the trapped men's strength was built up. But the regular supply planes that Skorzeny flew in began to attract the unwelcome attention of both the Russian ground and air forces.

Skorzeny did some swift thinking. Two hundred miles from Minsk there was a series of lakes which by now should be frozen over (according to Gehlen's experts). If Scherhorn could fight his way through to the lakes, there would be no need for runways. The planes of the rescue force could land safely on the ice.

In the midst of a snowstorm Scherhorn got moving. That first day, he radioed that he had made ten miles' progress. Skorzeny was overjoyed. Although he was occupied with his role in the Battle of the Bulge, he took a personal interest in the Scherhorn rescue attempt which went under the code name of "Operation Freischütz." The next day Scherhorn reported he had covered only six miles. But still he was moving. Mile by mile Scherhorn's pitiful columns crawled towards the landing zone. Their few trucks were piled high with the wounded, but the majority of the undernourished, weary soldiers had to slog on foot through the depth of the Russian winter, fighting not only blizzards but repeated attacks by Russian police units. Still they moved forward—mostly at a speed of three to four miles a day.

Time passed. Skorzeny's supply of planes was cut. Desperately he fought to obtain more transports. Gehlen washed his hands of the operation. He was by now convinced it was a Russian trick. Skorzeny persisted. Then, after fourteen weeks of marching and fighting their way through the depths of the Russian winter, Skorzeny received a radio message which made his heart beat faster. The advance party of Scherhorn's force had reached the lake area!

By this time Skorzeny was down to one supply plane a week. Now, with victory in sight, he was informed there was not even fuel for the single plane. Berlin said the flights must stop. That was that.

Desperately Scherhorn himself radioed, "Where are the planes? Send to fetch us. Hurry. We are running out of food."[2]

Another of the Gehlen-Skorzeny missions was more successful. Under the leadership of blond, curly-haired Lieutenant Walter Girg (who Skorzeny originally intended to turn down for his unit because of his lisping speech), a mixed group of Germans and "Ethnic Germans" from Rumania penetrated the Russian lines to carry out the High Command order that they should "bar the Carpathian mountain passes, reconnoiter behind the enemy, wreck his communications and help German civilians to safety."

It was a tall order, but twenty-three-year-old Lieutenant Girg was undismayed. He split his group into four and ordered each group to block a separate pass, which they did successfully for several days. Then they assisted several hundred ethnic Germans, who had been established in that part of Rumania for five hundred years, to escape from the Red Army. A few days later, however, Girg's luck seemed to run out. After successfully passing through the newly-captured town of Kronstadt disguised as Rumanian soldiers who were now fighting side by side with their new allies the

---

[2]Nothing is known of the fate of the Scherhorn group. Skorzeny ordered the Knight's Cross awarded to his subordinate who had found them. This was dropped by parachute and acknowledged in one of the last radio messages received from Scherhorn—*if it was Scherhorn!* Then silence.

Russians, Girg and four of his men ran into a Russian ambush.

A fire fight broke out and Girg was forced to surrender. The "spies," as the Russians rightly regarded them, were roughly stripped naked. Two of the Rumanian-speaking soldiers were brutally clubbed to death with rifle butts. Girg and the two remaining men were dragged to the nearest hill and told they were to be shot immediately. A half-naked Girg realized that this was his last chance. He had everything to gain and nothing to lose. The young officer who had already won two Iron Crosses and was soon to gain the coveted Knights Cross of the Iron Cross took a deep breath and lowered his head so that the Russian, cursing and shouting, should not see the sudden look of determination in his deep-blue eyes. Then he was up and running, naked as he was. The Russians gave a yell of rage. For a moment, though, no one fired.

Perhaps the sudden escape of a man already half dead (or so they thought) had completely surprised them. Then someone let loose a burst with his tommy gun. It missed. The next one didn't. Girg felt a stinging pain in his foot. But he did not falter. The Russians were after him, yelling angrily and firing—fortunately for him—wildly. So the strange chase went on until finally Girg threw them off and fell, wounded and completely exhausted into a swamp.

More dead than alive, he crawled and staggered through the night in the general direction of the German lines. Luck was on his side once more. Some time later, just as the first light of the false dawn began to flood the sky, he reached a German outpost near the small town of Morosvasacheli. He was saved!

In those last months of the war, Gehlen immersed himself in many other wild schemes. It was almost as if he deliberately attempted to keep himself fully occupied with a hundred and one plans in order not to have an opportunity to consider the defeat which he knew, better than most high-ranking German officers, stared Germany in the face.

One such scheme was Himmler's last-ditch secret army—the "Werwolf." In November, 1944, Himmler had cried out during the course of a speech given to the members of a German Volkssturm outfit that he was establishing a new unit that would "strike bravely to the rear of the enemy." Allied intelligence offiicers pricked up their ears. Was this the start of a German postwar underground movement? In fact, it wasn't. Himmler did not at that time even consider the possibility of Germany being defeated in the field, so why should he establish a postwar resistance movement? All that he intended was the formation of a paramilitary organization made up of some 5,000 eager young Nazis recruited from the elite of the Hitler Youth and Hitler Maidens who, trained by SS men, would sneak behind the Allied lines in civilian clothes to carry out tasks of a military nature. No more, no less.

He gave the command of this new organization which was soon to frighten Allied intelligence so much (one of Eisenhower's reasons for ordering General Patton to push into Bavaria was to prevent the establishment of an "Alpine Fortress" in the Alps from which this underground army would sally to attack Allied communications after the war) to a lazy, good-for-nothing SS police general, Hans Pruetzmann, who did very little with it. In fact, Pruetzmann's Werewolves, who took their names from that legendary figure which was able to change its male form for that of a wolf at full moon, carried out only one really successful operation: the murder of the Allied-appointed senior burgomaster of occupied Aachen, Dr. Franz Oppenhoff, in March, 1945.

Gehlen decided that Pruetzmann could do more with his young fanatics. For a long time he had studied the activities of the Polish Underground Army. Indeed, he had even infiltrated agents into it. Now, as the war began to draw to its inevitable close, he drew up a careful plan for the establishment of a nationwide German resistance movement, based on the Polish model. Through his contacts with Skorzeny and Schellenberg, who was becoming ever-increasingly Himmler's confidant, he approached the Reichsführer of the SS with his plan.

The pale-faced SS leader with his pince-nez and schoolmasterly appearance was thoroughly shocked by Gehlen's suggestion. "This is complete madness," Himmler thundered, in a way that made Schellenberg, who had transmitted the plan, tremble for his life. "If I were to discuss such a plan with Wenck (General Wenck, commanding officer of the vital twelfth Army fighting on the Elbe), I should be denounced as the first defeatist in the Third Reich. The fact would be served up to the Führer piping hot."

And Heinrich Himmler went on to denounce "high-class staff officers" who sat safely in evacuation areas conjuring up plans for the postwar period instead of getting to the front and fighting to the last as he, Himmler, intended to do. Schellenberg nodded dumbly, cynically reminding himself that Himmler was already throwing out peace feelers to the Western Allies. Later, when the SS Secret Service chief informed Gehlen of the outcome of his meeting with Himmler, Gehlen realized that the game was up. The war was lost and there was nothing he could do any more.

BOOK TWO

Beware of the devilry of secret service intrigues; don't ever drink from the poisoned cup of counterintelligence, for that poison is lethal.

German Colonel Heinz to Otto John, 1954

8

The end came for General Gehlen soon afterward. On the morning of March 28, 1945, General Guderian drove with his adjutant Freytag von Loringhoven from his HQ at Zossen to Berlin to meet Hitler. The major, sitting at the old warrior's side, knew that the meeting with the Leader would be a stormy affair. Guderian had told him, "Today I will tell him all!" Guderian had reached breaking point, but even Major von Loringhoven did not know just how stormy the confrontation would be.

A little later their car drove the bomb-littered streets of the battered capital to Hitler's bunker where, after being searched by guards, they were admitted to Hitler's presence. The noon conference could begin. General Busse began with his account of how he had been unable to counterattack successfully toward the beleaguered fortress of Kustrin.

Hitler began to show annoyance. "Why did the attack fail?" he yelled suddenly. Without waiting for a reply, he roared, "Because of incompetence! Because of negligence!" Unable to contain himself, he launched into an attack upon the whole General Staff. They were all incompetent, useless. The Kustrin attack, he yelled, was launched without sufficient artillery preparation. (Hitler, as a World War I soldier, was always much concerned with heavy artillery preparation for any attack.) Turning to Guderian, he cried, "If Busse didn't have enough ammunition as you claim—why didn't you get him more?"

Quietly, Guderian, careful to hold back his bad temper, answered, "I have already explained to you . . ." He never finished his sentence.

"Explanations! Excuses," Hitler interrupted. "That's all *you* give me!" And he ranted on about Busse's and Guderian's failings.

Suddenly the old tank man saw red. "Nonsense," he spluttered. "This is nonsense." His face red with rage, he bellowed that Busse was not to blame. "I've told you that," he cried. "He followed orders. Busse used all the ammunition that was available to him! All he had!" Frantically he sought for words to explain the feeling of inadequacy and rage that he had bottled up inside him for so long. "To say that the troops are to blame—look at the casualties!" he roared. "Look at the losses! The troops did their duty! Their self-sacrifice proves it!"

"*They failed—they failed,*" Hitler roared back, beside himself with anger, his Austrian accent so thick that he was hardly intelligible.

Now the die was cast. The two men were beyond reasonable discussion. All about them the senior officers were shocked into absolute silence; they had seen scenes enough in this room, but never anything like this.

Hitler slammed into the whole General Staff. His deep-seated hatred of the traditional Prussian military caste came to the surface. They were "defeatists," "fools and spineless fatheads." All the time they had misled and misinformed him!

Guderian took the opportunity of a gasp for breath on the part of the Leader to cry, "Had General Gehlen in his intelligence estimate misinformed him about the Russian strength?" And this time *he* answered his own question. "*He hadn't!*"

Hitler's raddled yellow cheeks flushed a deep red.

"Gehlen's a fool," he shouted back. He had consistently fooled Guderian into believing that his estimates were correct when they weren't.

And so it went on until Major Loringhoven tugged at his chief's coattails and dragged him away from the Leader, fearful that Hitler would order Guderian's immediate execution.

Hitler did not. But twenty minutes later, when both sides had calmed down a little, he asked Guderian to see him privately. The second interview lasted only a few minutes, and Guderian knew what was coming.

"Generaloberst Guderian," Hitler told the man who had once brought so much glory to German arms, "your physical health requires that you immediately take six weeks' convalescent leave."

His voice betraying no emotion, Guderian said simply, "I'll go."

It was all over.

Gehlen survived the dismissal of his chief by exactly thirteen days. On April 10, 1945, he was summarily dismissed from his post and placed in the so-called Leader's Reserve, which meant he had been sacked. He was replaced by Wessel, now a lieutenant colonel.

But the news no longer shook Général Reinhard Gehlen. He knew that Germany—or least *Hitler's* Germany—had lost the war, and he was already making plans for the future. One week before, he had met together with Wessel and Baun to plan one of the most unusual and daring changes of side ever recorded in a profession where double-dealing, changes of side, double-agents, treachery and complicated allegiances are the order of the day. But in the whole thirty-three-century-long history of espionage, there had never been quite anything like this.

The three men met in the nineteenth-century spa hotel at the medium-sized Saxon town of Bad Elster, as yet unthreatened by General Hodges's rampaging

First Army. Locked in a private room of the Kurhotel (which had now begun to show the signs of six years of neglect since the last fat-bellied, well-off guest had drunk the sour-tasting water which was supposed to be so good for a thousand and one complaints), the three long-time intelligence men began to discuss an amazing switch in allegiances.

Gehlen began the discussion with the statement that he felt there was still a future for them and their organization although their world seemed to be crashing to pieces all around them. Frankly, he told his old comrades, Germany had lost the shooting war. The question now was, how did they fit into the peace?

Stroking his long thin nose and speaking slowly as was his habit, he said he had been giving the subject thought for a long time now. For a while he had thought that Germany might be able to fight back against the victorious Allies in some kind of Werewolf organization. But Himmler had turned that suggestion down. And Pruetzmann was of no earthly use.

Now, however, he had been forced to go back to an old idea of his—eighteen months' old to be exact. He had borrowed it from one of his subordinate officers, anti-Nazi Major Count von Rittberg, who was responsible for the daily enemy situation report. Rittberg had not survived to carry out the plan himself for he had been shot as a traitor by the Gestapo, but he had confided to his friend Colonel Schwerdtfeger that "he was considering the possibility of somehow getting the complete Foreign Armies East documents files to the Western Allies with all their facts about the Russian Army, industrial potential etc., so that they could see the dangers presented by an ally of this kind and in this way prepare the ground for a separate peace with them."

Gehlen moistened his lips and looked at the tense faces of Baun and Wessel before he proceeded. Did they know what was coming? he asked himself.

Now, naturally, it was too late to think of making

any kind of separate peace with the British and Americans. However (and he lowered his voice before he completed the sentence), *there was no reason why they should not attempt to get their documents through the West to the Allies!* Before they could recover from their shock at this revelation, Gehlen went on hurriedly to explain that he had already ordered all his important files to be photocopied and packed away in forty steel cases, which could be loaded in trucks and sped away within a matter of two short hours if they had to evacuate their headquarters in a hurry—which was very likely.

Soon the war would be over. He predicted it would last—at the most—four more weeks. Within this period, he and his senior officers must see that the documents were transferred to the Western Allies.

Despite his sophisticated intelligence, Reinhard Gehlen had fallen for his own propaganda. He really believed that the West would soon quarrel with Soviet Russia and that soon Britain and the United States would need German help to continue the hot war against their former ally.[1] Soon they would all be "comrades" together. It was a pious hope, but one cherished by many Germans in those days, cut off by their own propaganda from the realities of the Great Alliance in which Soviet Russia was represented by the benign, pipe-smoking figure of "Uncle Joe." Few in the Allied camp realized just how much of a monster "Uncle Joe" Stalin really was, and it was going to take a great mass of the British and American peoples a

---

[1] More uncharitable commentators, mostly Communist, maintain that Gehlen became a turncoat for monetary reasons. I, personally, don't believe this. I feel he really felt he would be helping his own country in its future battle on the side of the Allies against Russia if he could get to the West with the vital information.

good many years after the war before they came to this realization.

But the three men in the shabby nineteenth-century spa hotel that day saw few problems in the amazing change of allegiance. Baun asked to whom they should offer their services and documents—the British or the Americans.

General Gehlen knew of the existence of plan "Eclipse," a top-secret British document which had been captured from them during the Ardennes battle in January. It maintained that "the only possible answer to the trumpets of total war in total defeat and total occupation. . . . It must be made clear that the Germans will not be able to negotiate in our sense of that word." Signed by Montgomery's chief of staff, Major General Sir Francis de Guingand, the plan seemed to indicate to Gehlen that the British might be more uncompromising than the Americans. Indeed, when he had shown the plan to General Heinrici, Commanding officer of the Vistula Army Group a few days before, the tough old soldier had groaned, "This is a death sentence."

As a result, Gehlen suggested they should offer their services first of all to the Americans who might be more flexible than the British. Both Baun and Wessel agreed, and so it was suggested that Baun should retreat with his unit into the Bavarian area for which the Americans were heading. Gehlen would follow him later.

Thus, the three men plotted that afternoon to turn over their whole massive *Apparat* to the advancing Americans. Not only would they offer them the forty steel cases, they would give them their comprehensive net of agents who would remain behind in the area to be occupied by the Russians. In addition, there was still some sort of network functioning in the Slavic countries that could be made use of, especially with the aid of American resources.

Baun was prepared to go even further. The middle-aged colonel was ready with an adventurous plan to leave behind depots of weapons all the way through Saxony, one day to be occupied by the Russians. These would be used by special sixty-man commando units who would actually take up arms against the Reds once they had arrived.

Gehlen restrained him. Under the present circumstances, he pointed out to Baun (whom he still did not like after three years of war together) that might be going too far. At the moment their primary problem was: just how were they going to make contact with the *Amis?* In his opinion, the first reaction would be to stick any German they captured into a PW camp.

For some time they discussed the problem. Finally they agreed that if they became separated in the course of the next few weeks, the first one to make contact with the Americans would offer the services of the Foreign Armies East in the name of the others. In the meantime, once they had to move their HQ, they would use the services of a professor of theology, Dr. Rudolf Gruber, in the Bavarian township of Eichstadt, as their "live letterbox." He would be the means of transmitting information from one to the other, using the code letters X W and Y, standing respectively for Baun, Wessel and Gehlen. With that, the conference broke. The great operation—the most amazing one of its kind in the annals of history—was on.

9

Fifteen days after that fateful meeting in the Saxon spa, the advancing victorious Red Army made it finally necessary for Foreign Armies East to start moving westward. They broke up into two groups. A smaller group set off for the town of Flensburg, in the far north of Germany, not far from the Danish border. Here Admiral Karl Dönitz, Commander in Chief of the Navy and Hitler's designated successor, was trying to establish a government to rule what was left of the battered Third Reich. The larger group, under the command of Lieutenant Colonel Wessel, had as its aim that section of Bavaria and Austria which German propagandists claimed was to be turned into the Alpine Redoubt, the site of Germany's last-ditch fanatical fight.

The two groups divided between them the forty precious steel cases with the files of the Foreign Armies East. Their orders were to bury them as soon as they arrived at their destinations.

As that beautiful hot April of 1945 came to an end, Gehlen's columns wound their way up the long serpentine into the Bavarian Alps, through lovely lush countryside which so far had had no taste of war. General "Blood and Guts" Patton's roving tank columns and those of General Patch's Seventh U.S. Army were still a long way off, and the German staff officers took their time, enjoying this "time out of war" after six years of combat.

Leaving the cold blue of the Spitzingsee (Lake Spitzing) behind, the column groaned higher and higher, most of the heavy trucks now in first gear until they reached Valepp. Here Gehlen halted and ordered his drivers to turn off to to the small hill town of Miesbach. When they were gone and safely out of sight, he, Wessel, and a handful of remaining staff officers clambered up the steep slopes of the mountain until they reached the lonely Alpine meadow named Elendsalm (the miserable meadow), rented by the Bavarian farmer Ludwig Priller.

Priller was still in the German Army, so his wife had given it over to middle-aged Rudi Kreidl to take charge of and work during his absence, and the latter was not often inclined to make the long trip up to the meadow with the picturesque wooden hut on its fringes. In other words, it was an ideal hiding place for Gehlen and his accompanying eight staff officers. So they settled in.

Gehlen fastened his family motto, *Laet vaeren nytt* (Don't give up), over the bunk in which he slept at night before departing with the rest in the early hours of the morning for the slopes up above the hut where they spent the day in talk and plans for the future. The steel cases were already hidden. Now all they had to do was to wait for the advancing *Amis* to reach them.

The days passed. April gave way to May. Still no Americans. Often Gehlen spent hours in his hiding place on the Apline slope searching the valley roads below for any sign of an enemy tank or truck. But without success.

Then one morning in the first week of May, he spotted a lone Sherman crawling cautiously down the valley road. Behind it, some half a mile away, came a second. They advanced exceedingly carefully, obviously tensed for the flat crack and tremendous, earsplitting roar of an enemy 88. None came, and the tanks passed on. The reconnaissance had arrived.

The next day the bulk of Patton's infantry started to roll down the valley road—truck after truck, half-track after half-track. Bunched close together and in a hurry, they were urged on by "Old Blood and Guts's" rallying cry which meant a lot to the sex-starved GIs: "On to Czechoslovakia and fraternization!" (General Eisenhower had strictly forbidden any dealings with the local German women and the soldiers were feeling the pinch.)

Gehlen let them pass, as he did with the second and third American waves. By this time the war had been over a full week. The German staff officers and their secret documents still had not been discovered by the Americans. Now Gehlen and his staff officers scrambled up the slopes above them well before sunrise, working on the assumption that the Americans would not mount higher up the mountain than they could travel in their jeeps. (They had already worked out that the average American would never walk when he could ride.) After sunset they returned to their lonely Alpine hut, confident that no American patrol would venture out after dark for fear of being attacked by the much touted Werewolves, who were still plaguing Allied intelligence officers, although Dönitz far away in Flensburg had forbidden the underground organization to carry out any further activities, to take effect from May 5.

Another week passed and Gehlen started to think about contacting his former enemies, still convinced that he and his officers had not yet been spotted. *But they had!*

Farmer Kreidl had known of their presence for almost a week now and he didn't like it. For days he had been observing them from a distance with his keen mountaineer's eyes, which were still sharp enough although he was no longer so young. He spotted the yellow gleam of Gehlen's golden cross (a Slovakian award) which he wore on his uniform jacket, and although he could not get close enough to identify the arm of the service to which the rest of the strangers belonged, he decided they were SS men. At that time, the heights of the "Alpine Fortress" were filled with high-ranking Nazi and SS officials who, sure that the Allies were after them, were hiding out till the heat was off. (Not too far from Gehlen, Skorzeny was similarly hidden on a height with a few of his officers, as was SS mass-murderer Eichmann.) Kreidl knew of this, and he was possessed—as he commented later—by a murderous rage at these SS men and the civilian with the "Golden Party Cross" (as he took Gehlen's decoration to be), who were hiding out on his meadow and endangering his life should the Americans find out. Finally he decided to do something about it and in the second week of May set off to tell the *Amis.*

The first GI he encountered did not understand the farmer's tale blurted out in his thick Bavarian dialect. But he did understand the word "SS." Swiftly he hurried the middle-aged German, dressed in the traditional Bavarian costume with a flat black hat adorned with the tuft from the tail of the local mountain goat—the *Gems*—stuck squarely on his shaven, stubborn head, to his company commander. The latter couldn't understand a word the excited farmer said either—save for the key word "SS." But he managed to obtain an interpreter in Bayrischzell, who was able to decipher the Bavarian's dialect.

Hurriedly a platoon was called together and thrust into jeeps. At forty miles an hour they set off on the Spitzing road and started thereafter the long drive up to the "miserable meadow," guided by an excitedly jabbering Rudi Kreidl, who was quite enjoying the new experience of riding in a jeep, side by side with a casual, gum-chewing GI.

The expected resistance did not take place. The Germans came out of their hut and surrendered at once as soon as they saw the U.S. formation. Gehlen, hands raised above his head, approached the nearest officer and, after asking permission to lower his hands, reached for his German Army paybook.

He showed it to the young American lieutenant, now completely bored by the whole business; indicated his rank which was written in it; and asked to be conducted to the nearest unit of the CIC (the American military intelligence corps). The lieutenant, a little more impressed now by the fact that he had apparently captured a German general, nodded and said he would see what he could do.

Thus it was that a little while later Gehlen, the man who knew more about the Russians than any other living person in the West and had a huge archive of the most vital information at his disposal, arrived in the little town of Miesbach, where a CIC outfit was located. He was led into the presence of another lieutenant, equally as bored as the first one. This one, however, spoke fluent German. In the German army fashion, Gehlen clicked his heels together as he entered and introduced himself. "I am the chief of the Department of Foreign Armies East in the German High Command."

The young officer, who had spent most of that long hot May 20 interrogating high-ranking German officers and officials who had been captured while hiding out in the mountainous area, looked up from his papers and yawned. "You were, General," he said lazily. "You were."

Reinhard Gehlen never forgave the CIC his treatment in that first casual encounter at the hands of its representative at Miesbach. After telling the officer that he had "information of value for your government," he was not received with open arms.

The American was not impressed. "All of you have," he commented cynically, and ordered the General and his staff to be taken away and placed in the nearest PW cage.

Fifteen years later, Gehlen's treatment on that day still rankled (even though he had been working with the Americans for fourteen years by then); and in a statement he allowed the German writer Wolfgang Wehner to make about the CIC in his book *Geheim* ("Secret"), we can see a reflection of his exasperation. Writing about the Miesbach outfit, Wehner maintains: "This unit was a typical product of the war. It had grown too fast, was staffed with the wrong people and if it did occasionally manage to carry out its assignment, it did so by chance."

And a friend of Gehlen's who wished to remain nameless also remarked: "He [Gehlen] had imagined the Americans would throw their arms around his neck with joy. The little worm in Miesbach did not do so and Gehlen was offended."

During the next two months that he was to spend in the PW cage Gehlen, onetime commander of the Foreign Armies East, was to be offended over and over again. He was no longer the general on the general staff, accustomed to instant obedience, smart salutes, respectful attention. He was simply another "Kraut prisoner of war" who had to line up with the rest to receive his food dished out to him by a bored cook on a tin plate. Now the stupidest, lowest-ranking GI in the whole of the U.S. Army could tell him—the man who had once held the power of life and death over so many people and had helped to control the destinies of armies—to "move it, bud—*and make it snappy!*"

In those two months in the cage, Gehlen was forced to take a rapid course in self-reeducation. He had to learn that his world had fallen apart and that he, like all the other gray figures around him, was a member of a beaten race; and a beaten race that was bitterly hated by many of their captors now that the newspapers were reporting the full and hideous extent of the atrocities committed in the Nazi concentration camps. He had to see that Goebbels had lied, consistently and deliberately.

There was no feeling of hatred among the GIs he had daily dealings with, for the Russians. The "Russkis," as they called them fondly, were their allies, and they had not the slightest intention in the world of fighting them. The war was over. All they were concerned with was enjoying the local girls (without being found out) and collecting the vital points which would get them on the boat for the "good old U.S.A."

There were some Americans in Germany, though, who did hate the Russians. One such man was Third Army Commander General Patton, soon to be military governor of Bavaria in which Gehlen found himself. That July Patton wrote in a letter home: "We have destroyed what could have been a good race and we are about to replace them with the Mongolian savage and all Europe with Communism."

Patton would not and could not hide his hatred of the Communists. Typical of his hatred was his remark to Marshal Zhukov, the conqueror of Berlin. During the course of the great military review in Berlin that September, a large number of huge Soviet tanks rumbled by. Proudly the barrel-chested, bemedaled "Hero of the Soviet Union" turned to the immaculate Patton and growled, "My dear General Patton. You see that tank. It carries a cannon which can throw a shell seven miles."

Patton listened attentively while the interpreter translated the dimple-chinned marshal's words, then he replied.

"Indeed," he said in that thin, high-pitched voice of his. "Well, my *dear* Marshal Zhukov, let me tell you this. If any of my gunners started firing at your people before they had closed to less than seven hundred yards, I'd have them court-martialed for cowardice!"

As an eyewitness reports: "It was the first time I saw a Russian commander stunned into silence."

But Patton was an exception. The attitude of most American soldiers in that first hot, heady summer of victory was best summed up by their commander in chief, the Supreme Commander, General Eisenhower, when he expressed the view that "the Russians are generous, they like to give presents and parties, as almost every American who has served with them can testify. In his generous instincts, in his love of laughter, in his devotion to a comrade, and in his healthy, direct outlook on the affairs of workaday life, the ordinary Russian seems to me to bear a marked similarity to what we call an 'average American.' "

So it was that as Gehlen lounged, bored and angry, in his prisoner-of-war camp in that beautiful summer of 1945, the world was set for an era of peace, controlled by the two new superpowers America and Russia, which would be able to live in peaceful coexistence for decades to come.

There would be no need for the services of General Reinhard Gehlen and his mysterious, all-powerful *Apparat*. In short, the thin, balding, jackbooted German officer had failed. The amazing plan hadn't come off. In the postwar world of the victors there was no place for him and his vaunted forty steel cases of information about an ally. Gehlen was a thing of the past. As the GI guards jeered, he was *"kaputt."*

10

On the morning of September 6, 1945, a desperate Russian, Igor Gouzenko, was walking the cold gray streets of the Canadian capital of Ottawa wondering if he had not just made the biggest mistake of his life. Together with his wife and infant son, he trudged the streets looking for someone to talk to. But apparently no one was prepared to listen.

He had already tried at the city desk of the *Ottawa Journal,* but the copy editor he had seen had turned him away brusquely, thinking he was just another "goddam foreign crank," thus missing the greatest story of his journalistic career.

Igor Gouzenko was not just another immigrant among the many who flooded the streets of the Canadian capital. He was a Soviet diplomat, admittedly a minor one, but at that moment one who carried with him priceless information, soon to set the whole Western intelligence network buzzing.

Igor Gouzenko, aged twenty-six, was a cipher clerk at the Soviet Embassy in Ottawa. His record showed him to be a card-carrying, disciplined Communist who had gone through the Komsomol, the Young Communist League, entering the Moscow School of Engineering from whence he had graduated to Soviet Military Intelligence. In short, he seemed to be an utterly reliable young Communist, ideally suited for his task of worrying in the code room at the Embassy, which was sealed off even from high-ranking members of the Embassy who did not possess a clearance.

Indeed, upon arriving in Ottawa in 1943, Gouzenko had been a convinced Communist, but his stay in the Allied country had changed all that. Not only had he and his wife Anna come to love Canada, which possessed so many riches in comparison with his starving, war-torn homeland, but he had also come to hate his superior, Colonel Zabotin.

Nikolai Zabotin, otherwise known as the likeable military attaché, was in reality the Soviet master spy in Canada. At the very time that Canada and Russia were fighting a major war in Europe. Zabotin was engaged in spying on his ally, seeking in particular— apart from their normal military potential—details of the American and British nuclear operations.

The news came as a shock to the young cipher clerk, through whose hands much of this information passed preparatory to it being forwarded to Moscow for decoding. But the years passed and Gouzenko did nothing until that fateful day in 1945, when he was informed that he was to be posted home.

For a while Gouzenko was paralyzed into inactivity. Then he had a second chance. His sailing was postponed. It was at this time that Anna, who shortly before had given birth to a son, went to work on him.

"This is your chance to do something for this country and yourself, and most of all for Andrei and the new baby," she urged in the privacy of their apartment. "Canada is to be our home. Let us not take everything and give nothing."

"What can I do?" Igor asked her helplessly.

Anna told him.

On the afternoon of September 5, 1945, three days after the war with Japan had ended, Gouzenko spent the hours selecting several hundred top-secret Russian documents, pertaining to their espionage activities not only in Canada but throughout North America. With the material hidden under his shirt, Gouzenko, frightened out of his life at his boldness and the terrible consequences for him if he were found out, locked the door of room 12, his office, behind him, and left the Soviet Embassy in Ottawa for the last time.

But nobody seemed to want his information.

On his first visit to the *Ottawa Journal,* he was told to go to the Royal Canadian Mounted Police. But Gouzenko did not fancy taking his tremendous story to the Mounties. He tried the *Journal* once more, and again they turned him down. Anna now took over, and with a selection of the vital papers in her handbag, she called at several Canadian Government offices, only to find the same lack of interest.

One high official told his assistant, "Tell the Russian to go back to the Russian Embassy with his papers." And with that the two young traitors and their infant son found themselves once more on the streets of the capital.

Now thoroughly confused and badly scared at what might at this very moment be happening back at the Embassy, the couple could think of nothing better to do than to return to their small apartment in the suburbs.

And they were right. When Gouzenko had still failed to report for duty by the afternoon of that day, a wave of apprehension swept through those in the know in the Soviet Embassy. A badly-frightened Colonel Zabotin called his secret espionage people together and hurriedly demanded to know if they knew anything about Gouzenko's absence from room 12.

They didn't. Zabotin, who was well aware what would happen to him in Moscow if he had slipped up, ordered an immediate search of their top secret files. It confirmed the old soldier's fears. A number of highly confidential and potentially highly explosive documents were missing!

Zabotin acted. It was an act of desperation and he knew that it meant his recall to Moscow once the Canadian authorities became aware of it, but he saw no other alternative. He sent one of his men with his chief assistant to Gouzenko's apartment on Ottawa's Somerset Street. They were to position themselves there in civilian clothes and size up the situation. Once they had come to a conclusive decision about Gouzenko, they were to act.

The two hulking embassy agents in their heavy gray overcoats set off at once and thirty minutes later were seated on a park bench on Somerset Street keeping the front door of the apartment building under tight observation.

By this time, Gouzenko, almost frantic with fear, had finally found someone who would listen to him. He had appealed to his two nearest neighbors for help. One of them—a sergeant in the Royal Canadian Air Force—had called the police; the other had taken in the frightened Soviet trio, and only just in time.

Late that same evening, the two Russians, aided by a further couple of hulky reinforcements, rapped on the door of Gouzenko's apartment. When the Russians received no reply, they forgot their diplomatic manners and immediately applied their hefty, discreetly gray shoulders to the door. It splintered and they were in.

Thus it was that the cops from the Canadian Police patrol car found the four "diplomats" busily engaged in ransacking the Gouzenkos' apartment when they hurried up the stairs to investigate the Air Force sergeant's call. As "diplomats," the crestfallen Russians were allowed to depart while the Gouzenkos cowered fearfully in the next apartment, but now at last the

Canadian authorities took the medium-sized twenty-six-year-old cipher clerk seriously.

The week-long interrogation of Igor Gouzenko started the next morning, and in the course of the next weeks would be attended and continued not only by British military and secret intelligence agents, but also by representatives of the U.S.A. What Gouzenko had to reveal was not only of vital importance to Canada (so much so that Canadian Prime Minister Mackenzie King could tell the Russian, "You have accomplished an historic act. The people of Canada and the world are your debtors"), but also to the United States.

Apart from information on Canadian troops, submarine warfare and the use of the new proximity fuse shells which had knocked the Japanese Air Force out of the skies in the last months of the war, Gouzenko's testimony revealed that there was a whole Russian spy network established throughout North America whose task it was to find out what they could about the atom bomb.

In the next months, agent after agent was arrested. They included a Labor Progressive member of the Canadian Parliament, Fred Rose, key civil servants, Dr. Raymond Boyer, French-Canadian millionaire and one of the foremost chemists in the world—*and* Dr. Nunn May, the British nuclear scientist!

This was the breakthrough. Weedy Dr. Nunn May had been working on atomic energy for several years and for the last two had been employed at the great experimental plant at Chalk River, Ontario. Not only had he obtained samples of uranium for Zabotin which the latter had found so interesting that he had ordered a special plane sent in from the Soviet Union to pick it up, but he had also given the Russians his store of knowledge on the theory of atomic energy. Together with the information supplied by German refugee Dr. Klaus Fuchs, this would soon be sufficient for the Russian scientists to construct their own atom bomb. Perhaps it is not suprising, therefore, that immediately after the cipher clerk's defection, the Russians ordered their agents in North America to lie low and take up some other form of less dangerous employment for the time being.

The grim-faced American officials present at the Gouzenko and Nunn May interrogations now realized that the Russians were not only eager to share top secret information for the purpose of defeating their wartime enemies Germany and Japan; they also wanted to use it against their current allies. For instance, the telegram sent by Colonel Zabotin to Moscow about Nunn May's disclosures, which fell into Canadian hands, contained a specific reference to the Hiroshima explosion. From this it was clear that the British scientist could not have thought that the Soviet Union would use the information the rest of the telegram contained except against its erstwhile allies, the United States and the United Kingdom. Why else would Russia need the information now that the shooting war was virtually over?

That September in Ottawa really heralded—at least for a few farsighted officials in Washington—the start of the cold war. What Churchill had vainly been trying to convince top American leaders from Roosevelt down through General Marshall to General Eisenhower for the last eighteen months or so was now a reality: the enemy of the future, once the Axis had been defeated, would be Soviet Russia. In Washington this handful of officials began to ask themselves what exactly they in fact knew about Soviet Russia. The answer was usually the same—*nothing!*

During the war, the American Army had sent an American military mission to Moscow under the command of Major General John R. Deane, whose main task it was to coordinate the military efforts of the two allies in Europe. Theoretically Deane was to have access to Russian military plans so that he could advise Eisenhower in Paris accordingly. In practice, it never turned out that way. Deane was hindered in a dozen different ways. Indeed, he never had any real success in learning Russian military intentions until as late as March, 1945, when it suited the Russians to let him know their future strategy. And as far as gathering any other information on Russia went, Deane's office proved a failure.

Otherwise, the United States had nothing. No organization, no group of individuals—nothing which could provide them with reliable information about their erstwhile ally. Four years before, Mussolini had joked about the American secret service that "it is the best in the world because no one knows where it is." And, as Roosevelt had glumly confessed to Major General "Wild Bill" Donovan, when he had asked that lawyer-soldier to form the first wartime intelligence service: "Bill, you will have to begin with nothing. We have no intelligence service."

Donovan's organization, the OSS (Office of Strategic Services), had had some outstanding successes in the course of its four-year wartime existence, but its efforts were directed solely against the enemy. Although on paper its beat was the whole world, ranging from China to Latin America, in practice it was limited to the major battle areas in Western Europe and the Pacific. Even if the OSS, which grew to cover not only intelligence, but counterintelligence, sabotage and commando activities, had wished to spy on Soviet Russia, it had only a handful of Russian linguists available and virtually no trained Soviet experts.

In addition, the OSS was a wartime creation that had hardly shaken itself down to serious work when it was wound up. Its ranks contained too many adventurers, playboys and unworldly college professors so that its losses were unreasonably high, in many cases, for the amount of information that it brought in. It lacked professionally-trained officers such as were available to the British, Russians and Germans.

As Hanson Baldwin, the military historian, has noted: "Much balderdash has been written about the 'brilliance' of the work of the O.S.S. Some of it was brilliant—particularly in Switzerland and some of the work in China and Southeast Asia—but much of it was inefficient, some of it stupid, and for a considerable part of the war, we were dependent upon the British for much of our secret information."

Thus, those few officials in Washington who were in the know about Soviet Russian intentions that fall were faced with the almost insurmountable problem of where to obtain reliable, detailed information about this potential new enemy in the light of the Gouzenko disclosures.[1]

Soon, however, a senior American officer three thousand miles away on the other side of the Atlantic was going to solve the problem for them.

---

[1] Igor Gouzenko went into hiding after the Nunn May trial. He never "surfaced" again. Presumably he is still living in some suburban Canadian community under an assumed name.

11

That man was Brigadier General Edwin Luther Sibert, G-2 to General Bradley, commander of the U.S. twelfth Amry Group in Europe for most of the campaign in Northwest Europe.

General Sibert, a handsome forty-eight-year-old former military attaché and West Point professor of military science, was relatively new to intelligence work. He had replaced Colonel "Monk" Dickson, Bradley's G-2 for the last two years, in August, 1944, and dogged by bad luck and a lack of "nose" for the intelligence situation, had been unfavorably compared with his brilliant predecessor throughout the European campaign.

At first he was diffident about pressing his views because of Dickson's experience. Later, when everything that came from Eisenhower's Supreme Headquarters emanated optimism, he tended to decry Dickson's pessimistic forecasts, so that the relationship between the First Army intelligence chief, Dickson, and Sibert, was never very good.

Sibert had started out very badly indeed. On August 12, 1944, Patton telephoned his boss Bradley to tell him, "We've got elements in Argentan. Let me go on to Falaise and we'll drive the British back into the sea for another Dunkirk."

Apart from the crack about Montgomery's Canadians' slowness in linking up with his own fast-moving

Third Army, Patton indicated by his call that he believed that the time was now ripe to bottle up the remaining German troops in western France at Falaise (later to be known as the Falaise Pocket).

Bradley vetoed the move. "Nothing doing. You're not to go beyond Argentan. Just stop where you are and build up on that shoulder. Sibert tells me the German is beginning to pull out. You'd better button up and get ready for him."

On Sibert's advice, Bradley believed that nineteen German divisions would stampede through Patton's lines, so Patton was stopped and many of the Germans got away, due to what Ladislas Farago, Patton's biographer, has called "one of the gravest intelligence blunders of the war".

Silbert stumbled again three months later when in November he accepted the suggestion of U.S. OSS agent Allen Dulles's chief adviser, German-American Gero von Gaevernitz, that he should recruit captive German generals who would try to contact their opposite numbers on the other side of the line and convince them to surrender. Sibert went to work swiftly and recruited a Lufwaffe general named Gerhard Bassenge who was prepared to organize a committee of captive German officers to start the contact operation, but Washington vetoed Sibert's suggestion. He was told that there would be no fraternizing whatsoever with these Nazi officers.

Sibert's greatest blunder was that he completely failed to warn his chief, General Bradley, that there was any possibility the Germans might ever again be in a position to counterattack on the Western Front.

As Bradley was later to write: "By this time I commanded almost three quarters of a million men on a 230-mile front. It was impossible for me even to scan the intelligence estimates of subordinate units. As a consequence, I looked to my own G-2 and to the

Army commanders to keep me informed on the enemy's capabilities."

G-2 Sibert slipped up, and as a result, the Germans were able to launch the Ardennes Offensive which resulted in 80,000 American casualties and came as virtually a complete surprise to the U.S. commanders. Later, Sibert's role in the prebattle intelligence was investigated and he came in for some ciriticism, but again he weathered the storm and by the time the war ended, he had established himself as chief of intelligence in the newly occupied American Zone of Germany.[1]

But the Ardennes reprimand rankled. The quick-minded, thoughtful intelligence chief still believed that if Washington had let him retain the contacts with the Germans which he had begun to make in November, 1944, he might well have received from them information helpful in his assessment of the enemy's pre-Ardennes intentions. For the realist Sibert, all means— even contact with the enemy—were justified if they helped him to form a better appreciation of the enemy's capability and plans.

Now, in the summer of victory, the enemy had been defeated and most of the general's time was spent in routine investigation of alleged sabotage of American Army installations, Nazi war criminals, and half a dozen minor issues which paled when compared with the vital assignments which had faced him during the war. General Sibert, established in his headquarters at Kronenberg, was bored.

While General Sibert was killing time in Western Germany, things were moving in the far north around

---

[1]In all fairness to General Sibert it must be pointed out that Eisenhower's own intelligence chief, General Kenneth Strong, the British officer who was the best Allied intelligence man in the West throughout the war, has written of Sibert's role in the Ardennes: "In my opinion, this criticism was unmerited and unfair. He behaved throughout with cool deliberation and never to my knowledge gave me bad advice during the whole battle."

the town of Flensburg which had been the headquarters of the last German "government" under sharp-faced Admiral Dönitz.

Even before Dönitz had been summarily arrested and flown off to far-off Mondorf in Luxembourg to await his trial as a war criminal, a delegation of Russian officers had appeared at Flensburg. Under the command of General Trussov, the four-man Russian team was more concerned with rooting out German secrets than representing their country at Flensburg while the Western Allies wound up the Dönitz "Government."

The Russians fastened onto ex-Major Borchers of the German Demobilisation Team, and insisted he tell them what he knew of the Foreign Armies East. Finally they got the information out of him that the man who would know would be "General Gehlen who is probably somewhere in the south."

The Russians then asked if the Foreign Armies East had any representatives at Dönitz's HQ.

Borchers replied, "Officers of the Foreign Armies East are still here." Whereupon the Russians ordered that Borchers should reappear the following morning at ten o'clock sharp with these officers. They wanted to question them.

Major General Rooks, Eisenhower's representative at Flensburg, got to hear of the Russian interest in Foreign Armies East. The man who had been sent to the North Sea port to wind up the Dönitz Government as soon as possible, despite Churchill's objections (the British premier presumably wanted to keep Dönitz in power as a bulwark against the Red Army, for there were still a good million German soldiers "interned" in the area), scented he was on to something interesting here. He ordered his own officers to find the Foreign Armies East officers still in Flensburg.

On May 19, four days before the Dönitz Government was finally wound up, mild-mannered General Rooks's officers arrested Lieutenant Colonel Scheibe of Gehlen's office. He revealed the presence of some of the steel cases containing the Gehlen documents to Lieutenant Colonel Austin of the U.S. Army.

By now, the Americans began to find this mysterious German Army organization Foreign Armies East, of which most of them had never heard up to this moment, highly intriguing. Like the Russians, they started to ask, "Who the hell is this guy Gehlen?" Finally, in the last week of May, the order went out: Find EX-GERMAN GENERAL REINHARD GEHLEN!

It took some two months before he was found. The CIC order circulated unsuccessfully throughout the American Zone of Occupation, until Colonel William R. Phillip of the G-2 section, commandant of Oberursel Camp, finally found it on his desk one fine day in the first week of July.

For a while Philip stared at the notice thoughtfully, then he remembered the case of the German general who had been handed over to him the previous month. The skinny staff officer with the deep-set blue eyes had repeatedly requested to be allowed to speak to a senior intelligence officer; he had (or so he stated) some information of the greatest importance to pass on. No one had taken him seriously—neither the CIC nor Philip himself. Was this the Gehlen they were looking for?

In the end Philip decided it was, and a few days later he had organized a meeting between the thin German ex-general, still clad in his gray-green uniform stripped of all badges of rank, and the highest-ranking American intelligence officer in the Zone—Brigadier General Edwin Luther Sibert.

Sibert took in the German's haggard, almost undernourished face which, despite the brilliant sunshine that had been shining all July, was deathly pale. Sibert had seen faces like that before—in the still, noiseless, slightly dusty backrooms of university libraries and the planning sections of higher headquarters. He realized that he was in the presence of an "egghead" and planner to boot.

He nodded to his aide who was going to do the interpreting, (as he recalls of that meeting: "Gehlen's English was not very good nor my German either"). "Tell him he can start," he ordered.

Gehlen needed no urging. He had been waiting for this moment for months now. Swiftly he plunged into a potted history of the activities of Foreign Armies East. Then he went on to give his estimate of the Soviet Union's present war potential. He predicted that the Russians would use all means in their power to turn those countries presently occupied by the Red Army, ranging from Hungary to Eastern Germany, into Communist states. The Russians wouldn't even hesitate to attempt a Communist putsch in the zones of the Western Allies—Britain, France and America—if they could bring it off. On and on he went, finding an unusual fluency of speech, engendered by the long months of frustrated imprisonment and the knowledge that this was his chance.

Sibert listened in complete silence, the only indication that he was listening to the monologue being an occasional movement of those sharp eyes of his. Then Gehlen paused for breath, his exposé presumably finished.

Sibert straightened up in his chair. "You know a lot about the Russians, General," he commented laconically and leaned forward to see Gehlen's reaction.

Gehlen's professional honor was offended. Quickly he assured Sibert that (in the latter's words) "he had some documents and files hidden away somewhere and he was the only one who knew where they were." They would prove his statements. He continued that he also had officers everywhere in Allied PW camps; if they could be collected together, he could use them and the network they had built up in the East to start their old job once again—*this time for the benefit of the Americans!*

Brigadier General Sibert did not bat an eyelid at this outrageous, unprecedented suggestion which implied using an enemy to spy on an erstwhile ally and friend. His sole comment was, "I'll see what I can do for you, General."

But a little later, when Gehlen was ordered by his accompanying officer to turn about and leave the room for the truck that was waiting to take him back to the Oberursel Internment Camp, General Sibert rose to his feet and, to the astonishment of the other American officers present, shook a surprised Gehlen's hand.

Today such a gesture means little but in July, 1945, when the newspapers of the Western world were decrying all Germans as Nazi barbarians who made soap out of their concentration camp victims, and each new day brought fresh and more terrible revelations of the extent of Nazi cruelty, it was a highly significant gesture indeed.

Gehlen walked out of the room as if he were treading on air. For the first time in months he felt something akin to happiness. *He knew now that he had made a convert of the American general!*

Sibert had learned over the last year as G-2 to General Bradley to be careful—very careful indeed. That summer he still remembered Washington's irate reaction to his suggestion that he should employ German officers in the Allied cause. This time he decided to feel his way cautiously before he reported to Washington. As a result, General Sibert did not report his meeting with Gehlen or the latter's amazing offer to his superiors. Neither Bradley nor Eisenhower was informed, nor even General Walter Bedell Smith, Eisenhower's red-haired, fiery-tempered chief of staff. For some inexplicable reason, he did tell General Kenneth Strong, Eisenhower's British intelligence chief, that he "was making arrangements to exploit captured German Intelligence archives using German officers for the purpose. Among these was General Gehlen." As Sibert himself said later: "I only informed my superiors of Gehlen's value for us later when I was certain of it."

Proceeding very cautiously and under the strictest secrecy, he ordered that certain of Gehlen's officers should be released from their PW cages temporarily in order to dig up the hidden suitcases with their vital documents. One by one they returned with the mission completed and handed the documents over to Gehlen, who in the first week of August was finally able to present a complete and detailed exposé of the Russian Army and its war potential as it stood at the end of World War II.

Now Sibert was fully convinced. He acted immediately. He informed Bedell "Beatle" Smith. We do not know the chief of staff's first reaction to the news, for he is long since dead; but we do know that the man who one day was to be head of the CIA had told his close friend General Strong in the final days of World War II that "though he would always remain my personal friend, I should bear in mind that the United States regarded Russia as the country of the future and his official co-operation would be with them. Britain was old-fashioned and out of date. The war had finished her and the Americans must ally themselves with the nations of the future."

Surprisingly enough in the light of this attitude, Smith, who always maintained that "someone had to be an S.O.B. around here (he meant Supreme Headquarters) and it might as well be me," did not explode into one of those famous rages of his. Instead, he quietly got in touch with certain people in Washington who might be interested in what Gehlen had to say.

They were. So, right under the nose of General

Eisenhower, whose major wish now that the war had been won was to coexist peacefully with the Soviet Union, "the nation of the future," General Gehlen, Lieutenant Colonel Scheibe, Major Horst Hiemenz, Major Albert Schoeller, and Gehlen's old friend Colonel Heinz Herre and a Herr Stephanus were smuggled out of occupied Germany. Some time in that August of 1945, the five Germans arrived in Washington. They were going to stay there for nearly a year.

12

The German officers who were to be sent to the States were hastily fitted out with threadbare civilian clothes instead of their gray-green Wehrmacht uniforms. But the U.S. Army Quartermaster Service could not find civilian suitcases for them and they had to improvise as best they could with whatever they could lay hands on in the camp. Colonel Stephanus, for instance, had to make do with a violin case in which to carry his bits and pieces, and the whole group of them, Gehlen couldn't help thinking, "looked like a music group or something similar."

They flew to the States in General Bedell Smith's own plane, but in spite of the fact that this was the first trip for any of them to the States, their mood was depressed save for an amusing half hour in the Azores where they were forced to land to refuel. Assuming that the chief of staff himself would be on the plane and knowing the red-haired general's equally red-hot temper, the base commander hastily assembled a guard company which presented arms to the Germans hidden in the big four-engined plane (their conducting officer would not let them get out during the stopover).

Neither was their mood relieved when they arrived in Washington. After undergoing a health test, they were driven from the airport to their destination in a sealed Black Maria. As General Gehlen recalls in his memoirs: "Naturally this type of 'reception' disappointed us, especially as in the next few days nothing happened and our nervous tension began to rise." He was forced to use "my whole eloquence to keep my comrades balanced." Nor did it help to discover that the "Truman Hotel," as they called the camp some ten miles outside Washington which housed them, was bugged.

Gehlen reported the mikes to the young officer in charge of them, a Captain Erikson, whom he found *sympathisch*.

Captain Ericson cried, in his fluent German, "This is unbelievable! I'll find out who did this!"

It turned out that the culprit was the camp commandant, curious to know who these strange prisoners in civilian clothes were in the midst of a camp dedicated to grilling high-ranking German officers for military information. Erikson must have "pulled brass" because the bugging and other harassment ceased from then on.

Still, the Gehlen group was getting nowhere. Occasionally they were cross-examined about their activities in Russia, but only by minor officials or low-ranking officers, and even when these were ready to cooperate with their wartime German enemies, they were prepared to do so only to a very limited extent.

The big break for Gehlen came in February, 1946, when Soviet troops suddenly occupied the northern part of Iran. That month one of the examining officers exploded in Gehlen's presence and snapped, "The American doesn't like to be taken for a sucker!"

As Gehlen later recalled: "The occupation of North Iran was for the Americans a decidedly unjust, illegal act and led to the sudden realization that the Soviet Union was not developing—as they believed—into a peaceloving nation."

Thereafter the Americans were prepared to listen to and accept his suggestions about a new anti-Soviet intelligence service, based on his own former organization. The group was taken out of the camp and allowed to wander around Washington seeing the sights like the many thousand other "rubbernecks" who flooded the nation's capital that spring. One wonders what many of the veterans spending a few days in Washington on their separation leave would have said if they had learned that the shabby, skinny little man in the crowd of sightseers at, say, the Capitol, was a lieutenant general in the army they had just defeated preparing now to spy for the victors. But they did not know. The only men who knew were a handful of very influential civilians whom General Gehlen still protects to this very day. In his memoirs, written a quarter of a century later, all that he says about that period of his life after the Soviet take over in Iran is: "All in all this stay of several months in the USA was useful to prepare us—not only in our special field but also in human relationship—for our mutual operations later on so that we could gain confidence in one another—something which is vital for this difficult and discreet activity."

One highly discreet and purposely vague paragraph, not one word more, to describe the amazing espionage operation which was planned in Washington that spring between the deadly enemies of a few months before.

We know little of what went on in those long months that Gehlen and his associates spent in Washington. Understandably, no one on the American side particularly wishes to be connected today with a deal that had strong undertones of conspiracy about it, especially as it was concluded with a man who had served Hitler loyally for twelve years. Allen Dulles, for instance, who undoubtedly had a hand in the negotiations with the Germans, never once so much as mentions Gehlen in his entire book on espionage,[1] although Gehlen became one of his chief collaborators when Dulles was later appointed head of the CIA.

What is definite is that Gehlen and his ex-officers

---

[1] *Craft of Intelligence.*

were subjected to examination by a committee of G-2 and OSS experts. Under the leadership of "Wild Bill" Donovan, who had fought with New York's 69th Regiment in France in World War I, and gained his nickname there on account of both his martial and amorous ability, the committee was made up of men such as G-2 General Strong, OSS's Allen Dulles and its strategic analyst, Professor Sherman Kent; Brigadier Magruder; New York lawyer Loftus Becker; ex-banker Walter Reid Wolf; and perhaps half a dozen leading soldiers and civilians loosely or intimately connected with intelligence work.

These men were in the main, like Dulles, Republicans and from wealthy backgrounds. They had helped fight one war against the Germans, and were not prepared to see the new peace endangered by what they were readier to see as the "Red Menace" than their Democratic fellow-citizens, especially those surviving "New Dealers" in high places who had still not recovered from their flirtation with Communism in the heady, "progressive" attitude of the late thirties and early forties.

Now they were prepared to listen to this pale, intellectual-looking ex-general, who two months before had been their deadly enemy but who bore with him detailed evidence of the "true" intentions of the former ally. For them, his revelations must have confirmed the belief that many of them had held ever since the early twenties that the "Communist conspiracy" really existed.

But they were careful. To this day very little is known exactly about where Gehlen stayed during this period of interrogation and cross-examination, and even ten years later, *Time* could report that "lips snapped shut" at the Pentagon at even the slightest mention of Gehlen's name; during that year Gehlen ceased to exist —at least for the outside world.

Most commentators on his life at that time conclude,

however, that Allen Dulles and G-2 General Strong had a decisive say in Gehlen's employment. (One cannot rule out the possibility that J. Edgar Hoover played a role in that decision as well; the FBI, which was traditionally anti-Communist, was represented at some of the negotiations.)

All that we really know is the outcome of that year's evaluation in Washington, and this comes from circles close to General Gehlen, who naturally would want to present his activities in Washington, which some Germans might regard as being opportunist, if not worse, in the best possible light.

This outcome was as follows: the new espionage organization which Gehlen would form would be exclusively German; it would not do anything that might endanger or harm German interests; and if and when Germany ever again became a sovereign state, the Gehlen Organization would have the opportunity to revert to this new state. As for the Americans, the OSS would finance the new organization and have the right to direct its intelligence activities in unearthing information needed by the United States.[2]

In any event, ex-General Gehlen returned to his ruined homeland in the second week of July, 1946, with the order to revive his old Foreign Armies East department—or what was left of it—and set it to work to gather as much information as possible, both military and political, on Russia and the other Eastern Bloc states. "Organization Gehlen," which was going to monopolize espionage against Russia and her satellites for the next decade and a half, had been born.

---

[2]To some extent it is clear that Gehlen did not leave the United States in 1946 with such a clear-cut mission as was later maintained by his friends and advocates. That summer Baun, who was already working for the Americans, noted after a conversation with Wessel: "Gehlen would also be prepared to work under you [Baun] if you make it."

At the start, Gehlen proved a disappointment for his new masters who, if the rumor is true, were paying with Chesterfields and Lucky Strikes, a much more stable currency than the mark in those far-off black-market days. A year had passed since the Foreign Armies East had fled westward before the advancing Russians, and when he tried to contact his carefully planted agents on the other side of the Iron Curtain, Gehlen found they had either been captured, disappeared, or were not interested, being too concerned in those hungry years with the simple, overwhelming task of finding food to keep body and soul alive.

However, Gehlen was ever resourceful and, forgetting for the time being the plan to set up a network of agents in the Iron Curtain countries themselves, he concentrated on sheer routine work on the same lines as had first brought him results in 1942, when he had been posted by General Halder to Foreign Armies East. He gathered together those of his former staff who were prepared to work for him in Schloss Kranzberg, located in the lonely Taunus forest not too far from Wiesbaden, and in a hunting lodge in the same area; there he planned his first operation.

Its essence was simplicity and careful interrogation, followed by detailed analysis on the part of his old-time staff officers. In 1942, he had proved to Halder that the large-scale accumulation of a host of minute details—which in themselves were unimportant and valueless—could yield an exciting and worthwhile intelligence dividend once they had been subjected to the trained mind of the professional staff officer, capable of making a meaningful whole out of the myriad pieces of the jigsaw puzzle.

But where would he find the equivalent of the many hundred thousand Russian prisoners of war who had been available to him in 1942, his officers wanted to know. After all, they had been the first people to open up Soviet Russia to the German intelligence; cajoled, threatened or bribed into giving little snippets of information here and little snippets of there.

Gehlen had an answer for his staff officers that summer. It was simple. *"Die Plennis."*

"Plennis" was the name that the ragged, starved hundreds of thousands of German PWs in Soviet Russia had given to themselves, taking the word from the Russian term for prisoner of war, just as the Anglo-American PWs in Germany had once called themselves "kriegies," from the equivalent German word, *Kriegsgefangene.*

Now with increasing frequency, these former German soldiers were returning to the defeated Germany. Day in, day out, the bell that heralded their crossing of the zonal frontier range at such camps as Friedland in the north, and out they came, swarming from the beflagged, flowerbedecked trains, staring wide-eyed at their weeping relatives, some of whom had not been seen for years.

Before they could be reunited with their families, however, they had to report at the camps to receive civilian papers, ration cards, civilian clothes—when they were available—and a few worthless marks.

Shuffling forward in their thick winter-felt boots (if they were lucky), or in cloth rags (if they were unlucky), they would move from one blanket-covered table to the next, receiving a ration card here, an identity card there from the officials with white armbands, until finally they came to a table in one corner of the huge, echoing hall were a sharp-featured civilian with no armband but with all the characteristics of an ex-regular army officer sat holding his pencil poised to take down their answers. They had arrived at the representative of the Gehlen Organization!

More often than not, these ragged ex-prisoners had nothing to tell their interrogator. Confined in the wastes of Siberia or down in the bowels of some Don coal mine, the plennis had seen and heard nothing save hard work and even harsher words from their Russian guards; their sole concern, where their next bowl of watery soup or straw-filled hunk of black bread was coming from.

But some of these emaciated men had heard and seen things of importance. By learning Russian, and keeping their ears open while working in the Russian officers' messes, or driving their Soviet masters about, they had heard things not intended for their ears. Others had been employed in top-security Russian ports and factories or near military installations, where the former panzer soldier might note a different type of tank from the old T34 that he had fought in battle, or the ex-Luftwaffe pilot hear a howling aircraft engine which sounded like no propellor plane he had ever flown during his military flying career.

Often these men who had valuable information were wary of the strange civilian with his pencil poised ready to take down their answers. But the skilled interrogator soon disarmed them and dispelled their suspicions. He would ask them about any traitors they had known in their camps. It was an opening gambit that always worked. Most of the plennis were only too eager to name names; stool pigeons and opportunists were universally hated by the ex-prisoners. Dutifully the Gehlen man would note their names (possibly these men might one day turn out to be Soviet agents, they consoled themselves as they took down the unimportant information).

With this completed, the Gehlen man would lean forward confidentially and, using the familiar "thou" form common among soldiers, would whisper out of the side of his mouth that although he was working for the *Amis,* what he was doing was really in "Germany's interest." And if this appeal to the man's patriotism did not work, the Gehlen agents' offer of *Ami Zigaretten* usually did.

In those days, an American Camel or Chesterfield

was worth two and a half dollars, and tobacco-starved plennis would all but have sold their own mothers to get their hands on an *Ami Zigarette* after years of smoking black Russian tobacco wrapped in bits of coarse newspaper. And if these informants had really outstanding information, the Gehlen man was empowered to offer them a can of Spam and a loaf of American white bread, unbelievable luxuries in the Germany of that time.

Soon the first pieces of significant information started to appear among the flood of routine details which the Gehlen field workers sorted in their Taunus headquarters.

One day a Gehlen agent came into conversation with a ragged, yellow-faced ex-Wehrmacht corporal who produced from his "rucksack," made of an old Russian sugar sack, a strange-looking cigarette lighter. The Gehlen ex-officer's eyes fell on it at once. It seemed to be made of stone, a reddish-brown stone.

Taking the ex-corporal to one side after the main body of plennis had moved on, he asked him where he had gotten his "souvenir."

Proudly the ragged prisoner explained that he had found the stone on the refuse dump of a "secret factory" which the German PWs were not allowed to enter. It had been his job, however, to transport the waste from the factory with his little horse and cart to a nearby special dump. During one such trip it had struck the bored German PW that the reddish-brown stone had a strange property: you could strike sparks off it like you could off flint.

With all the time in the world and spurred on by the shortage of matches, the corporal had fashioned a cigarette lighter out of the stone and, in the months that followed, had managed to smuggle the lighter from camp to camp. He had even managed to get it through the final search by the Russians before they had been released. Now he wanted to keep this single souvenir of his years in Russia to show his children in the days to come.

But Gehlen's agent did not allow him to keep his souvenir. He was curious about the properties of this strange stone which, although it was not flint and was relatively soft, could give off sparks when struck.

He offered the man twenty cigarettes for it.

The prisoner refused. It was all he had left from all those dreadful years in Russia. Gehlen's man raised his bid, but the corporal remained firm. In the end, the agent offered a whole carton of Camels. In those days this was the equivalent of a fortune. In 1946, you could buy a woman for a week with all you could drink and eat for two hundred Camels. His faded eyes suddenly bright with greed, the corporal accepted the extravagant offer, grabbing the shiny carton before the other man changed his mind.

That same night the stone was sent off to the Taunus.

Gehlen's staff and their American associates were just as puzzled by it as the corporal had been. As they had no facilities to examine its chemical properties, it was flown to the United States a few days later.

Time passed. Then one day, Gehlen's organization received a curt note requesting them in future to forward radioactive material only in specially sealed lead containers.

The ex-corporal had been walking around for months carrying a piece of radioactive material! More important, Washington knew now that Russia was well advanced in the nuclear race; the treachery of Nunn May, Fuchs, and half a score of American traitors was already paying dividends.

By the end of 1946, Gehlen felt that he had exhausted the information he could obtain from the plennis. After all, their position in Russia had been a passive one; they had not deliberately sought information. In-

Young Gehlen at the cavalry school in Hanover in the late twenties.

The newly-married Captain Gehlen with his wife Herta, daughter of a long line of Prussian military aristocrats.

Sergeant Hans Putzer, who led Gehlen's first commando paradrop behind the Russian lines in 1942. The mission failed, as the Russians were waiting at the dropping zone. Twenty-two-year-old Sergeant Putzer and two Russian renegade associates escaped and struggled back nearly 800 miles to the German lines. The journey took over three months. Putzer was awarded the Iron Cross.

A Gehlen agent at work, planting information at a "dead letter box" from where it would be taken a stage further by another agent.

Martin Bormann, Hitler's secretary, was believed killed in Berlin in 1945, yet he has been sought ever since all over the world, from Soviet Russia to South America.

Towering, scarfaced Colonel Otto Skorzeny of the SS, who in 1943 rescued Italian dictator Mussolini from Allied captivity in a daring airborne operation. In the last years of the war he aided General Gehlen with his subversive operations deep in the heart of Russia.

General Reinhard Gehlen, head of the Foreign Armies East, inspecting Russian auxiliaries during World War II. The officers around him are Russian renegades, who were part of his plan to raise a large anti-Communist Russian army to fight against their mother country.

BUNDESARCHIV, KOBLENZ

The results of Hitler's refusal to accept Gehlen's forecast that the Russians would attack in East Prussia in January, 1945. Raped and massacred peasants in one of the villages which changed hands many times in the bitter fighting.

IMPERIAL WAR MUSEUM, LONDON

British paratroopers staring down at a Werewolf man they have just shot because he fired at them. In the latter stages of the war, General Gehlen was concerned that this Nazi partisan army should be built up into a powerful postwar force to plague the Allies. His efforts did not meet with success.

Patton was one of the few U.S. commanders at the end of the war who was outspokenly anti-Russian. At this time, Eisenhower, the Supreme Commander, still hoped he could get along with the Russians.

TIROLER KUNSTVERLAG

Left: This picture illustrates the type of terrain, which was too rugged and forbidding to encourage the advancing men of Patton's armies to enter, where Gehlen thought he and his staff officers would be safe.

Bottom: The lonely alpine hut in Bavaria where General Gehlen hid out at the end of the war until he was betrayed to the Americans.

DER SPIEGEL

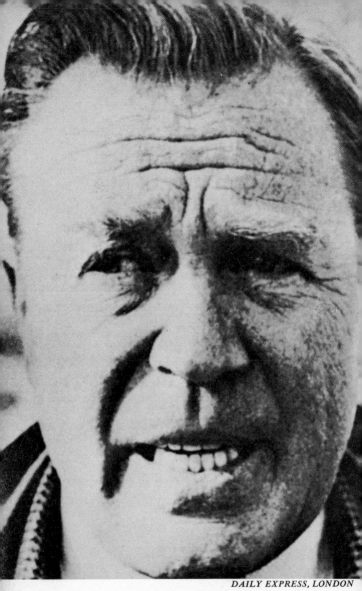

Otto John, head of the BFS, whose fight with Gehlen for the control of Federal Germany's intelligence services ended with John's defection to the East.

Left: Stefan Bandera, the head of the Ukrainian anti-Communist movement and ally of General Gehlen. He was assassinated by Soviet professional killer Bogdan Staschinski in Munich.

Bottom: General Luther Sibert, General Omar Bradley's Chief of Intelligence at the end of World War II, and the man who brought Gehlen out of the PW camp behind Eisenhower's back in July, 1945, and gave Gehlen the opportunity to start his amazing postwar career as the spy of the century.

ULLSTEIN

Top: One of the rare photographs, taken by a Soviet agent, of Gehlen, here swimming in a Bavarian lake; behind him in the boat are his bodyguards. It is rumored that magazines like *Time* and *Newsweek* offered thousands of dollars for such pictures in the fifties.

Bottom: Another Soviet picture. Gehlen in his later years, disguised behind dark glasses and wearing a mustache. Behind him is his favorite Mercedes.

Top: Two of Gehlen's foremost enemies. Wilhelm Zaisser (first on the left), the "General Gomez" of Ernest Hemingway's *For Whom the Bell Tolls,* was head of the East German Secret Service in the fifties. Next to him (in uniform) is Erich Mielke, his successor and Gehlen's foremost opponent.

Bottom: The retired spymaster, General Gehlen, today.

CHART I THE GERMAN ESPIONAGE SETUP IN RUSSIA, 1942-1945

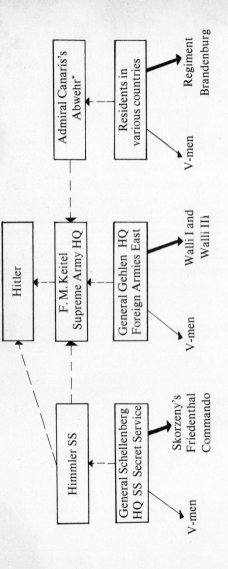

Legend:
* = Army's espionage service
━━➤ = Military operational arm in enemy territory
──➤ = Agents (V-men, literally "trusted men") in enemy territory
---➤ = Information going back to Hitler

CHART II THE FIGHT OF THE GEHLEN ORGANIZATION AGAINST THE SSD, MID-1950s

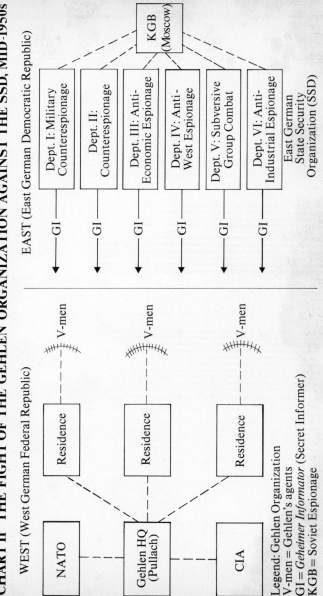

WEST (West German Federal Republic)

EAST (East German Democratic Republic)

KGB (Moscow)

Dept. I: Military Counterespionage

Dept. II: Counterespionage

Dept. III: Anti-Economic Espionage

Dept. IV: Anti-West Espionage

Dept. V: Subversive Group Combat

Dept. VI: Anti-Industrial Espionage

East German State Security Organization (SSD)

GI

GI

GI

GI

GI

GI

V-men

V-men

V-men

Residence

Residence

Residence

NATO

Gehlen HQ (Pullach)

CIA

Legend: Gehlen Organization
V-men = Gehlen's agents
GI = *Geheimer Informator* (Secret Informer)
KGB = Soviet Espionage

CHART III THE STRUCTURE OF THE BUNDESNACHRICHTENDIENST

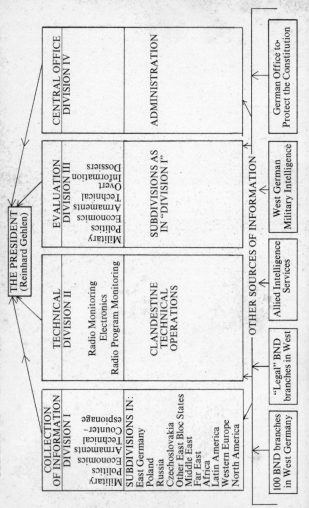

THE PRESIDENT
(Reinhard Gehlen)

COLLECTION OF INFORMATION DIVISION I

Military
Politics
Economics
Armaments
Technical
Counter-espionage

SUBDIVISIONS IN:
East Germany
Poland
Russia
Czechoslovakia
Other East Bloc States
Middle East
Far East
Africa
Latin America
Western Europe
North America

TECHNICAL DIVISION II

Radio Monitoring
Electronics
Radio Program Monitoring

CLANDESTINE TECHNICAL OPERATIONS

EVALUATION DIVISION III

Military
Politics
Economics
Armaments
Technical
Overt Information
Dossiers

SUBDIVISIONS AS IN "DIVISION I"

CENTRAL OFFICE DIVISION IV

ADMINISTRATION

OTHER SOURCES OF INFORMATION

100 BND branches in West Germany

"Legal" BND branches in West

Allied Intelligence Services

West German Military Intelligence

German Office to Protect the Constitution

stead, they had had it forced upon them. Besides, their numbers were beginning to dry up and, although there were still many thousands of Germans still imprisoned in Russia, they were now coming into the camps only in dribs and drabs.

His masters, although they were well satisfied with what he had obtained from the PWs, were more interested in events closer to home. The American zonal authorities' relationships with their Soviet opposite numbers on the other side of the River Elbe, which marked the border between the western and eastern zones, were becoming more and more difficult; and the American Military Mission in East Germany was not doing a particularly good job of supplying details of what was going on there. There was talk of mass collectivization, the establishment of an East German paramilitary formation, a persecution of all anti-Communist opposition—all signs that the Russians seemed to be transforming their zone of occupation into a Communist satellite. But the American authorities in the West did not know for certain what was going on and they *had* to know if they wanted to plan their own strategy accordingly.

Gehlen was given the order: "Find out what's going on over there." The time had come to change over from passive to active intelligence. Reinhard Gehlen now had to build up his first postwar network of agents if he was going to do the job the *Amis* expected him to do successfully.

13

By the spring of 1947, there was already a steady stream of civilian refugees flowing across the border of the Russian Zone of Occupation into those controlled by the British and Americans. In those days there was no Wall, only a three-hundred-mile-long wire barrier, complete with minefields and "death strip," running the length of Germany and separating the country into two great halves. At that time, it was still comparatively easy to flee the Soviet Zone, either by taking a train into East Berlin and from there a streetcar or subway to West Berlin; or by struggling across the "green frontier," as it was called, the rugged wooded areas, which the Russians found it hard to guard, and which could usually be safely passed during the night.

As a result, the refugee camps that dotted the border area were filled that spring with haggard, poorly clad fugitives from the Russian Zone of Occupation, who were only too eager to give vent to their hatred and anger at the Russians and their German underlings. Under the patient questioning of the Gehlen men (and women too;) the general now found it was necessary to employ women to obtain information from the female refugees), the men and women who had "voted for democracy with their feet" and had sacrificed everything they had in their flight, began to talk. A myriad of details of what was happening on the other side of the Iron Curtain was duly noted and forwarded to HQ. Collectivization, nationalization, troop movements, repression of non-Communist political parties, erection of new concentration camps, a special political prison at Bautzen—the interrogators could scarcely take down quickly enough the wealth of detail which came pouring from the bitter lips of these refugees who now had to start life anew with what they had managed to carry across the border in their shabby rucksacks. But Gehlen, back at headquarters, analyzing the daily reports, knew that these admittedly firsthand accounts were not enough. By the time the information reached him it was already dated—perhaps even out of date. He needed up-to-the-minute information and he could only obtain that from sources *on the spot*.

The order went out to the Gehlen field workers: try to find out addresses and names of those refugees left behind who might be prepared to work for us.

Speedily his field workers started to obtain names of likely agents who could be asked to West Berlin, to the small obscure hotels and bars generally frequented by the Gehlen men, and invited to join the Gehlen Organization, whether for money or sheer patriotism.

Names began to pour in, ranging from high-ranking Soviet Zone officials, whose apparent acceptance of the Communist regime was only a cover for a deep-rooted hatred of the new masters in the Kremlin, to do-nothings prepared to jeopardize their own kin for money—or preferably in the days of the black market—for cigarettes and coffee.

Within a matter of weeks, Gehlen had built up his first *"V-Apparat"* which was based on the "tipper" and the "researcher." The researcher, a full-time member of Gehlen's staff, worked in the refugee camps, where he was continually on the lookout for tippers, who might suggest a name for the new spy ring. Neither of these people ever learned what happened to the tip, whether it had been accepted or not, for it was passed on to the next person in the *Apparat*—the "recruiter."

The recruiter would make the actual contact with the potential agent and, if he found him suitable, engage him as a "V-man"—a *Vertrauensmann*.[1] This completed, the recruiter would probably never see the V-man again. From now on, he would deal with the Gehlen Organization direct, reporting and receiving instructions by means of "dead mailboxes" (holes in walls, tree stumps, certain dusty reference books in public libraries, for example,) agreed upon in advance.

In his turn, the V-man would also be expected to build up his own private spy ring of V-men, as well as *Quellen*, or "sources," agents who would penetrate the enemy's espionage or secret police organizations, or would spend their time verifying and double-checking information obtained from other sources, and, in a few cases, agents employed in sabotage—so-called *S-Quellen*. Once the V-man had succeeded in building up his organization, he would now receive the title of *V-Mannführer*, or "leader."

As the cold-eyed spymaster back in the West saw it, this form of organization would prevent anyone knowing too much about the work of other members of the Gehlen Organization. Each V-Group would be limited in its numbers so that if any one cell was broken by the enemy, its members could reveal each other's identities and that was about all. Even if the head of the cell betrayed the name of the man who had recruited him, it did not really matter much; by then the recruiter would be safely lodged somewhere in the West where the secret police could not arrest him, and already busily engaged in building up another ring to replace the one that had just been broken up. With the

---

[1]Literally "confidence man"; a term borrowed from the old wartime secret service, meaning basically a "trusted man."

abundance of names that the tippers were bringing each new day, he did not need to fear any lack of new agents.

The young V-man, who four years before had been a fighter-pilot himself in the German Luftwaffe, wandered—apparently aimlessly—through the woods, bending every now and again as he found a fresh mushroom to add to the collection he already had in his bag. It was a warm afternoon and beads of sweat collected along the base line of his blond hair. But the sweat was not just the result of his warmth; it was also caused by the overwhelming knowledge that he could be discovered any moment now!

The place was the Russian airfield at Schönwalde, not far from Berlin. For weeks now, the V-man had been hearing strange noises from the direction of the field. Once he had actually seen a strange shape hurtle across the summer sky, filling the air with its harsh whistling sound. It was gone almost before he saw it, but it had seemed to him that the plane, or rocket —or whatever it was—had no wings. In any event, it had been like no plane he'd ever flown or seen during the war.

His curiosity had been aroused, so he had contacted the man who had recruited him in the west, a retired Wehrmacht colonel, and told him that he intended to find out what this strange Russian machine was. But to do that, he needed a camera, preferably a Leica.

The colonel had warned him. Better not risk his head, especially if he were discovered near an airfield with a camera hidden in his clothes, but the ex-pilot's curiosity had been aroused and he persisted. Far away in the safety of the West, his recruiter had given in, and a few days later the V-man received his Leica. He could make the attempt.

Now, with the camera hidden beneath his jacket, he wandered ever closer to the field, his eyes apparently set on the ground in search of the brown, sticky, gleaming heads of the mushrooms among the moss, but his ears permanently cocked for that strange whistling sound which would herald the approach of the plane. It was a good cover he had chosen, and he knew it. Normally anyone found wandering about the countryside in such a slow manner, especially in the neighborhood of a military establishment, would be suspect; but not a mushroom picker.

As the afternoon wore on, the V-man felt his shirt sticking to the small of his back every time he bent down, and he longed to take his jacket off, but he dare not; he needed it to cover the camera. He licked his cracked lips for the hundredth time and told himself he would treat himself to a barrel of beer, even the weak zonal stuff, if and when he ever got away from here. Slowly he circled the field. There seemed not a soul about. It was Saturday afternoon, and everybody who could, would be in Berlin. But still he kept up his pretense; at this very moment someone might be watching him through binoculars from the barbed wire enclosure which marked the field.

Then abruptly, there it was. The howling noise!

He swung around as quickly as he dared. A gleaming silver shape shot through the hard blue summer sky at a tremendous speed. He had never seen anything like it in all his wartime flying career. It was going to land.

The agent threw a quick glance around him; the countryside seemed deserted. He dropped his bag and flung himself behind the nearest tree. It was poor cover, but the best available. With hectic, nervous fingers he fumbled with the camera. The plane—he recognized it was a plane now—was coming in to land. He could see the undercarriage coming down. Hastily he focused. Then there it was; huge and silver in his lens. Crazily, panting as if he were running a race, he clicked the shutter. With a shattering whine and rush of wind, the silver bird swooped over his head and was gone, disappearing behind the trees.

The young ex-pilot sat down suddenly. He was trembling all over. He breathed out hard. *He had it —he had it!*

Then suddenly his mood of triumph vanished as quickly as it had come. He could hear voices. Russian voices!

Cautiously, noting automatically that his hands were trembling, he raised himself. Less than twenty yards away, hidden from him all the time by a grove of pines, he saw to his horror that there was some kind of bunker with a thin aerial sticking up from its roof. But there was nobody in sight. Whoever was speaking Russian was inside the bunker. He made a quick decision. Raising his camera, he took a quick shot of the strange, almost completely hidden building. Then realizing his luck wouldn't hold out much longer, he hid the camera, seized his bag of mushrooms and hurried away, while he still had a chance.

One day later the agent's photos and information were in Gehlen's office, causing heated discussion and worried frowns among the U.S. liaison officers attached to his HQ.

What the ex-pilot had photographed was the first Soviet jet fighter—the MIG-15, which had been developed by Russian designers Mikoyan and Gurevich from information about the German Me-262s captured by the Russians from the German Dessau manufacturing plant in 1945. For the first time, the U.S. Air Force realized that the Russians had a serious rival to their own first operational jet-fighter the F-86 —the Saberjet.

Once the news hit Washington, an immediate order flashed back to Gehlen: "Get more details." In particular, the Air Force generals wanted to know details of the plane's fuel and electrical systems, as well as its armament and speeds.

Gehlen did not hesitate. Another group of agents were set to work to find out what Washington wanted to know about the Russian jet-fighter.

Thus it was that a slow Russian military freight train chugging its way through Saxony was stopped a few weeks later near the industrial city of Chemnitz. It was night, and Russian soldiers guarding their precious freight were tired, but in the rear guard-car, a young private popped his head up inside the tower from which he could survey the length of the train in front of him.[2] The night was pitch-black. He could see nothing. There was no sound save for the steady puff-puff on the steam locomotive. It looked like a routine halt to him. He yawned and then disappeared back to his bunk. They'd probably be moving on again in a few more minutes. Perhaps trouble up the line. The overworked, under-repaired tracks were always causing trouble, he knew that.

Seconds after he disappeared, a stealthy figure, dressed in black from head to foot, clambered onto the car some fifty feet away which contained fuel. Swiftly the man unscrewed the cap on top of the car. Hastily a beer bottle, attached by a piece of rope, was lowered into the darkness below. It was empty, and the man could hear the faint gurgling sound as it filled with liquid from the car. Then finally the sound died away, and the beer bottle was full. With nervous fingers he dragged it up. He pulled off the rope and snapped the cap shut. Dropping to the ground lightly, he ran along the gravel track to the tense,

---

[2]During the war the Germans had attached a guard-car to most of their trains. It had a kind of tower with slitlike openings from which the train guards could fire on partisans, etc. The Russians borrowed the idea from the Germans.

waiting engineer. A few whispered words were exchanged and he handed the man the carton of Lucky Strikes. There was the clank of gears, and noisily the train began to move forward again. The man in black watched it for a moment, then he disappeared into the shadows.

The long supply train gathered speed. Minutes later it had disappeared altogether and the Gehlen agent was sitting in the waiting car which would take the precious beer bottle across the frontier that same night.

Now that the Gehlen men knew what kind of fuel the MIG 15, the Russian top-secret jet used, they were eager to find out about its construction. For this, Gehlen had his HQ staff check through their files for the names of former plennis who had once worked in Russian aircraft factories. In particular, he wanted the names of those who had been employed in the Tiflis plant, where, he suspected, the MIG was built.

They were able to find a score of such men who had now returned home and were living in West Germany. One by one these men were visited by the Gehlen agents, who after introducing themselves as employees of the U.S. Military Government, using the papers and ID cards that the Americans were now allowing them to carry, asked the former plenni to send everyone else out of the room prior to questioning.

In most cases they drew a blank. The former PWs had been too hungry or too concerned with simply keeping alive to worry about the nature of the metal used in the Tiflis plant. But then they struck luck.

The most unlikely ex-PW turned out to be the one who gave them the vital information. He was a Bavarian farmer, living in a remote Upper Bavarian village, who spoke with such a thick dialect that the Gehlen man could hardly understand him. Sitting together in the farm kitchen with its rough wooden table and

four hard-backed chairs, its only decoration a cruci-
fix on the whitewashed wall, the Gehlen man tried
to get the ex-plenni to refresh his memory about the
months he had spent in the Russian airplane factory.

The agent decided that it was no use trying to hedge
with the simple-minded, unshaven farmer; he had to
put it to him directly. According to the dialect-speak-
ing Bavarian, he had worked in the machine shop with
some form of light metal. "Did its surface gleam or
was it dull?" the Gehlen man asked.

The farmer looked at him stupidly and rubbed his
heavy, unshaven chin.

"Were the edges sharp or smooth? Did it get a sort
of white covering when you left it out in the rain?" The
Gehlen man tried one approach after another, but apparently all were in vain. The farmer stared at him
in blank incomprehension until finally the Gehlen man
gave up.

Then the Bavarian spoke in his thick, slow dialect.
"I never looked at the stuff all the time I was there,"
he said. "But you wait a minute." While the Gehlen
agent stared at him, he rose slowly to his feet and
stomped heavily into another room, where he could be
seen searching through the objects contained in a
roughly hewn unpainted farmer's chest. "What the devil
is he looking for?" he asked himself, puzzled. A little
while later he had his answer.

The farmer returned with what looked like a bowl.
He placed it on the bare, food-stained wooden table
in front of the agent. "There's your metal," he said
proudly.

"*What?*" the agent croaked, hardly daring to believe his ears. Apparently, the then-plenni had shaped
the bowl from the metal used to build the MIG 15
because he was sick of eating his daily ration of thin
Russian soup from an old food can. Secretly he had
taken a piece of the precious metal when no one was
looking and had shaped it lovingly when everyone else

was having their midday break. Thereafter no Russian had ever suspected that the stained, scratched bowl was anything other than a mess-can. As a result, the Bavarian farmer had been able to get it through the last Russian search before he had been released to the West.

The agent recovered quickly. For what seemed to the farmer in the poverty-stricken wood-and-plaster farmhouse the huge sum of fifty marks, the bowl changed hands and Washington's chemists were soon hard at work trying to establish the alloys in the metal.[3]

So the secret war went on, with Gehlen's agents in the Russian Zone of Occupation, aided by a large number of Soviet citizens who hated their masters, notching up victory after victory.

They discovered that Russians were secretly training a large force of East Germans for "police duties" which included training in the use of heavy artillery and tanks. They discovered the exact location and strength of virtually every major Russian Army formation in the Zone, and discovered those among the Soviet officers and officials who were dissatisfied with the Communist regime; those who hated the thought of returning to Russia, and regarded East Germany as an ideal jumping-off spot for defection to the West.

Thus it was that as the forties began to draw to their close and West Germany was made into a sovereign state again as a result of the cold war, the Americans, and in particular the newly created CIA, started to regard Gehlen the former Nazi general, as their

---

[3]When the MIG 15 turned up in Korea, the American authorities already knew much about its weaknesses and strengths, but they were still prepared to pay North Korean pilot Kum Sok No the enormous sum of $100,000 on September 21, 1953, for delivering an intact MIG to them.

primary source of information about what was going on in the East. Gehlen and his organization were established now as the "eyes of the CIA." beyond the Iron Curtain. *He had arrived.*

14

While all this was going on, the character of the Gehlen Organization was changing. Slowly, Gehlen was beginning to realize that he could no longer operate solely with the aid of the staff officers from his old organization, Foreign Armies East. The ex-staff officers had neither the knowledge to analyze the flood of economic information he was receiving from the East, nor did they have the political background necessary to help them understand and interpret the complicated political machinations of the Soviets behind the Iron Curtain. Too many of them were apolitical staff officers who regarded themselves as "military technicians" and felt no need to learn anything more about the changing postwar world.

As a result, Gehlen had to begin hiring new personnel—economists, political analysts, political warfare experts, and former SS and SD[1] agents who were not so chary about getting their hands dirty as were the professional officers. By 1949 military titles were dropped altogether in the Pullach HQ of the secret organization.

Here, in a walled-off community which had once belonged to the organization run by the former deputy of the Führer, Rudolf Hess, and guarded by heavily armed GIs, the two hundred Germans employed by

---

[1]Nazi Security Service

Gehlen lived a completely sealed-off life. They had their own mess, stores, living accommodation and even schools for their children. Everywhere, a practice which had been frowned upon by the old Army was introduced. Wives, children and intimate friends were encouraged to take jobs at Pullach to avoid having to employ office personnel not closely linked to the members of the organization.

Gehlen, who had now dropped his military title of general and called himself Dr. Schneider (a good cover as there were then about two thousand Dr. Schneiders in West Germany), knew that the system smacked of nepotism, yet it was better than having his security compromised by strangers. Accordingly, he allowed his own son to work in the organization's labs, and encouraged his secretary to marry his own cousin.

Pullach, the mysterious high-walled settlement just south of Munich, had become one big family, but not a very pleasant one; the new men who had come to join it had brought with them the hard, brutal, unscrupulous methods of their former organizations, well aware that Gehlen's influence with the *Amis* protected them from any unpleasant queries about their political past.

Naturally Gehlen knew about their pasts, and that by now some twenty percent of his staff was drawn from the SS and SD. Later he was to comment on the many charges made by Soviet propagandists that his organization was a Nazi one: "it's all a propaganda campaign with which the Communists hope to discredit me." But there was no denying that by this time he was employing people like Wilhelm Höttl, ex-SD chief Kaltenbrunner's orderly and associate of mass-murderer Eichmann; former SS colonel and liaison officer between Himmler and wartime German spy chief Admiral Canaris; Kirschbaum; ex-SS Brigadier General Franz Six, who had been congratulated and promoted by Hitler himself for his "outstanding services" with the SS in Russia. As *die Deutsche Zeitung* was to write many years later: "It is evident that the Americans were forced to close their eyes when it came to making political decisions about the personnel of the Gehlen Organization."

He knew too that some of their practices in the Russian Zone of Germany were nothing short of blackmail. For instance, he learned of the case of a young school principal who had agreed to help a colleague who had fled to the West. One day the principal was invited to West Berlin, where a couple of agents were introduced to him by his ex-colleagues. The four men set off on a tour of the local bars, with the two strangers paying each time for the drinks but insisting that the principal sign his name to the bill. When he inquired why, they told him they needed the signature for their "expenses". A few weeks later the principal received a letter from the strangers. In it they threatened that if he did not help them in their espionage activity, they would turn over the signed bills to the Russian authorities; the latter would conclude that he had been working for Gehlen and that the bills were payments for services rendered.

In another case of blackmail, a former Wehrmacht officer who was now living near a large East German city was told that he *had* to work for the organization. The ex-frontline soldier brusquely turned down the "offer"; he wanted nothing to do with spying. It was too dangerous. The V-man who had approached him grinned unpleasantly and asked him if he had felt that way near Leningrad in '41. The ex-soldier asked him what he meant and the V-man replied that he had information that during the war in Russia, he had been part of groups of soldiers employed in mass executions of harmless Russian civilians. With another unpleasant grin, he added that the Reds certainly would like to have that kind of information, wouldn't they?

The ex-soldier did not reply. He knew he was caught.

And while the nature of the personnel employed in the organization changed, so did its structure too, now that the Americans were paying in hard dollars for its services (some rumors set it at five million a year) instead of the groceries and cigarettes of the early days.

In essence, the Gehlen Organization at this time (its members called it the "Org," or "firm") was built up on a vertical plan, with the "central office" in Pullach under "General Director Dr. Schneider" running a series of "branch offices" all over West Germany. Some of these were disguised in the conventional way as "export-import" firms, others really did operate commercially, such as the ball-bearing plant offices in Düsseldorf or the carpet factory at Karlsruhe. These branches then worked the "residences"—full-time agents—in the East, who, in their turn, ran the V-man cells, which were usually limited to three to five agents and a somewhat larger circle of informants.

This business cover, dreamed up by Dr. Schneider, was excellent. The individual branches (some of which ran for years) paid taxes, issued a balance sheet and used normal automobiles like any other small firm, making them in no way different from similar firms in the same town. Unlike Pullach, which Gehlen knew would attract Soviet agents like flies once they became aware of its existence, the branches would go unobserved, so that agents could go and come without observation. If, however, a branch was discovered by the enemy's intelligence, then the branch would simply declare itself bankrupt, and that was the end of that particular collecting point for information. In a matter of days a new branch would open elsewhere in another town and under another totally different name.

And as a final precaution, Gehlen insisted that the couriers who took the information from the outside agents or branches to the Pullach "Head Office" should never know the source of that information. The couriers would collect the material either from a "dead letterbox" or from a "living one"—a middleman, who simply acted as a transmitter of material but never was active in the field.

As Gehlen saw it, the whole organization should be an unbreakable chain with invisible links. Thus it might happen that one East German office or organization might have two or three Gehlen V-men working and spying in it, but each would be doing so unknown to the other; they would all be working for different branches and residences. If one were captured, the others could continue their nefarious activities, secure in the knowledge that their captured "colleague" did not even know of their existence. And by this time, Gehlen, with ample money at his disposal, was well able to do just this. In fact, he *had* to do so because his agents were now reaching up to the top hierarchy of the new pro-Communist state, established in East Germany in October, 1949—the German Democractic Republic.

In April, 1945, when the war was still on and Russian soldiers were not yet masters of the capital city, Berlin, a Soviet plane landed not many miles away from the besieged city with a handful of Germans on board. This motley crew of Germans, some young, some old, some in Russian uniform, some in the badly fitting clothes of Soviet officials, were the men whom the Russians had already chosen (although the war was not yet over) to be the future "German" government of their section of the beaten country. Unlike the Western Allies, the United States, in particular, who were concerned solely with punishing the Germans for their "crimes against humanity," the realistic Communists, who had suffered most of all at Nazi hands, were not looking backward; they were looking forward to the future when they would need the Germans, if only to be their puppets. The main thing—East Germany was a Soviet satellite!

In the immediate postwar years these men, all long time German Communists, who had spent many yers in Soviet exile and were loyal servants of their Russian masters, carried out the Russian strategy skillfully. As they saw it, the Eastern Zone must appear to be a "democratic" state so, unlike West Germany which later banned the Communist Party, they did not ban the opposition parties. Indeed, they encouraged them to participate in running the country with the rest of the members of the "Anti-Fascist Democratic Front," created by the Soviet Military Administration.

Within the framework of the new German government of the Democratic Republic, then, there were not only Communists represented and the Socialists who had been forced to join them in 1946, but also members of what were thought in the West to be conservative parties. Admittedly, for every conservative in office or in a position of some importance, there were two Communists to watch him and "guide him along the right path"; but the fact still remained that there were non-Communists in positions of high authority all over the new republic in the first years of the 1950s, when the cold war was reaching its peak and the Americans badly needed information about Soviet intentions behind the Iron Curtain.

Gehlen was not slow to utilize this unique opportunity. Through agents in East Germany as well as through politicians in the West, who still managed to keep in touch with the members of their parties in the East, he cautiously approached a large number of people. Many were too scared to agree to help him. Others seemed to have believed the lies that the Soviet authorities had told them about free elections and the rights of democratic representation, and refused angrily to have anything to do with him. But there were some who agreed to help.

One such man was tubby, bespectacled, jolly Herman Kastner, a sixty-four-year-old former professor of law. Kastner had had the courage to defend enemies of the Nazi regime in the courts during the Hitler period and as a result had been arrested by the Gestapo. After the war he had formed the conservative, middle-class Liberal Democratic Party in Soviet-occupied East Germany, and instead of fleeing like so many of his colleagues when it became clear that it was becoming a Soviet satellite, he had soldiered on. In fact, the Soviets were proud of their potential opponent. Kastner became very friendly with the political adviser to the Soviet Military Administration General Semyonov, and with his aid quickly advanced in the hierarchy until finally he achieved the astounding position of Deputy Premier of the German Democratic Republic—astounding *because Herman Kastner was already working for Gehlen!*

It is not exactly known when Kastner was recruited, but it is pretty clear that an old friend from the days when they were both persecuted by the Nazis convinced him that "you helped a lot of people under Hitler. You've got to do it again. Above all they must get to know in the West what's going on over here."

The friend did not specify who "they" were, but the ex-professor was no fool; he could guess who they were: Gehlen and his American employers. Naturally a man of his caliber was not going to lower himself to the role of a skulking back-street agent. Kastner preferred to limit himself to supplying information about economic and political events in the East, with now and again a few juicy tidbits about the "upstart, uncultivated" (as he saw them) Communists in the government, which included the detail that the East's "hanging judge," "Red Hilde"[2] read in the Talmud by candlelight with Bach music playing in the background

---

[2]Hilde Benjamin, longtime Communist and anti-Nazi, who became the state's chief justice and the terror of the anti-Communist opposition.

every evening after she had passed the death sentence.

For over a decade Kastner continued to pass information to Gehlen's men in Berlin, smuggled out weekly by his second wife, who hid the documents in her girdle and bra as she passed the smartly saluting East German police in her husband's official car on the way to "visit a friend in hospital." Then, early in 1959, he was dismissed from office. His information was no longer so important. Indeed, Gehlen began to suspect that Kastner was deliberately being supplied with false information or slightly "bent" pieces of news by the Russians in order to hoodwink the West. Kastner was dropped, his life coming to a nattural end without his espionage activity for the West ever being openly discovered.

"Brutus," another of Gehlen's key men in the East, was not so lucky. For Brutus, whose real name was Walter Gramsch, a balding, medium-sized man in his early fifties, had decided to spy on one of the toughest, most frightening men in the entire history of the German Communist Party—Ernst Wollweber.

15

Ernst Wollweber had a long career of aggressive political activity behind him which had started in the last year of World War I. In those dark, hungry days of 1918, pockmarked young Wollweber, who at seventeen had joined the Socialist youth movement and then transferred to the revolutionary Spartacus League,[1] organized a group of young terrorists to sink cement-filled barges in German canals so that naval shipping could not leave the North Sea ports.

Later, when in the first week of November, 1918, the German High Sea Fleet prepared to leave their harbors for one last desperate battle with the British, Stoker Wollweber incited the crew of his ship, the *Helgoland* to mutiny. The revolt caught on and spread to the other naval ports. One week later, with the High Sea Fleet paralyzed and its officers powerless, Stoker Wollweber, who hoisted the first red flag ever to be seen in Imperial Germany, rode triumphantly into Bremen in a truck of laughing, victorious revolutionary sailors. The Empire was *kaputt*.

On leaving the Navy, sharp-eyed Wollweber, who had now become a full-time member of the Party, used his rough tongue to whip the tough longshoremen of the Communist-controlled Seamen's International into shape. And if they did not obey its dictates blindly, Wollweber was not averse to pulling off his jacket, roll-

---

[1]It later merged with the German Communist Party.

ing up his sleeves and "convincing" his opponent with his bare fists.

Some time in the early thirties he went to Moscow to attend the top Soviet school for espionage and sabotage, and gained the reputation (presumably with the aid of practical exercises) of being the "best saboteur" in the world. But his real chance to put into practice what he had learned in Moscow came after the Nazis came to power in 1933. While most of the other top men in the German Communist Party fled the country and saved their skins or allowed themselves to be taken off to concentration camps by the Gestapo, Wollweber went underground and began to organize a Communist resistance.

He managed to avoid capture for a year. Then he escaped over the border one night to turn up some time later in Denmark. For the next few years his movements are vague, because he always traveled under an assumed name and with fake papers. But his enemies could not deny that his organization was a force to be reckoned with.

His sabotage organization, made up of a handful of Swedish, Danish and German Communists, all of them ex-longshoremen or sailors, effectively sabotaged or sunk over a score of Axis ships or those supplying the Axis powers. Wollweber's principal sabotage trick was simple but highly successful. It consisted of placing an explosive charge in the bilge between the holds and then fixing the timing mechanism so that it went off when the ship was safely at sea and the saboteur who had placed the charge had had time to change his place of employment (if he had done the job while working under the cover of a longshoreman).

So it came about in the late thirties that the Italian and German Ministries of Marine were plagued with a host of unexplained sinkings of vital tonnage; a mystery that was only going to be solved at Wollweber's trial later in Sweden.

Between 1937 and 1939, Wollweber was in charge of the "Organization Department" of the Comintern's Western Bureau. This sabotage outfit had its headquarters in a building on Copenhagen's main street, operating under the cover of a light engineering firm on the third floor, *while on the floor below, the Gestapo maintained one of its secret agencies under the guise of a radio company!*

In 1940, however, the Germans invaded neutral Denmark and Wollweber had to flee to Sweden. Here he continued his sabotage activities for nearly two years, devoting his work mainly to cutting the German railroad traffic through Sweden which that country had been forced to accept under Nazi pressure.

In January, 1941, he was finally caught by the Swedish police when he was linked to the attempted sabotage of a Finnish ship, the *Figge*. The details of that trial, at which Wollweber was sentenced to three years' imprisonment, were quietly forwarded to German intelligence by Swedish officers in their pay, including a frustrated Air Force Colonel Stig Wennerstrom, one day to become a Communist spy himself.[2] The Germans were pleased that Wollweber had finally been put out of circulation for a while and immediately applied to have him repatriated to Germany at the end of his sentence.

Wollweber knew what that would mean. Death in the rat-infested Gestapo cellars! For a while he despaired, until a friendly Swede, Dr. Harry Soedermann, a well-known criminologist known among the local crooks as "Revolver Harry," suggested a way out. Just

---

[2] Colonel Wennerstrom, who had been passed over by the authorities for promotion, decided to offer his services to the Russians so that he could "play a larger role in modern affairs." They made much of him, "promoting" him to major general and bestowing upon him three Soviet decorations. He was a useful contact and forwarded them excellent information on his own country as well as on NATO.

before his sentence was due to expire, he was to provoke a fight with one of the guards and hit him. This he did and, as "Revolver Harry" had rightly predicted, his sentence was lengthened by an angry judge who would not "tolerate this kind of thing." Twice Wollweber managed to prolong his stay in jail in this manner until finally Moscow stepped in to save him.

The Russian party bosses claimed that Wollweber had become a Soviet citizen way back in the early thirties. Then they filed a firm demand to the Swedish Government for Wollweber's extradition. According to their ambassador in Stockholm, Wollweber had embezzled state funds. The Swedes had no alternative. The "embezzler" was handed over at the end of his sentence to the Russians who naturally set him free at once.

In 1945, Wollweber, now putting on weight, returned to East Germany and immediately offered his services to the Soviet Military Administration. But the man who with his bald head and comfortable paunch looked like a caricature of a complacent, solid citizen, did not want a desk job. He had still not lost his taste for aggressive conspiracy. The Russians hesitated. They knew their Ernst. In 1946, they appointed him to the post of deputy director of the Department of Fleets and Harbors. But Ernst Wollweber had not been content just to supervise shipping, the working of the ports and the training of ships' officers, radio operators, and jobs of that kind. He wanted something which was more active.

Soon after he had established himself in his new office, he began to train ten percent of the recruits in his sea-officers' schools as potential saboteurs. There they learned all the old tricks that Wollweber had used in his marine sabotage days in the thirties, and a few new ones needed to cope with the new developments in shipbuilding. They were taught, for instance, how to mix sand in with the lubricants used in diesel motors, or how to fix sextants and compasses so that they put a ship hopelessly off course.

In the years that followed, these saboteurs spread out all over the world to carry out their nefarious duties. In the early fifties, a whole series of large British liners, for instance, could report the outbreak of mysterious fires. Even the two biggest ships afloat—the "Queens"—were not proof against these outbreaks. The mysterious fires and other forms of menace spread to the Royal Navy. Military vessels from destroyers up to aircraft carriers were hit by fires, damaged cables, complete breakdowns of electric systems, ruined boilers. British intelligence was powerless to deal with the outbreaks which could not always be traced to disgruntled seamen, who sometimes adopted this means of preventing their ship from leaving port. They sensed instinctively that they were up against sabotage, but they could not pin it on any one particular individual or organization.

Far away in Pullach, "Dr. Schneider" thought he could, however. For him the mysterious series of marine and naval acts of sabotage could only be the work of Ernst Wollweber, of whose record Gehlen was well aware; in his files Gehlen had a complete dossier on the Communist sabotage boss dating back to his 1940 Swedish trial (Sweden had been one of the countries covered by Foreign Armies East during the war). In addition, Gehlen had an ace up his sleeve. He had had an agent in the Department of Fleets and Harbors ever since 1947, one year after Wollweber had become its deputy director.

That man was Walter Gramsch, born in 1897, and a convinced Socialist all his life. When in 1946, Otto Grotewohl, the head of the eastern section of the German Socialist Democratic Party, agreed after four days of "discussion" (at the end of which he was, according to some sources, almost a physical and mental wreck) to merge his party with the Communists, Walter Gramsch was shocked. One year after the Soviet take-over of East Germany, he still hoped that there was a chance of establishing a democratic—and naturally socialistic—government sometime in the future. That was why he had remained in the East, instead of fleeing like so many of his colleagues had done in the face of Soviet threats and terror.

What was he going to do now? Should he cross the "green frontier"? Should he try to make a new start with his SPD comrades in the West? Walter Gramsch had been in a similar position once before, when the Nazis had taken over in 1933. Then, too, he had been forced to choose: either run away, or stay and hide your true feelings about the new regime. He had stayed; and in 1946, he stayed once more.

Capitalizing on the training he had received during the twelve long years of Hitler's domination, he concealed his real attitude toward the new Socialist Unity Party(SED), which had been formed from the Communists and the Socialists. As a result, the man who had, in the jargon of the day, a "clean vest," because he had not worked for the Nazis, was gladly accepted into the ranks of the new Communist bureaucracy. Swiftly he established himself as an efficient, loyal, hardworking official and began to make headway within the Directorate of Fleets and Harbors, going from one responsible post to another.

Sometime in late 1946, one of Gehlen's "researchers" got a tip from a refugee from the Soviet Zone that Walter Gramsch was not all that he seemed to be. Beneath his cover of absolute loyalty to his new master, he concealed a burning hatred of the whole Communist system. The researcher pricked up his ears. A man in Gramsch's position would be invaluable to the "firm." He passed on the information to his own particular "branch" and they set about making contact with their new potential agent.

The details of how that contact was actually made are still classified; all we know is that when Gramsch was asked by the Gehlen man what his cover name should be, the balding, hard-jawed official in his early fifties replied laconically, "Brutus." To his particularly cynical turn of mind, it seemed a highly suitable cover. *"Et Tu, Brute?"*

Brutus proved a highly competent source of information. Not only did he deliver details of Wollweber's sabotage school at the Sea School located in Klein-Machnow, and of their final training course at Ladebow, but he also forwarded them a profusion of highly classified material about Soviet merchant shipping, naval movements and security arrangements in the Baltic Sea.

The latter were particularly important. Gehlen and the CIA were already running in agents to lonely landing sites behind the Iron Curtain along the Baltic coast (where Gramsch assured them they would meet no importuning Soviet or German guards). With the aid of high-speed motorboats of the old German *Kriegsmarine*, manned by their former crews now working for the U.S.-controlled Mine-Removing Commando, these agents were dropped during the night hours, carried out their assigned tasks, and brought out a few days later with the material they had been able to gather.[3]

Brutus's aid went even further. By the early fifties, the American embargo on suppies of "strategic goods" to the Communist countries was hitting the expanding Communist economy hard. Many of the new processes

---

[3] One of the Germans involved was probably Wilhelm Ahlrichs, of whom we shall hear later, whose major claim to fame is that he was responsible for "Operation Pastorius," the landing of nine Germans in Florida by submarine in World War II to spy and sabotage in the United States.

and the machines that went with them had been developed in the West, not only in the NATO countries but also in such places as neutral Sweden and Switzerland. Yet if these latter countries delivered machines to the East, they risked losing their attractive and lucrative export orders to the United States.

East Germany in particular, was hard hit by the embargo. Prior to the war, the eastern part of Germany had been a primarily agricultural region. Now, under Soviet orders, it was to be turned into the East's major industrial power after the Soviet Union itself. To achieve this, East Germany needed machines. But where were they to come from?

Wollweber thought he had the answer. Using his contacts with old buddies from his longshore days in Hamburg, Bremen and Lübeck, he arranged for them to load goods bought in "neutral" countries without asking too many questions, and at the same time used their knowledge of the weaknesses of the local customs men to "grease" the transit of the forbidden freight eastward.

Brutus's information soon brought an end to the scheme. Longshoremen who sympathized with the soon-to-be-banned Communist Party of West Germany, were quietly rounded up and deposited behind bars. Neutral businessmen were firmly warned that if they continued to deal with the East, they would be placed on an international blacklist which would ensure that they never sold another machine or machine part west of the River Elbe.

With all the aces in their hands, Gehlen's men even played a malicious joke on the still unsuspecting Wollweber. Gramsch, alias Brutus, had discovered that the Communist Saboteur had spent a great deal of money to buy a large factory and its machine park in a West European country. Apparently it was his intention to use the factory as a base for future shipments eastward, after quietly forwarding its present stock of machines in the same direction. Aware of Wollweber's plan, Gehlen's agents allowed his front men to ship half of the parts to the East. *Then they clamped down on the other half!*

As a result, Wollweber was left holding a large number of incomplete machines, bought with precious foreign currency, and was still unaware that he had a traitor in his own camp who was sytematically sabotaging all his ambitious plans (by then half of the machines had arrived safely in the East).

For nearly seven years Gehlen was able to play this cat-and-mouse game with the burly sabotage boss, who one day was to become his most hated enemy as head of East Germany's own intelligence service. His efforts and those of many like him began to make themselves increasingly felt in the East. As Georges Penchenier could write in 1954 in the French newspaper *Le Monde*: "For the East Germans, he [Gehlen] is Enemy Number One, who is responsible for the constant sabotage in the mines. . . . He is the instigator too of the attacks on the Soviet forces of occupation and the anti-governmental campaign." A few years later, the London *Times* could echo the same sentiments when it wrote: "Gehlen . . . has already provoked insurrections, disorders and sabotage in East Germany." And even *Neues Deutschland,* the official East German paper, which was naturally loath to admit that the national security service and its counterintelligence department were failing, commented in 1953: "The Gehlen Organization has had several successes in the German Democratic Republic."

It was the understatement of the year, for in that year Gehlen was already ordering Gramsch and all other key agents in the East: "Report all war production measures in the German Democratic Republic, whether they are undertaken by the local authorities or the Occupation Power. Division of the labor force of the country into the various branches of production. Results of police or political measures taken by the local authorities and the Soviets on the attitude of the local population."

But there were, inevitably, failures. The number of agents captured by the Russians or their German underlings grew rapidly as Gehlen put more and more of them into action. Cases such as the one below began to be reported with increasing frequency in the East German papers:

JUDGE: Your mother knew about your espionage activities?

SPY WOLF OSTERREICH: Yes, she knew.

JUDGE: And your brother?

OSTERREICH: My brother was also an agent of the service [Gehlen's]. He was ordered to the German Democratic Republic with orders to commit economic sabotage.

JUDGE: There was also another member of your family in the Republic.

OSTERREICH: Yes, my other brother.

JUDGE: Now we have met this charming family, tell us a little about your uncle.

OSTERREICH: Since the spring of 1953 my uncle has also been a member of espionage organization.

JUDGE: Your mother too?

OSTERREICH: My mother too.

JUDGE: And your wife?

OSTERREICH: Yes, my wife too.[4]

If the situation had not been so serious—Osterreich was fighting for his life—there would have been something ludicrous, almost absurd about this family which (according to its head) was an intelligence unit of its own. But then the Osterreich family was made up of amateurs of whom the *Sunday Times* of London wrote at the time: "The West German Intelligence agencies

[4]*Neues Deutschland,* December 23, 1953

recruit an army of amateurs among the East German refugees. . . . Their vast resources enable them to keep a stable of agents which can be replaced easily when they are arrested by the Communist authorities."

Yet although Gehlen and his full-time agents, recruited from the SS and SD, were becoming hard-boiled by now and could forget the arrest of yet another amateur with a half-apologetic shrug of their shoulders, they could not risk the capture of their key men. So that when just after noon on October 29, 1953, a sweating, frightened courier came running into the Gehlen main office in West Berlin crying, "We're in a mess! They're arresting our men by the score," Gehlen sprang into action.

As soon as he learned at Pullach of the massive crackdown on his organization behind the Iron Curtain, Reinhard Gehlen knew that "Grell" had indeed defected and was now singing. Forgetting about the score of lesser agents whom he knew Grell would implicate, he radioed Berlin: *Evacuate Brutus and family immediately!*"

16

But who was "Grell"?

He was the most unlikely of secret agents in a profession naturally given to recruiting agents who would not stand out in a crowd. Despite his fearsome-sounding real name, Hans-Joachim Geyer (pronounced as *Geier,* the German word for "vulture"), was a short, bespectacled, tubby North German in his fifties. For most of his adult life Geyer, writing under the pen name of Henry Troll, had earned a comfortable living regularly turning out cheap novelettes, filled with crime, murder and gore; and in doing so had amassed a tidy little fortune.[1]

In May, 1945, the swarthy, squat little Red Army riflemen in their mud-colored uniforms brought Henry Troll's nice little world of make-believe crashing violently down about his ears. For the first time in his life Henry, who looked like a nice roly-poly bank clerk, encountered reality. In this world, when the gunman fired, his enemy really got hurt; and the blood that spurted from his body was real.

For several years Henry could not get over the shock. His "literary" production came to an abrupt

---

[1] At the time of this writing (1971), the West German TV is featuring a series of Geyer's "John Kling adventure stories." One wonders if Geyer is still alive to collect the royalties and fees from it.

stop. In addition, the Russians had discovered that he had joined the Nazi Party way back in 1928, so that they regarded him as a dyed-in-the-wool Nazi. He was turned out of his fashionable villa in the rich Berlin suburb of Falkensee and had to live with his wife and three children as best he could from what he could afford to buy on the black market.

In the late forties Henry started writing again—for a West German publisher—and soon the hard marks began to pour in, just as they had in the old days. But then Henry decided to join—of all things—the Gehlen Organization. He would change the fantasy world of his office for the reality of the outer world.

Today we do not know what prompted him to make this amazing move. The money wasn't so interesting. He could support himself and family well enough now from his royalties. He had no proven hatred of the Russians (as we shall soon see) that might motivate him to work against them. Perhaps his imagination ran away with him, nudging him to have some physical part in the kind of cloak-and-dagger activities he had been writing about for twenty years. In any event, he joined the organization in 1952 and was put to work in West Berlin under an agent named Alfred Paulberg.

The new operative, whose cover name was "Grell," which can be translated as "vivid" (again not a very apt name for such a basically colorless personality), worked in West Berlin as a "researcher," while his family remained behind in their East Berlin apartment —a cardinal blunder, and possibly the means that the East Germans used to force him to work for them.

For several months he proved a loyal and hard-working Gehlen staff member, so much so that overworked Polster (Paulberg's cover name) made him his assistant, and gave him the important task of guarding the spy cell's files at night. The double agent—by this time he was already working for both sides—had a skeleton key made for the door of the wooden closet which housed the files, and each night busily photographed the vital documents with his mini-camera.

Night after night, week after week he did this, with the names of Polster's agents and the details of the information they had collected being regularly forwarded to the Ministry for State Security on the other side of the Iron Curtain. And Polster, who had already inflated his "branch" to six times the size of a normal one, did not suspect a thing.

1952 gave way to 1953. Grell was beginning to like his new job. For the first time in his whole life he was really living an adventure, and with apparently little danger to himself. Then in mid-October, 1953, his boss asked him to interview applicants for a new secretary he needed. Obligingly, Grell set about finding a suitable girl for the supposed industrial concern which was the organization's cover. Naturally he did not want to interview the girls in the office until he was sure that he had found the most suitable applicant, who could then be told that she wasn't working for a commercial firm but an espionage outfit. So he decided to interview applicants in a West Berlin restaurant.

The little talks went well until one blond girl whom he interviewed was struck by the strangeness of an interview being conducted in a restaurant. The more she thought about it as she left the polite and exceedingly charming fifty-year-old Grell, the more she was convinced that he was some sort of representative for a white slave outfit. In that year there had been a lot of such cases in Germany. Finally she went to the police and reported her suspicions.

The local police took the would-be secretary for another spinster who saw "sex maniacs" in every harmless middle-aged businessman, but there had been a lot of press criticism of the Berlin police's conduct of white slavery cases of late and they felt they had to make at least a show of investigating the complaint.

At 10 A.M. on the morning of October 29, two plainclothesmen called at the boarding house where Grell lived in West Berlin. The double agent had not yet returned from his nightly labor of guarding—and photographing—the top secret Gehlen files. All that his landlady could report was that he was out of the house most nights; that was the only suspicious thing about her polite lodger. The two detectives tipped their hats and went on their way, deciding that there was nothing to the whole business.

Grell panicked when his landlady told him that the police had been asking after him. All that the elderly woman could report when Grell arrived one hour later was that two policemen had been inquiring about him. She knew nothing about the branch of the police from which they came—whether they were political police or not—and an extremely frightened Grell did not waste time asking. From his twenty years of writing "thrillers," he knew that time was of the essence once the police started inquiring about you.

As far as he knew, the two men had been counter-espionage agents. Perhaps they were already in his office checking through the contents of the closet together with a worried Polster. Throwing all his remaining microfilm into a grip, he opened his window and jumped out into the back garden. He knew from his writing days that the "cops" (as he was calling them in his own mind now) always watched the front of a house, but often forgot the back. He was right. There was nobody about. Cautiously the tubby middle-aged double agent crept round to the front of the house. In all the books he had written, the police agent always lolled "casually" under the nearest lamppost "idly perusing a newspaper." There was no one under the nearest lamppost to his boarding house. Nor was there any "figure with his hat pulled well down over his forehead" sitting in a parked car opposite. The street was deserted.

Grell did not need a second invitation. Hurriedly he scurried to the nearest subway station and took the first train going eastward. Minutes later he had disappeared from West Berlin and this history forever.

But his arrival in East Berlin did not go unnoticed. On the following morning, the East German papers, including the official *Neues Deutschland,* carried banner headlines, which this time were not devoted to a new record in the production of tractors or bags of cement, but the mass arrest of "West German Fascist agents and mercenaries of the CIA." According to the Communist papers, some three hundred agents had been captured by nightfall on the previous day and more arrests were still to come. Later it was demonstrated that the East German claim was highly inflated, but even the right-wing West German *Die Welt* of November 10, 1953, had to admit that Grell had taken with him the photographic record of the names and addresses of some sixty-five Gehlen agents.

One by one, some of Gehlen's most capable operatives were hauled in and transported away in the middle of the night in best Gestapo manner, handcuffed between two heavyset, leather-coated secret service agents to face torture, imprisonment and worse. Ex-Wehrmacht Major Werner Haase, for instance, who worked in Gehlen's West Berlin office. The spy, who was a trained engineer, had hit upon the brilliant idea of trying to lay a secret telephone cable between his agents and his HQ in Berlin.

At one point in the south of the former German capital, the two sectors, Russian and American, are divided by a sluggish stream known locally by the contemptuous name of "cow's ditch." Here there are few houses save for a weekend cottage or two and the little homemade sheds used by the Germans when they go gardening. It was an ideal spot to begin the hidden cable. Accordingly, Haase, who had been decorated in action several times during the war and was known for his bravery, decided that he would run the cable through the sluggish, slime-filled stream. The problem was how to do it.

Eventually he constructed a kind of toy boat which would carry the cable across to agents waiting on the other side in Soviet territory, who would immediately link it up to their own system. Then East and West would be able to communicate without the danger of couriers and the chance that the latter might be picked up as they crossed the zonal frontiers. It was a brilliant idea, as we have already said, but Grell's defection put an end to it before it even started.

The cable-laying operation was planned for the night of November 13. That evening Haase received the signal from the other side that his agents in the East were ready and waiting and he could go ahead with the task that had to be completed before dawn. Believing that everything was in order, the ex-major drove down to the lonely site after dark and began to prepare his little boat. But no sooner had he reached the bank of the sluggish stream, laden down with coils of wire and his boat, than two men sprang out of the bushes.

With a curse Haase went down in the wet grass. Vainly he tried to fight off the other men. To no avail. They were stronger, and he was hampered by the load he was carrying. In a matter of seconds he was over-powered and bundled into a car which carried him through the unguarded sector exit into the East. One month later, ex-Major Werner Haase was sentenced to life imprisonment.

But at the last minute, Gehlen's operators did manage to save Gramsch and his family. He was spirited away just in time. The man who, next to Kastner, was Gehlen's agent *par excellence* and by now a close personal friend of Wollweber[2] was snatched away under the very noses of the East German counterintelligence agents sent to arrest him.

So just like Grell, the man who had denounced him, Brutus disappeared from history, spending the rest of his life in the obscurity of a medium-sized German town, his identity always concealed because of the fear of reprisals, his career as a politician ruined.

We do not know Gehlen's reaction. The Grell disclosures and the hurried evacuation of key agent Gramsch could be regarded as a major disaster for the "Organization," since it would be many a long day before Gehlen and his employers the CIA would again find a man of Brutus's caliber. But by the end of 1953, after seven years of increasingly successful work for the Central Intelligence Agency, Reinhard Gehlen, West Germany's spymaster, could afford to ignore such failures. Besides, he was now preparing to change masters once again.

---

[2]Soon Wollweber himself was to fall from grace and during the course of the discussions and inquiries which led to his going, his friendship with Gramsch was often cited as an example of his "softness"—perhaps even his "collaboration"—with the West.

17

An American news magazine was the first international publication to make the world at large aware of the fact that Reinhard Gehlen was preparing to change allegiances. In its issue of July 12, 1954, *Newsweek* wrote under the heading of *Gehlen Future* (and after discussing a little of the "mystery man's" past): "On December 11, 1953, Gehlen himself appeared before a secret meeting of *Bundestag*[1] deputies and scored a considerable personal success. However, a bitter-behind-the-scenes struggle is being waged in Bonn as to the future of the Gehlen group. Some of it may be transferred to the E.D.C.,[2] if there is an E.D.C. There are also two plans.

"1. Make the organization the G-2 (in German nomenclature I-C) of the *Amt Blank*.[3] This course, naturally, is supported by Blank himself. It is strongly supported by parliamentary leaders, too.

"2. Put the group under Chancellor Adenauer's office. *Bundestag* members strongly oppose this because there would be no direct parliamentary control.

"Nevertheless, last March a tentative agreement was reached to put the Gehlen organization under the chancellery and the Finance Ministry agreed to foot

---

[1]The West German Parliament.

[2]The European Defense Community.

[3]The nucleus of the future West German Army, named after its boss Theodor Blank.

the cost between $4.5 million and $5.5 million per year. Adenauer is now reported to want to delay any decision."

Gehlen had, in fact, been considering the future of his organization for over a year now and, as *Newsweek* rightly reported, he was determined to return to the German service if he could. Since 1949, West Germany had been an independent state, and since 1950 it had had a planning office devoted to the reestablishment of a new German Army, if the Americans could ever get the French to agree to such a new force. This "Amt Blank," run by forceful ex-trade union leader Blank with the active support of Chancellor Adenauer, was already filled with former associates and employees such as his old wartime chief Heusinger;[4] and the latter reported to Gehlen that one day soon his old dream would be achieved—the reestablishment of a German Army.

Throughout 1953, then, with the prospect of a new German Army just around the corner, Gehlen was preoccupied with the problem of what exactly his role would be in this new organization. Friends like Heusinger, for instance, assured him confidentially that naturally he would be its new chief of intelligence. But Gehlen was too much a realist to believe this entirely. He knew he had many enemies in Germany and abroad. There were, among others, enemies in both government and opposition circles who believed that he was deliberately spying on them as part of his duties with the CIA and passing on his reports to wily old Chancellor Adenauer, always eager to get "more dirt" on his political enemies within and without his party. As one British secret service agent commented cynical-

---

[4] Although Heusinger claimed later that he had been employed as a "free-lance writer" after World War II, it is reasonably certain that he became an employee of his onetime subordinate for a while in the late forties.

ly: "Under the old set-up the Americans got the top copy and the Germans got the first carbon; now it's the other way round." He knew that the capital of the Federal Republic was full of malicious little stories about "Adenauer's FBI."

According to one story, a prominent politician had written to him as follows:

My dear General Gehlen:

I have reason to believe that my telephone wires have not yet been tapped by your service. All of my prominent colleagues in the *Bundestag,* I understand, have had their wires tapped for a long time. As I feel I am just as important as any member of the House, I wish to protest and I demand that the situation be corrected forthwith!

[True or not, politicians in Bonn were lifting up the receiver and beginning their conversations with *"Grüssen Sie* Gustav"—"regards to Gustav"—under the mistaken impression that Gehlen's first name was Gustav.]

Another bitter little story had it that a prominent politician was invited to dine at the house which Gehlen now kept in Bonn for his dealings with the West German government. Just as the important guest sat down to dinner, his eye fell on a neat little card next to his plate. It read, according to Gehlen's enemies: *"Do not hesitate to speak frankly. The butler will be shot after dinner!"*

But it was not only the anecdotes and the indiscretions which worried Gehlen and made him despair of ever being able to stop working for the *Amis* (as he called his employers behind their backs in the derogatory postwar term for the Americans) and return to the German fold. There was something else: the presence of two capable men, who were already holding high office in the Federal Government's intelligence services.

The one was ex-Lieutenant Colonel Heinz, chief of Military Intelligence (*MAD*) and formerly member of the wartime German Abwehr. Heinz had been a terrorist or soldier most of his life, graduating from the early post-World War I "Free Corps,"[5] through the frontline soldiers' organization, the Stahlhelm (Steel Helmet), into the Nazi Party, and from there finally into Admiral Canaris's Abwehr, where he took over the paratroop-commando outfit the Brandenburgers, which operated behind enemy lines during World War II.

The other was Doctor Otto John, of whom we shall hear more in due course.

Colonel Heinz had stayed in Berlin through the battle for the capital in April-May, 1945, and after its capture had been made mayor of the small town of Pieskow for several months in 1945-1946. This despite the fact that he was a known right-wing reactionary and former Nazi. (Perhaps the explanation might be that Heinz had become or already was a double agent during the war.)

In 1949, when West Germany was established, Heinz, who by this time was attached to the staff of Adenauer's military adviser Count Schwerin, applied for the job of head of the newly created Office for the Protection of the Constitution, a kind of FBI and counterespionage unit in one. But he was disappointed. A former refugee who had spent the last six years in England, Dr. Otto John, received the coveted post; a decision which started a smoldering feud between the

---

[5]Groups of ex-World War I officers who fought against the Poles in Silesia when the area was handed over to the newly created Poland by the Treaty of Versailles, and against left-wing elements in their own country.

two men, both of whom had once belonged to the Abwehr.

One year later, however, Heinz's chance came and he was appointed head of the new Military Intelligence Service which had been set up within the framework of the Amt Blank. Here he now encountered the dislike of Reinhard Gehlen, still an employee of the CIA.

Thus, by the early fifties, a strange kind of three-sided rivalry had been set up within the three major intelligence outfits operated by Germans in Federal Republic. One side of the triangle was made up of Heinz's MAD, the other by Gehlen's Organization, and the final and third side consisted of Otto John's BFV.[6]

But who was this third man in the triangle—Doctor Otto John? Otto John was a tall, broad-shouldered, blond, handsome lawyer who was at that time in his early forties and looked more like a boxer than the legal expert he in fact was.

He had come of solid middle-class stock and had right from the start of his life the knack of making friends in high places, including Louis Ferdinand of Prussia, grandson of the last German Kaiser and friend of President Roosevelt, who admired the wealthy young prince because he had come to America to work on the production line at Ford. Another friend was a half-Jewish schoolmate called Wolfgang Höfer, of whom we shall hear more later. Another was German professor and philosopher Theodor Heuss, one day to be West Germany's first postwar President, a useful contact indeed.

Otto John was of average intelligence, but he managed to graduate from university with a doctorate in law. It was this qualification which took him into the new German civilian airline company Lufthansa as

---

[6]*Bundesfassungsschutz*—Office for the Protection of the Constitution.

a legal adviser, which job took him to the various capitals of Europe. In those days just prior to the outbreak of World War II it was an ideal job for a conspirator who had to make contact with the outside world; the ordinary citizen was not then allowed to travel abroad because of Nazi currency restrictions. It was not surprising, then, that John was approached sometime in 1938—through his aristocratic friends—to do a little courier work for anti-Nazi groups within the Reich. And the happy-go-lucky, handsome young man, whose great interests seemed to be drinking and horse-riding, surprisingly enough agreed to carry out various missions to such capitals as Madrid, Lisbon and Stockholm.

In the middle of the war, the anti-Hitler plotters threw in their lot with dark-faced, highly intelligent Admiral Canaris, head of the German Secret Service the Abwehr, who now also wanted to get rid of Hitler; and to his surprise, Otto John found himself pitchforked from the somewhat genteel, amateurish world of the "gentlemen conspirators" with their ancient aristocratic names, into the tough, rough professional world of Canaris's Abwehr.

It was a change of circumstances that was to have a fatal influence on the rest of his life. Canaris was at that time hated by the rival SS secret services, and his organization was already effectively infiltrated by double agents working for the Gestapo and the SS. It was not surprising, therefore, that when the July, 1944, plot to kill Hitler failed, the Nazis were able to round up most of the conspirators—by virtue of their agents within the Abwehr—almost at once.

On that July 20, when the bomb that exploded in Hitler's East Prussian HQ failed to kill him, Otto John was at Berlin Army Headquarters in the Bendlerstrasse. Here he learned that the plot had failed and his beloved brother Hans had been arrested.[7] For sev-

---

[7] He was later executed by the Nazis.

eral hours—or for several days, according to the particular chronicler of that period of chaos and catastrophe in John's life—he evaded arrest by the Gestapo before flying to Madrid on a regular daytime Lufthansa flight. As easy as that.

That July 20, 1944, was a day he was not to forget. Of all the major conspirators, he was the only one to escape. While the rest faced the terrifying rage of the badly scared Führer in the person of the bitter, cynical chief prosecutor Dr. Roland Freisler, and that final terrible moment of agony of being strung up in a Berlin cell with a meathook stuck through their chins, and the movie cameras whirring (so that Adolf Hitler could enjoy the moment of their death), Otto John escaped to the sun-drenched peace and safety of Portugal. It was a turning point in his life. From that day on, his whole life changed. He was forced to renounce his own nation. He became a refugee—a traitor too, in the eyes of many of his contemporaries who remained behind in Germany.

In conversation with his friends, he returned to that day over and over again, spelling out those long leaden hours of July 20 in ever new forms, as if with a haunting need to relive its every moment. But one thing was certain: on that day an undying hatred of all who were even remotely connected with the men who had murdered his beloved brother was born within him, a hatred that would never leave him.

In November, 1944, John was spirited out of Portugal by the British Secret Service and taken to the United Kingdom. Here he worked for the British propaganda group responsible for trying to convince the German Wehrmacht that it was beaten. In May, 1945, when his job with the station—Soldatensender Calais—was terminated, John decided to stay in England, interrogating German PWs interned there, and preparing legal documents for the Nuremberg trials.

In 1946, he returned to the British Zone of Occupation in British Army uniform to help prepare the cases against military "war criminals," in particular von Rundstedt and von Manstein, two of Germany's most respected generals.

The von Rundstedt case was abandoned when the ancient field marshal became too ill to stand trial, but John definitely assisted in the capacity of legal interpreter and translator in the case against von Manstein. It was a cardinal mistake, but a mistake that John was blinded to because of his hatred occasioned by the murder of his brother in 1944. German traditionalists, in particular those regular army officers who one day would be a power again in a new Germany, called him a traitor and vowed vengeance. John ignored them, describing himself as the "broom that's going to sweep the Nazi pigsty!"

For three years John continued to have his headquarters in London, working during this time both for British Intelligence and in his private legal practice. In 1949, Otto John decided to return to the new Federal Republic. But before he left England for good, he made a snap decision, one that greatly surprised his friends. Instead of marrying his longtime girl friend Gisela Mann, whom he had met during the war when he had been working for Soldatensender Calais, he married her mother: Lucy Marleen-Mankiewicz, a German refugee who had earned her living in London since 1933 by giving singing lessons.

With this lady he returned to Germany, and through her and his own connections he managed to land a plum job—he became president of the new BFV, the German intelligence agency dedicated to preserving democracy in the fledgling West German state: an appointment that caused a wave of anger and resentment among more conservative circles in the country. "After all, the man was a traitor," so they gossiped,

"And in the light of his surprising marriage, an opportunist of the worst kind to boot!"

By the beginning of the new decade then, the stage was set for a fierce contest for power between Heinz, Gehlen, and John, and for one of the most bizarre stories in the entire history of modern intelligence, which has not exactly been lacking in bizarre stories.

18

Surprisingly, it was the amateur Otto John who got in the first blow against the two professionals, Heinz and Gehlen. It was directed against Colonel Heinz, the obviously more vulnerable of the two, with his record as a wartime terrorist.

Assiduously John set his men to work collecting evidence that would incriminate the middle-aged colonel. It was not difficult to find details of his long association with right-wing movements and such reactionaries as the writers Ernst Jünger, Franz Schauwecker, and Ernst von Salomon (the latter had actually let his political principles involve him in a political murder). Nor was it hard to show that Heinz, despite his Nazi past, had actually worked for the Russians during his period as mayor of Pieskow.

It was not so easy to prove that the chief of Military Intelligence, as he had since become, was now working for the Russians or their East German satellites, which John believed he was. But did not the fact that he had been *persona grata* with them in 1945 prove that he had already worked for them as a double agent during the war?

Yet he did learn that Heinz had been approached by the East German Ministry for State Security in 1952, or at least an attempt made to contact him through an ex-secretary of his. The woman, instead of reporting the approach to Heinz, reported the incident to the local Berlin office of the BFV. It, in its turn, passed on the information to John and *not* to Heinz. The incident gave John food for thought and he redoubled his efforts to prepare a dossier on Heinz.

Then John found what he was looking for: Heinz's dealings with a Dutchman named Jan Eland.

Jan Eland was a former agent of the Dutch intelligence who lived in postwar Berlin on the then-exorbitant pension of $1,250 per month. But even that kind of money did not keep him in the style he was accustomed to with girls, champagne and riotous living. He was forced to shop around for additional sources of income and he found them in his old trade—intelligence. In 1946, he set up a kind of private intelligence agency to sell information to the highest bidder. *His partner was Colonel Heinz!*

As it happened, John knew Eland too. During his numerous trips to Germany in the late forties before he decided to return for good, he had met him several times in the company of the Dutchman's secretary Else, who was the widow of a close friend who had been killed in the war. Therefore when in October, 1951, Heinz was forced to have Eland arrested because the latter was blackmailing him, John knew he was onto something. He bided his time, however, until Eland came out of prison in 1953. Then, according to German press sources, he met the broken ex-prisoner twice in his office in Cologne. After that, he handed the Dutchman a little money and put him on a train for Switzerland, where he died in November, 1953, in a Zurich hotel. As the German Press reported at the time, he was writing a book for a Swiss publisher and, according to the weekly news magazine, *Der Spiegel*, it would include the stories of several prominent figures on the contemporary intelligence scene.[1]

---

[1] Later it was reported that the Swiss police were investigating the case as one of murder, though nothing apparently came of their investigations.

With the material obtained from the unfortunate Eland, who was soon to die "from an overdose of sleeping tablets," and through Eland's lawyer at his trial, a certain Helmut Kelch, who was also sued by Heinz later as an "accessory to blackmail," Otto John was able to complete his dossier on Heinz. A few days later it was on the desk of his boss, Adenauer's "gray eminence," Dr. Hans Globke. The latter brought the information to the notice of Adenauer, who passed the matter on to Theodor Blank. With effect from October 1, 1953, Lieutenant Colonel Heinz was suspended from his office. Six months later he was discharged completely.

We do not know Heinz's immediate reaction when he learned that John was the agent of his downfall. Perhaps he had been too long in the shady business of intelligence with its plot and counterplot to feel unduly betrayed. Or perhaps he already knew that Otto John would not survive his downfall by very long himself. As he told a newspaperman much later, "Eventually John would be dealt with in the same manner by his former ally General Gehlen himself."

The dismissed secret service boss contented himself with sending John a letter in which he repeated the cryptic warning he had given the former once before. It read in part: "Beware of the devilry of secret service intrigues; don't ever drink from the poisoned cup of counterintelligence, for that poison is lethal."

But an overconfident John chose to ignore that warning. He knew what Gehlen thought of him and there was no personal contact whatsoever between the ex-General and the ex-resistance man; yet their two organizations worked together well enough. Indeed, there was even some talk in the middle fifties to the effect that the two organizations had worked together to get rid of Colonel Heinz.

Now that he had brought about Heinz's withdrawal from the competition, Otto John tried to make contact with the remote spymaster in Pullach, although he and Gehlen had completely different concepts of the future of Germany. For John, Germany of the future had to be a neutral no-man's-land; for Gehlen, it had to be a strongly armed force, completely integrated into the Western alliance against the Russians and their "lackeys."

As John described his efforts in his memoirs: "I was happy to note that our cooperation with our American colleagues was particularly friendly and well developed. For that reason I took special care to cooperate with Herr Gehlen, the head of the espionage organization of the same name belonging to the American Army."

Some time in that year, Gehlen visited John at his office in Cologne and invited the latter to return the compliment by coming to Pullach. John did so and was welcomed to a small, intimate dinner with Gehlen and his staff. After the meal Gehlen raised his glass and, with his cold eyes directly on the younger man, said in toast, "We want to forget the past. Here's to the future."

John pretended surprise at the strange toast. But he knew what Gehlen was referring to—his part in the Manstein trial. As he wrote later: "I had nothing 'to forget,' but I knew well he meant my part in the trial against the former Field Marshal von Manstein, who at that time was still in an English jail and whom Gehlen admired as a great soldier."

John considered for a moment, then he smiled, his broad, handsome face lighting up as he did so. He raised his glass and cried *"Prosit!"* warmly. Then he rose and, crossing over to Gehlen, pressed his hand.

The two men were friends—*or so Otto John, in his naive, amateurish way thought.*

By this time, Gehlen's men had established themselves in all the leading posts within John's organization. In spite of his bitter hatred for the men who had been associated with the executioners of his brother—ex-members of the SD and SS—John was forced to accept them into the ranks of the BFV for the lack of any other available agents. These men were invariably easy meat for Gehlen's own former SS and SD men. Together with such agents as John's vice president, Albert Radke, who had formerly belonged to the Gehlen Organization for which he had worked for five years, they really ran John's outfit.

Nor was it too difficult for them to conceal their real activities from their chief, who was really an amateur and "dilettante" (as Gehlen characterized him) in the spy game. John was not interested in what he contemptuously called "spy novels"; he wanted to know the "pyschological motivation" of the men and women they suspected of extreme right- or left-wing activities. Cynically they gave him what he wanted, all the while preparing an intimate dossier of their boss's private and public life for Gehlen in faraway Pullach. And what a dossier it was! John was *"ein Mann der Engländer"*—a paid stooge of the English Secret Service. Worse, he was a Russian agent too and had been working for them since 1942, when he had turned over "a detailed tactical map of German air defenses" to Guy Burgess, the British diplomat who had long been in the Soviet employ and later defected to the East.

His private life did not escape the work of the nasty-minded agents within and without his own organization. According to them, John was an inveterate drunkard and, in addition to being quite a ladies' man (which seems to have been true), was also a homosexual (a pretty remote possibility).[2] And so it went

---

[2]According to the *Ruhr-Nachrichten,* in an article published shortly after John's defection, he had been indicted

on, this sordid record of a man's forty-odd years of life, in which invariably there will be some skeletons that will have to be hidden away securely in one's own mental closet.

In March, 1954, Sefton Delmer, chief reporter of the British paper, the *Daily Express* and John's former boss at Soldatensender Calais, came to Bonn to write an article on "How Dead Is Hitler?" Although John did not want to be associated with a newspaper which was radically anti-German, he did agree to meet his old boss for a couple of drinks.

The couple of drinks developed into a couple more (John had been a heavy drinker for several years now) and the tubby, bald journalist with the piercing dark eyes relaxed. Leaning forward over the table, he said softly, "I've talked to a lot of well-informed people here in Bonn. . . . It won't be easy for you here in the Federal Republic." He hesitated for a moment.

John looked at him a little bewildered and wondered what was to come. Delmer's face hardened. "You've got more enemies here than you think. But I'll tell you something. The *Daily Express* and Lord Beaverbrook [owner of the paper] will always be at your disposal if you need help."

John pooh-poohed the warning as he had done Heinz's more cryptic one. A month later he flew to Washington to be briefed by the FBI on how to fight Communism. That job done, he was given a lavish month-long tour of the United States at government expense. And all the while he was in the States, shaking

---

in prewar Berlin for homosexual activity but had been saved because the Berlin Chief of Police was himself a homosexual. The paper commented: "British Intelligence had learned about this inclination, but to this day nobody knows for sure whether it used this knowledge to press John into its service." The inference is that Burgess, who was a homosexual, presumably made the contact in Madrid in 1942.

hands with such prominent cold war warriors as Edgar Hoover and, more crucial, CIA boss Allen Dulles, far away in Pullach, Dulles's employee Reinhard Gehlen was getting ready to plunge a dagger into John's unsuspecting back.

Otto John returned to West Germany in late June, 1954, to learn that his days as head of the BFV were numbered. During his absence, his new "friend" Gehlen had deposited a voluminous dossier on the desk of Secretary of State Globke. Its title was *"This Is Otto John."* Dr. Globke, who owed Gehlen many a favor, was only too eager to present it to his chief, Dr. Adenauer.

Adenauer was shocked. He had never liked John, whom he regarded as an agent of the hated British.[3] Now the fat Gehlen dossier seemed to label the chief of his internal security office a lady-killer, homosexual, and drunkard into the bargain. It was too much for the strict Catholic and moralist Adenauer. As already noted, the German Chancellor was never given to many words. His sole comment before he left on his summer vacation was, "I never want to see that fellow [John] again."

John naturally heard that Adenauer had decided that he was through. But there was more to come. Just before he was due to leave Cologne to attend the reinauguration of his friend, President Heuss, followed three days later by the ceremony celebrating the tenth anniversary of July 20, 1944, he was called by a

---

[3] After the Americans had captured Cologne in March, 1945, they had appointed Dr. Adenauer as chief burgomaster. When Cologne later came under British jurisdiction as part of the British Zone of Occupation, a British brigadier relieved Adenauer of his post on the charge of "incompetence." Adenauer never forgave the British this "insult." As a result, anything British or concerned with the British was automatically suspect in his eyes.

fellow conspirator of those wartime days, Father Laurentius Siemer.

On July 13, 1954, his old friend called him to complain bitterly that a mutual friend, the former German Chancellor Dr. Brüning, was being spied upon by John's organization; indeed, Brüning dare not even venture from his office to go to the nearest call box to telephone. As the Catholic priest said, "This is impossible, Dr. John, that you should do something like this for Dr. Adenauer!"[4]

"Father Laurentius," John protested, "I give you my word that there is no truth to this! Nobody in my office would do a thing like that, even behind my back. But I don't know whether Dr. Brüning isn't being watched by someone else. I'll check into it. And if you're right, it really is scandalous!"

At the other end, the elderly priest took a deep breath, apparently appeased. "I believe you," he conceded. "I think Dr. Brüning is a decent man. But he's observed something going on. And after all, he's experienced how the Gestapo was after him one time."

John felt as he put down the phone that he would have liked to have gone to Brüning on the spot and clarified the matter there and then. But he knew he hadn't time to do that; there was other work to be done before he could go to Berlin.

But that telephone call had its effect. It added to the mood of deep despair into which he had been plunged after his return from the jaunt to America. He knew that the game was up. Gehlen and his other enemies had proved too powerful for him. When he left Cologne to fly to Berlin a few days before the Heuss ceremony, Dr. Otto John was obviously at the end of his tether.

---

[4] It was well known that Dr. Brüning was regarded by Adenauer as a potential rival for the office of West German Chancellor.

His mood of despair was heightened by a chance meeting with a pal of his schooldays at the Realgymnasium, the half-Jewish Wolfgang Höfer, now Captain Hoefer of American Military Intelligence. By an amazing coincidence, Höfer had been assigned by his outfit to spy on John. But his old friend of Wiesbaden days could not hide his unpleasant assignment from Otto; over the dinner table in a little Berlin restaurant, he told John everything: how he was suspected of being a secret Russian or East German agent by the CIC Military Intelligence and how he was being watched by several Western intelligence agencies. This was all the confirmation John needed. He knew now that his career in the Federal Republic and all his grandiose plans were finished.

On the afternoon of July 20, 1954, ten years to the day of seeing his life in Nazi Germany fall to pieces, he attended the ceremonies to commemorate that fateful day and its dead.

It was an unpleasant, hot summer afternoon, and it triggered off the final chemical change in Otto John's personality. At the ceremony he sobbed loudly at the memory of his beloved dead brother. Then his sadness turned into rage and he denounced two of the other mourners as "Gestapo agents." Now he was beginning to see spies everywhere. But his mood did not end there. He even succeeded in denouncing his old schoolfriend Prince Louis Ferdinand, to whom he had owed so much. It was clear even to the most casual observer that Otto John had finally reached breakingpoint.

That evening he returned to the hotel and, taking off his suit, threw himself on the bed. But still he could not rest. He dressed again and told one of the hotel staff to tell his wife he was going out for a beer; he would be back in time for dinner. Ordering the hotel car, he drove off—and never came back!

This is not the place to go at length into the amazing—almost unbelievable—story of what happened to Dr. Otto John next. There are many versions, all contradictory to Otto John's own, which states that he drove off to visit another old pal, Dr. Wohlgemuth, who at that time had a practice in both sectors of the divided city (an ideal cover for a Soviet agent). Together they had a few drinks and then a few more —and more. Next morning when John woke up, it was to find himself in a darkened room. As he describes it in his memoirs: "It was like a bad dream. Through the door to the next room I could see three robust men in blue uniforms and a little way off a well-built woman in a white uniform apron. On her head she had a white hat and there was a dark brown leather bag next to her. Her head hung down. She was sleeping. The men were smoking. One read a newspaper, another a book. The third observed me. Through a door open a little to another room, I could hear men speaking Russian. Suddenly, I was wide awake."

Otto John was a prisoner of the Russians in East Berlin!

That was John's story. What probably happened was that when a drunken John complained to his old friend and Communist sympathizer Wohlgemuth that he simply could not carry on fighting against the reactionary forces present in West Germany and did not want to go back there, the doctor helped him to cross into East Berlin, probably with the aid of Max Wonsich, an agent of the East German Ministry for State Security. But when the little group arrived in East Berlin, they were not received with open arms as John had obviously anticipated.

Naturally, the East German Intelligence Service would have liked to have made use of John, but he was no good to them in East Germany. They needed him in Cologne, as boss of the BFV. Yet to everyone's consternation, John balked. He had had enough of Gehlen, Adenauer, and the rest of the intriguers and their ex-Nazi backers. He was *not* going back!

Dr. Wohlgemuth panicked. He knew that when his part in John's "defection" became known, he would be finished in West Berlin. He excused himself from the little conference and rushed back to the West to pick up his nurse and favorite girl friend, Annemarie Wehres (he was running a stable of five mistresses at the time). Before dawn he was in East Berlin once again and the great scandal could break.

It surely did. Next morning the papers were full of the alarming news of Dr. John's defection, the major one of its kind in West Germany since the war. The German public was shocked. So was the American Army. Where had John gotten his tip-off that he was being shadowed so that he had had time to make a bolt for it?

Swiftly the leak was traced back to John's old school buddy Wolfgang Höfer. For two days he was grilled intensively by his former colleagues of the CIC and then, when they were finished with him, he took his service .38 and blasted his brains out in his room at the Berlin Bachelor Officers Quarters.

When John heard the news, he broke down. Then, recovered, he commented laconically, "Höfer was destroyed by the CIC's abuse of him." Reinhard Gehlen's was even shorter and more to the point. Asked in Bonn to comment on John's disappearance eastward, he said in that dry manner of his, "Once a traitor, always a traitor."[5]

---

[5] A few months later, John "escaped" westward again with the aid of a Swedish journalist friend. He was arrested by the West Germans and sentenced to four years' imprisonment. Since his release, he has lived in Austria where his main concern is the attempt to prove his innocence.

Gehlen had won the three-cornered duel at last. The way was free for him to take up the coveted key post of chief of the West German Intelligence Service.

19

On April 1, 1956 (April Fool's Day once again), fourteen years to the day since he had taken over Foreign Armies East, and nearly nine years after he had begun working for the Americans, Reinhard Gehlen transferred his whole organization to the new Federal German Republic. Although it is known that the CIA objected strongly to losing their expensively paid "eyes and ears" behind the Iron Curtain, Gehlen was determined to change masters now that Germany once again had its own army, the Bundeswehr. Over the border in East Germany, Wollweber, the head of the Ministry for State Security was none too pleased either. It was bad enough to have his old enemy Gehlen working for the Americans, but it was even worse to think of him employed by the "Bonn warmongers," as he saw them.

Wollweber quickly mobilized his propagandists who, with the aid of the excellent dossiers available for such purposes in the East, set about discrediting "Hitler's spy general," the "gray hand" of Bonn, or "the gray general" as he was variously called. In Holland, France, East Germany, and naturally other Communist countries, books appeared, which were written specifically to denigrate Gehlen and prove that his organization was dominated by former Gestapo and SS men. These books were so thoroughly and con-

174

vincingly documented that it was clear that their sources were located in the Berlin Ministry for State Security.

But it was not only the Communist countries which opposed Gehlen's appointment to the key position of chief of intelligence in West Germany. There were many in the West who did not relish the idea of this position for a man whom they regarded as little better than an opportunist, who had been ready right from the start to work for the enemy for money. Among West Germany's Socialists there were those who thought him too "American," and by this they really meant he was little better than a "creature of the *Amis*."

Gehlen immediately set about assuring the Socialist parliamentary opposition by means of an interview with a West German journalist that he was neither the creature of the Americans nor a tool of the government Conservative Party. He told the journalist, in one of the few interviews he has ever granted to the press: "If the opposition came to power tomorrow, our service would continue to work as if nothing had happened. . . . In addition, our reports are not only presented to the ministry responsible for our work, but also to the Chancellor and his secretaries of state—and to the heads of the opposition parties in parliament. We pass on our information to Ollenhauer" [the then head of the Socialist Party].[1]

After appeasing the socialists, Gehlen still had to face the Allies in NATO. It is reliably reported that both the French and British protested about his appointment and there is evidence that there were those in the American camp who objected to Gehlen taking over the responsible post in which he would be removed from American control. According to these

---

[1] In actual fact, Gehlen agents were shadowing Ollenhauer's nephew at that time on Gehlen's express command as a suspected Communist sympathizer!

sources, their antagonism was caused primarily by the "Trudeau Affair."

General Arthur Trudeau, U.S. Army, had gained a good reputation during World War II in the Pacific, when he had helped to plan MacArthur's offensive against Manila. After the war he had risen steadily in rank until in 1954 he was appointed head of G-2 (intelligence) at the Pentagon. But the Pacific veteran kept his new and highly responsible post for only a year. Abruptly and for no apparent reason, he was dismissed from it well before his tour of duty was over and posted to the staff of General Lemnitzer in the Far East, where he took up a comparatively minor position.

His friends at the Pentagon were shocked. Why had this highly respected and efficient officer been treated so shabbily? they wanted to know. Rumors began to run through the brightly lit corridors of the Pentagon. Politics were behind it, said some. Others thought it was the CIA. Some thought that the Kraut general— Gehlen—had a hand in the G-2's sudden dismissal. Eventually a group of Trudeau's friends and former associates confided in John O'Donnell of the *Daily News*. They gave him what they knew and allowed him to put the story together as best he could and "leak" it to the public.

According to O'Donnell, what had happened was that during the visit of the first West German Chancellor, crusty Dr. Adenauer, to the United States in 1954, Trudeau had fallen into conversation with him at a reception. Foolishly enough—for Adenauer was a convinced "cold war warrior" and a loyal believer in Gehlen's work—Trudeau had confided his doubts about having an American organization, the CIA, pay money to a "Nazi general" to ferret out information for them about the Communists.

Evidently Trudeau's outburst came to the ears of

Allen Dulles, perhaps via his brother Foster, who was an intimate of the shrewd German Chancellor and like him in many ways. Allen Dulles, head of the CIA, had one of his rare rages and took the affair directly to Eisenhower himself. The President was forced to act, although Trudeau was an old comrade of his and defended by the Army chief of staff as well as the Secretary of defense Charles Wilson himself. Trudeau was dismissed from his post and sent into exile.

Those who remembered the "Trudeau Affair" in the United States now tried to collect other evidence to show that Gehlen was unsuited for the post that he was desperately trying to obtain. In addition to employing a goodly number of ex-Nazis in his organization, they pointed out, he also had a man on his staff who had actually attempted to sabotage American industry and military installations during World War II.

They referred to Wilhelm Ahlrichs, already mentioned during the course of the Baltic operations, who was one of the organizers of "Operation Pastorius," perhaps one of the most audacious operations launched by the German Secret Service during World War II. It entailed—among other things—landing two teams of German-Americans, one in Florida and one off Long Island, by submarine. The scheme misfired, and most of the men ended in the electric chair, except the one who had betrayed them before they could start on the spying and sabotage mission Ahlrichs had planned for them.

Once the war was over, Ahlrichs had spent a long time in the United Kingdom as a "guest of His Majesty's Government," revealing everything about the Pastorius Operation, which also included introducing German spies into Britain and Ireland. After he had been suitably "squeezed out," Ahlrichs returned to Germany to work for British intelligence before being passed on to Gehlen when he had outlived his usefulness.

Now, although Ahlrichs was principally employed in the Baltic by virtue of his naval experience, as well as his intelligence background, he was still suspect by many Americans in the know as the man who had deliberately set out to subvert basically honest German-American citizens of the United States to spy against the country which had adopted them so generously.[2]

But in spite of all their efforts, the opponents of Gehlen's appointment in America had no success. After what appears to have been almost six months of deliberation (for apparently after the middle of September, 1955, the CIA no longer cared to use his services), Gehlen was appointed head of the new West German *Bundesnachrichtendienst* (BND), the intelligence service. The combination of Allen and Foster Dulles plus cunning old Konrad Adenauer had proved too forceful for all his enemies in both East and West.

Reinhard Gehlen's long and hard march to power, made secretly against the background of a defeated and thoroughly compromised nation, and in the pay of an "enemy" power, had achieved success. On that April Fool's Day in 1956, he became—with the stroke of a pen—one of the most powerful men in the most powerful state in Europe save Russia.

In that year, Reinhard Gehlen, the new Ministerialrat (ministerial councillor), who was feared and hated by many millions east of the Iron Curtain and a goodly number west of it too, was a medium-sized, middle-aged man who shunned publicity. He rarely showed himself in public. Indeed, popular rumor had it that there were only two pictures of him in existence, one as a young, thin-faced wartime staff officer, and the other as an aging civilian swimming in a Bavarian lake,

---

[2]Ahlrichs worked for Gehlen until 1959, when Polish counterintelligence caught him apparently photographing Polish warships in the harbor at Gdansk (formerly Danzig).

while two men—presumably his bodyguards—watched over him in a rowing boat from a discreet distance.[3]

Outside the tight little world of Pullach, little was known of his habits and personality. He seems to have had a vague sense of humor; every summer, when he went sailing on the Bavarian Starberger Lake, he would smoke a cigar whose band bore the inscription "Secret Service." But even that mild witticism was no more than a calculated risk, for whoever read it took it to be some kind of personal joke.

As for his office, we know that it was a sparsely furnished place, adorned solely with a picture of the wartime head of the German Secret Service, Admiral Canaris, and the death mask of Frederick the Great. The only unusual thing about the room was the packed suitcase always standing in the corner. It was ready for a hasty retreat to an emergency "secret HQ" on the Atlantic coast in the country of "a friendly power" in the event of war.

He dressed very conservatively, rather in the fashion of a retired English colonial officer, preferring discreet tweeds and striped ties. He even went so far as to drink tea. His favorite reading was files and books filled with facts; he had no time for novels or similar "silly rubbish."

German writer Jürgen Thorwald describes a visit to Gehlen's HQ one night in the fall of 1955, which gives something of a picture of him at the time.

"It was already dark when I arrived in the outer office. A cultivated, polite young man appeared out of the shadows and said, 'The doctor is waiting for you in the street in his car.'

" '*The doctor?*' I enquired.

---

[3] There were more. I have been able to locate six postwar photos of the ex-general. Two of these from Eastern sources have obviously been snapped by agents from behind the Iron Curtain.

" 'Yes,' he replied smilingly, 'that's what I call my chief with whom you have an appointment. He wants to take you to Schwabing [the artists' quarter of Munich] for dinner.' "

Thorwald realized that the mysterious young man who had not introduced himself was referring to Gehlen. A little bewildered, he followed him out into the dark fall street.

"When we arrived on the street," Thorwald goes on, "there was no car. But after walking a couple of hundred meters behind the young man, we came to a car hidden under the trees, its lights extinguished. It was a dark-colored Opel Kapitän. The door next to the driver's seat was opened and for a brief moment I caught a glimpse of its interior. Its sole occupant, looking up from behind the steering wheel, was about fifty, a thin man dressed in a dark-gray suit. He looked at me carefully for a moment, then offered a gray-gloved hand.

" 'Gehlen,' he said. No more. But it was sufficient . . ."

That night meeting in a lonely side street in fog-bound Munich was typical of the style that Gehlen now cultivated. The initial reserve which had been drilled into him as a young soldier as the only one befitting a Prussian officer had now developed into a phobia for concealment. His children, by this time well into their teens, were drawn into the circle of subterfuge and deception that surrounded their secret service father. His son Felix-Christoph invariably introduced his father to friends under a different guise, while, as already remarked earlier, his daughter took her high school diploma under an assumed name. Even his neighbors took a hand in the game.

According to the general, who revealed the incident in an uncharacteristically talkative moment: "One day I was phoned by someone in the local drugstore.

He was pretty excited. He'd observed a suspicious automobile. Its occupants had asked for me."

Gehlen had reacted at once. He notified the local police in the small Bavarian town of Berg, where he was living at No. 29 Waldstrasse, in a house bought for him by the CIA. They drove out to find the "suspicious automobile," which turned out to belong to the B.B.C., which wanted to do an interview with the German Secret Service Chief. The Englishmen were quietly directed to another village, where there was no hope of finding Gehlen.

German-American writer Joachim Joesten has described to what lengths Gehlen could take this desire for secrecy, in his book, *They Call It Intelligence*.

As the middle-aged author recalls it, he was traveling with his family in southern Germany in the spring of 1951 when he accidentally stumbled on Gehlen's Pullach headquarters.

"My family and I were staying, or rather, we had planned to stay, for a few days in Munich. The city just then was full of tourists and every hotel in a price class acceptable to us had the 'No Vacancies' sign out. So we decided to look for accommodations in one of the small towns of the city's periphery. We got back into our handy little Renault car, with our luggage piled high on top, and drove out of town in a southerly direction. After an 8-mile drive through the scenic Isar Valley, we came to a pleasant little village called Pullach. There was a fairly good hotel in a reasonable price class that looked almost deserted. So we put up there and left our car parked outside on the trim little village square.

"Before going to bed we took a stroll through the neighborhood. A short distance from the hotel there was what looked like a large estate, shielded from view by tall shady trees. A high barbed-wire fence ran around it and the wide driveway that gave access to it was barred on one side by a spiked grille and on the other by a moveable boom. We saw no guards around, but noticed a gatekeeper's lodge.

"Out of pure curiosity, we approached the gate and looked through the bars seeing nothing but trees and a curving stretch of driveway. The only noteworthy thing about the place was the profusion of warning signs. First, there was 'No Parking' beside the gate-keeper's lodge, and on the grille, a 'No Trepassing' sign also forbade 'Soliciting.' Finally, there was a notice saying 'Turn off Your Headlight. Turn On Interior Light.' We decided it probably was a U.S. Army compound and forgot about it.

"The next morning when I stepped out of the hotel to start the car, I saw that there had been mischief during the night. Somebody with a sharp knife had neatly slashed all four tires; they were flatter than pancakes!"

Joesten had taken this to mean that the local Bavarian townsfolk did not like him because his little Renault bore French license plates. It was not until several years later that he "learned that the Gehlen Organization maintained headquarters at Pullach." A picture of the entrance gate that appeared in a German magazine clinched the matter. "We had been prying quite unintentionally into Germany's best-kept secret of that time."

As the ex-*Newsweek* editor admitted ruefully later: "And then I realized that those slashed tires were the Gehlen way of telling us: No snooping newsmen wanted around here. *Get going!*"[4]

---

[4]For a while, when he learned what was really going on behind those locked gates at Pullach, Joesten felt like billing the U. S. Army for the tires, but (as he says) "somehow I never got around to doing it."

But despite his horror of any kind of personal publicity, which was only partly occasioned by the fear that Wollweber's men might try to assassinate him (it was rumored that "Dr. Schneider" always carried a loaded revolver in his pocket when he left his home for work), Gehlen knew that he possessed immense power. He had "branches" by now in virtually every large city in Germany—and many small ones too—and official representatives in every country where the Federal Republic had an embassy or a consulate. His HQ in Pullach ran a good hundred cover firms (*he was perhaps the only secret service chief who actually sold refrigerators*).

His agents, calculated by some sources to run to ten thousand men and women of nearly half a hundred different nationalities, were everywhere, spying and reporting on the potential enemy but also on friends and fellow citizens.

It is recorded that the West German Vice Chancellor of the middle fifties was shadowed by a Gehlen man as he slipped into a Parisian brothel during the course of an official visit to the French capital. The Gehlen man even went as far as to note down the price, the length of stay, and the type of female preferred by the heavyset, aging minister and forwarded these details to Gehlen, who passed them on to the strict Catholic, Chancellor Konrad Adenauer. His comment was a sigh and the remark, "Did it have to be a mulatto!"

The extremely pale-faced ex-officer with the rapidly receding hair, who was now running a little to fat, but whose middle-aged, benign appearance was belied by those cold, calculating blue eyes, now had a budget of —officially—some one hundred million marks at his disposal (other sources said it ran as high as four times this sum annually). With it, he knew, he could buy and sell people as he wished. High and low—money talked. It is rumored, for instance, that when one of his agents reported that a certain publishing house was preparing a book on the wartime activities of his first boss, Dr. Globke, the intimate adviser of Chancellor Adenauer, and a man who had been connected with drawing up the racialist "Nuremberg Laws" directed against the Jews, Gehlen did not hesitate to "buy" the manuscript. For the sum of $8,000 it "disappeared" from the printing plant and turned up a short while afterward on the desk of a delighted Dr. Globke who, ex-lawyer as he was, soon found a way of stopping publication.

But in spite of his enormous power in those middle years of the fifties, which was aided by the "cold war" raging then between East and West, Gehlen did not regard himself as more than a "military-intelligence technician," whose job had very little political significance—at least for him.

Just as he had been able to work with the Nazis, then with the Americans, now he was prepared to work with either of the main West German parties—conservative as well as socialist. Yet although Gehlen undoubtedly felt that his attitude was correct, and in the tradition of the German General Staff which had always insisted its officers should refrain from "meddling" in politics, there were dangers inherent in it. A "technician" like Gehlen could become the unwitting tool of political extremists —in particular, because of his family background and military training, those of the right. Indeed, one could maintain that after a decade and a half of espionage, with its blackmail, treachery, double agents and overruling principle that everybody had his price, Reinhard Gehlen's moral sense had become blunted. He had come to accept this dark, unsavory world in which he spent most of his working life as the real world; one without principle, charity, or decency.

20

But unknown to Reinhard Gehlen, who now felt himself at the height of his power and in control of an enormously effective apparatus that delivered most of the intelligence about the East that both NATO and the CIA used in their decision-making, a new enemy had appeared on the horizon: a man who would contribute greatly to the general discrediting of the BND.

This man was the new chief of the East German Ministry for State Security, Erich Mielke, a veteran of the Communist Party, born in 1905.

Mielke was a completely different type from Gehlen. There was nothing of the reserved military intellectual about him with good manners and good taste. He was an old party bully who had learned to use his hamlike fists and hard knees in the brawls between the Communists and Socialists (and naturally the Nazis) which were a daily occurrence in the working-class Wedding district of Berlin during the twenties and early thirties. Even his own comrades called him behind his back (his temper was explosive) *der brutaler Ede* (" brutal Eddie").

The nickname dated directly from one hot summer's day in 1931. On that August 9 day, against the background of an important political decision being made in the Prussian Parliament, two prominent Communists Kippenberger and Walter Ulbricht—one day to be head of the East German state—decided that two local police officers should be "removed." The men in question were police captains Anlauf and Henk. The man who was to carry out the task was tough, swaggering Ede Mielke.

On that sultry summer day, with the dogs lolling in the dirty gutters, their tongues hanging out panting for breath, and the undernourished children of the unemployed workers picking at the melting tar of the streets, a "spontaneous demonstration" of Communist workers marched a little wearily up the Berlin Kaiser Wilhelm Strasse, chanting their slogans and bearing their usual hastily painted signs.

For police captains Anlauf and Lenk, this was routine duty. They had been trying to pacify and disperse crowds like this for years—for their whole life, it sometimes seemed to them. Together with a few police, they positioned themselves at the corner of Kaiser Wilhelm Strasse and Bulow Square, and waited for the hot, sweating, more than bedraggled mob.

Moments later they were there, and the police were swamped by the unwashed screaming men and women who had not stopped—as was expected—when they hit the police line. Tempers flared. Rubber clubs came down on unresisting skulls. Irate, screaming short-haired women scratched policemen's faces. Men spat and bellowed abuse. And then suddenly, in the midst of the melee, shots rang out. The fighting stopped at once. The crowd drew back. Lenk staggered backward, holding his chest, the blood dripping through his clenched fingers. Anlauf lay sprawled on the hot cobbles in the extravagant posture of the violently done-to-death. As if hypnotized, the suddenly silent crowd watched as Lenk staggered to the entrance of the Babylon Cinema. And then there was a great sigh as the police captain clutched at his chest for one last time before he sank down the wall onto the tiled floor of the entrance. He, too, had been murdered.

The crowd surged forward. Unnoticed, a man stuck

a pistol deep into his pocket and began to walk rapidly away from the scene. That man was Erich Mielke, one day to be the head of the East German Secret Police. The legend of "Brutal Eddie" had been born.

In that year, Mielke fled Germany to Belgium, where "comrades" supplied him with false papers that enabled him to ship from Antwerp to the Soviet Union. Nothing is known about him for the next three years until 1936, when he turned up in Spain as training officer with the International Brigade during the Civil War, probably arriving with the same group of German Communists as Wilhelm Zaisser, portrayed as General Gomez in Ernest Hemingway's *For Whom the Bell Tolls* and one day himself to be head of the East German Ministry of State Security.

In Spain, Erich Mielke gained himself the unenviable reputation among his comrades in the battalion of being the *Genickschuss-Spezialist* (specialist in delivering the "coup de grace" at the nape of the neck), before fleeing to France in 1939.

The French interned him as they did most of the survivors of the Spanish Republican Army who had fled to France. But unlike most of his ex-comrades, Mielke did not fall into the hands of the Gestapo when the country was occupied by the Germans in 1940. He had already made his arrangements and escaped from the French internment camp without too much difficulty. Somehow or other he managed to get back to the Soviet Union, where we again lose track of him for nearly five years, when he turned up in the summer of 1945 in the newly occuped Soviet Zone of Germany.

There an unpleasant surprise was waiting for Mielke, who by this time was a Soviet citizen. Hardly had he obtained a job in the zone's Ministry of the Interior, which included, among the other departments, the police force, when one of his own employees brought a charge of double murder against him. Chief Inspector Erdmann brought the fact to the attention of the Berlin attorney general, a Dr. Wilhelm Kühnast, that Mielke was still wanted for the 1931 murder of Lenk and Anlauf.

Kühnast, who was himself a member of the Communist Party, was decidedly embarrassed by the disclosure, but he nonetheless placed his devotion to duty above devotion to party; he ordered that Mielke as well as Party Chief Walter Ulbricht be arrested.

The Soviet commandant of Berlin, Major General Kotikov, exploded when he heard what the attorney intended to do. Kühnast was ordered to Soviet HQ and told to drop the charges—*at once!*

Having little alternative, he did so, but he refused to surrender the Mielke dossier to the Russians, who were forced then to frame the obstinate lawyer. In May, 1947, Kühnast was suspended from his office and placed under house arrest as an ex-Nazi, thief, and sexual offender.

For fourteen months he was kept under house arrest, although the Western authorities tried to arrange for his release, only to be told by a cynical Russian spokesman that "they might as well order the moon released from the sky."

In 1948, the West decided to take matters into its own hands. On a hot day in August of that year, Dr. Kühnast, accompanied by two East German plainclothesmen, was being escorted through a series of streets close to the sector boundary. During the course of that "walk," Kühnast summoned up the last of his strength and broke away.

A cry of rage sprang to the lips of his captors. Too late! Just as they were about to recapture him, Kühnast pelted across the demarcation line. Angrily they drew their pistols. Kühnast threw himself onto the sidewalk and started yelling at the top of his voice. "Conveniently," at that particular moment, a West Berlin prowl car drew up at the corner. Four heavily armed policemen threw open its doors and ran swiftly to the screaming man, now struggling with the sweating East German cops. It was all over in a matter of seconds. The East Germans were overpowered and led away in handcuffs. Dr. Kühnast was free at last.

But the Kühnast accusations had little influence on Erich Mielke's career in East Germany. Rapidly he rose up the ladder of promotion until, in 1950, he was appointed secretary of state in the Ministry for State Security, first under Zaisser, and later under Wollweber.

When Zaisser was fired, Mielke retained his job. Then, when in 1957 Wollweber was forced to resign because of the chain of events set in motion by the 1956 Hungarian revolt, Mielke succeeded him as Minister for State Security; an event heralded cynically by one West Berlin newspaper with the headline: *It Could Happen Only in Pankow* [Soviet HQ]—*Double Killer in Minister's Chair.*

Erich Mielke did not measure up to the standards of his former bosses Zaisser and Wollweber in either intelligence or ability, but he did possess one quality that neither of them had: hard, brutal calculation.

One German writer who knew him well at that time, wrote of him: "He is the prototype of the heartless 'apparatschik' [who] knows no feeling of pity or consideration. He is the personification of cool calculation: I am the hammer; you are the anvil. *I strike and you will be struck.*"

Another East German who suffered a cross-examination at his hands in those days portrayed him as follows: "He was noticeable for his self-satisfied and arrogant behavior. . . . And it was clear that he liked himself in his uniform [General of the People's Police]. I watched him and he watched me . . . I have seen a lot of faces in my life, but seldom one that was so completely expressionless."

As soon as Gehlen became aware of the change of command in the intelligence service on the other side of the Iron Curtain, he automatically began to interest himself in his new opponent. A former captain of the East German intelligence, Max Heim, who had fled westward, was able to report: "He [Mielke] has an enormous desire to be noted. For that reason he likes to give long speeches and pass on stupid slogans. In addition, he is a loyal follower of the Ulbricht line and even mistrusts his closest colleagues."

The news pleased Gehlen and confirmed his belief that Ernest Mielke in no way measured up to the standards of his predecessors in the ministerial post. The information that the new minister had a weakness for luxury and the easy life, including a collection of fast, expensive cars and motorboats at his villa on Lake Wollsetz, which had once belonged to Hermann Göring himself, helped confirm Gehlen's picture of him. Even his plebeian interest in the working-class sport of soccer and his many side bets on the results of the games made Gehlen conclude that "Brutal Eddie" was in no way a danger to be feared by his highly trained, expert, long-established organization.

He was to find out in the next few years that he had greatly underestimated his opponent in the East. For Erich Mielke, in addition to already having an agent (of whom we shall hear much later) located in a key position within the Gehlen Organization, was prepared to eradicate BND agents inside and *outside* the borders of the German Democratic Republic. With the aid of the Soviet-run KGB (the Russian State Security Organization), which collaborated intimately with him,[1] Mielke did not hesitate to carry the underground war across the frontier into West Germany, not only with an esti-

---

[1] It is reliably reported that Soviet star spy Colonel Abel trained German agents for Mielke in East Germany after his release from U. S. imprisonment.

mated two thousand agents a year,[2] but also with hired killers prepared to murder on command. The age of the "licensed killer" had begun.

But far away in Pullach on the bright morning of April 1, 1956, Gehlen and his associates were too full of their own immediate triumph to be worried about the future. On that morning, when the first of the fifty American "liaison" officers appeared at the spy headquarters and asked to see the latest bulletins, one key German employee looked at him wordlessly for a moment before saying arrogantly, "Can you see what flag is flying outside?"

The young American turned almost instinctively and stared out of the window at the flagstaff. Flapping in the light breeze was a new flag. "Old Glory" had been hauled down and replaced by the flag of the German Federal Republic. He flushed red and, without any further comment, turned and left the office. Behind him the Germans began to laugh. The days of the *Ami* bosses were over.

Reinhard Gehlen was in full charge at last.

---

[2]In 1959, 2802 agents from the East were arrested or uncovered by the West German authorities.

BOOK THREE

What happens now? He bolts, and he takes
half your secrets with him for good measure
and suddenly you're the guilty ones and you're
blushing like a lot of virgins holding your
hands over your fannies and not talking to
strange men.

John le Carre: Small Town in Germany

21

The man in the shadows felt his heart begin to beat more rapidly. There was the sound of brakes outside. That would be him!

A moment later, the rattle of keys at the outer door of No. 7 Kreittmayrstrasse confirmed his suspicion. The other man was having difficulty finding the hole; his left arm cradled a large bag of tomatoes and he couldn't quite manage the job with one hand. Then he did it. The door swung open and a knifeblade of afternoon sun slid into the dark hallway and illuminated the ancient elevator cage. In the shadows the man pressed his body hard against the wall. Soon he was going to have to do it.

Suddenly he felt his whole body tense. His hand, which gripped the pistol so hard that his palm was damp with sweat, was white at the knuckles with the effort. His breath started to come in short, sharp, painful gasps. *In a moment he was going to have to kill someone!*

The other man had completed his complicated fumbling with the outer door. As security-conscious as ever, he locked it carefully behind him. Now there was no sound save for his heavy, elderly breathing and the distant rattle of one of Munich's ancient blue-painted streetcars. The city had not yet woken up from its midday doze. Blinking a little in the darkness of the hallway, he stumbled to the elevator door.

"Having trouble with the door?" the man in the shadows said. His voice seemed miles away, unreal, as if it belonged to someone else.

The elderly man turned, startled. "No," he stammered automatically, swinging round to face the man in the shadows. "But what are—" His voice broke off in mid-sentence. He saw the object in the stranger's hand. It was a newspaper, yet . . .

He did not have time to consider the object any further.

"Bandera?" The man in the shadows rapped out the word hard and brutal.

The elderly man's face turned pale. It was a long time since he had been called that name—at least by strangers. For years he had been known as Herr Stefan Popel by his neighbors and casual acquaintances. Bandera . . .

The man in the shadows did not wait for an answer. The look on the other man's face told him all he wanted to know. He whipped the newspaper away from the pistol. Cocking it, he pressed the trigger. Bandera, alias Popel, raised his hands in panic, as if he could ward off the bullet with his bare flesh.

But no bullet came. Nothing save a faint hiss like gas escaping from a leak. Bandera seemed more surprised than scared. His eyes opened wide with amazement. *What was all this about?*

The next moment he knew. A pair of invisible hands fastened themselves around his throat. He gagged. Deep down in his body his stomach suddenly seemed to be on fire. A faint groan escaped his lips. His eyes rolled upward while his body started to sag at the knees. A second later he slipped down to the dirty floor of the dark hallway.

For one long moment the thin young man in the shadows stared down at the man whom he had been trained so thoroughly to kill, then he turned and hurried away. The door clanked behind him. Once outside in the fresh air of the deserted street, he broke the little phial containing the antidote and breathed it in gratefully. Moments later he tossed the glass fragments into the nearest gutter and strode away in the fall sunshine. In an instant he had disappeared into the city. No one had seen the slim, handsome young man come and no one had seen him go. It was the perfect murder, just as they had promised him in Moscow it would be.

So, on that day of October 15, 1959, Stefan Bandera died as violently as he had lived. As a young Ukrainian patriot, Bandera had fought as a partisan against the "Reds" at the end of World War I, and when eventually he had been forced to flee his native land, he had continued that battle with cold-blooded bitterness. But in the years between the wars there were many Russian refugee organizations in the West, and Bandera's was one of many such minor and generally ineffective groups. Only the start of the German's Barbarossa campaign against Russia in 1941, made him hope that there was still a chance for him to return home.

In 1942, he finally returned to Russia as an employee of the Germans. He and his fellow exiles seized the heaven-sent opportunity with eager hands. Before the Germans could stop them, they declared that part of their homeland occupied by the Germans an independent state. Hitler was enraged at the news. The new republic was strangled at birth. Bandera and some of his fellow leaders were swiftly thrown into German jails. But not for long. Several months later, they were again working for the Germans, but this time as spies, counterespionage agents and saboteurs.

This led Bandera to his first contact with the staff officer of Foreign Armies East. But Bandera was no fool. As soon as he realized that Nazi Germany's defeat was just around the corner, he deserted his erstwhile friends and went underground, only turning up again at the end of the war when he knew that the breakdown of relations between the Americans and Russians would ensure that he would not be deported eastward to a final exit dangling at the end of a Soviet rope.

In those middle years of the war, Munich became a central gathering point for Bandera's followers and many like them, plus the new wave of Russian refugees who had fled the Red Army stationed in East Germany. Radical refugee organizations shot out of the Bavarian soil like mushrooms. Some were little more than discussion clubs or cultural meeting places for those who wished to keep up the old customs and languages, but others, like Bandera's OUNR (Organization of Ukrainian Nationalist-Revolutionaries), or the anti-Communist NTS, were deliberately dedicated to actively aggressive anti-Soviet missions within the Soviet Union itself.

And in those years which saw the start of the cold war, they did not lack backers. It is reliably reported that both the French and British paid these, and other similar organizations, to carry out their sabotage and spying activities deep inside the Soviet Union and Poland. But their main source of funds was from their old employers of the Foreign Armies East, now the Gehlen Organization, and the CIA.

Bandera and the rest were successful. From 1945 right up to 1952, they were able to carry on armed revolt in the border areas of East Poland and the Ukraine, which required carefully planned and massive Polish and Russian army actions before they could finally be put down. Thereafter they continued their resistance in those areas and other parts of Eastern Europe on a more individual basis in the form of spying and sabotage under the direct command of their (in the case of Bandera's organization) K-3 Department,[1] which supplied the agents to Gehlen for training and instructions.

---

[1] Called harmlessly enough, "Department for Relations with the Homeland."

According to a former Gehlen agent, Ossip Werhun, who fled to the East, and gave a "press conference" in 1962, these agents not only spied and carried out acts of sabotage, but also provoked anti-Soviet incidents and even revolution. Werhun said that "in 1956 Gehlen sent a group from Bandera's organization to Hungary to incite counterrevolution. They sneaked in by way of the Austrian-Hungarian frontier. A man named Vladimir Lenek oranized the crossing. . . . In 1959 another group of them disguised as citizens of the Federal Republic attended the World Festival of Youth and Students at Vienna. Lenek directed the group whose task it was to provoke anti-Soviet demonstrations. Another group under the direction of their security chief Kachouba had as its mission the recruitment of members of the Soviet Delegation for espionage activities."

Whatever the truth of Werhun's statements may be (and we shall have occasion to record more of them later), one thing is clear. By the early fifties, the Soviet authorities were thoroughly alarmed by Bandera's activities, and those of similar organizations, not only in the Slavic countries but also in East Germany.

At a staff meeting of the Russian State Security Service held in 1952, and attended by East Germans, it was decided with almost panic-stricken urgency that *every* measure must be taken to rid Russia and the Eastern Bloc countries of Bandera's agents. At that conference it was suggested that the only effective method of dealing with people like Bandera was to kidnap or murder them and that the best base of operations for these licensed killers would be the German Democratic Republic.

Thus it was that Bogdan Staschinski made his appearance on the international espionage scene as the first "licensed killer," à la James Bond, known to us.

Bogdan Staschinski's career in the Russian State Security Service had started early and innocently. As a nineteen-year-old student, he had been caught in 1950 traveling without a ticket on the train he was taking to the next large town in his native Ukraine, where he was studying mathematics in order to become a teacher. The trembling young student had been hauled up in front of an official of the State Security Service, who apparently knew that Staschinski's family were all convinced Ukrainian Nationalists and anti-Communists. At first the official threatened the young man with expulsion from the university if he didn't do what the Security Service wanted; the frightened young Bogdan asked what that was.

The answer was simple. The hard-faced man behind the desk said he wanted the Ukrainian to spy on his parents and, in particular, on his sister, who was connected with the pro-Bandera partisans hiding out in the local forests.

A thoroughly shaken Bogdan agreed to carry out the mission. And did so with remarkable success. He discovered the name of the partisan who had murdered a pro-Russian Ukrainian writer, Yaroslav Galan, and delivered it to his new employers. The murderer was duly "liquidated" and Bogdan received a reward: a monthly salary and the offer of a full-time job with the Security Service.

In the light of his overwhelming distaste for his job, it is hard to understand why he accepted the offer in 1951. Perhaps it was his youth and innocence. Perhaps it was fear. But he must surely have known after several months of spying on his own parents and immediate family to what lengths his employers could force him to go. In any event, within three years of the day the ticket collector had discovered the shaken youth traveling without a fare, Bogdan Staschinski was already training to be a licensed killer.

In 1954, after visiting a spy school in Kiev, Bogdan was sent to East Germany where a Soviet agent working closely with the local Ministry of State Security began to transform the twenty-three-year-old Ukrainian into a German. His teacher, with the frightening name of Sergei Demon, did his work well. Within a year, Bogdan was living in East Berlin as a German citizen and working as a Polish interpreter with the East German Import-Export Agency.

He liked Berlin. He liked the bars and cafés and the chance to go across to the well-stocked stores of the Western Sector every now and again; and he had plenty of money in his pocket to satisfy his liking for good food and clothes—and girls. It was during this period that he met Inge Pohl, an East German hairdresser, some two years younger than himself. It was love at first sight and soon thereafter the two of them were inseparable companions.

In 1956, Bogdan had already visited West Germany under Demon's "fatherly" guidance and made contact with a Russian agent in the ranks of the Munich Ukrainian Nationalists, a journalist named Bissaga, whose job was to shadow Lev Rabets, the chief editor of the Ukrainian exile newspaper for which Bissaga worked. Now, with Bissaga's aid, and using the identity of a dead German, Siegfried Drager, Bogden started to make contacts within the exile groups. It didn't take him long to find out that there were intense rivalries among these groups, and that certain of their key members, such as Rabets, worked as "tippers" for the CIA and Gehlen. Dutifully he passed on the information to Demon, his mind full of the blond German girl, Inge Pohl.

In September, 1957, Bogdan was called to Demon's office in East Berlin and told solemnly by his trainer, "The hour has come. A comrade from Moscow is here."

The young counterespionage agent said nothing, but he felt a sense of uneasy foreboding. *What hour?* he asked himself. But he did not translate his thoughts into words. In the few years he had been with the organization he had learned to keep his opinions to himself, especially if they were potentially dangerous ones.

A few moments later the two men were called into the presence of a high KGB official. For a while the three engaged in relatively harmless chatter. Bogdan, about whom the Moscow official seemed to know everything, including the matter of the unpaid fare, congratulated him on his work in the West. In particular, he was pleased with the way Bodgan had shadowed Rebets in Munich. Then slowly the benign smile left his face. Working himself up into a kind of artificial rage, he began to speak fast and furiously about Rebets, "this parasite" who as "a dangerous subversive" had to be "liquidated."

Bogdan felt himself grow cold as he listened to the older man. A small, frightening premonition was beginning to unfold itself at the back of his mind, like some deadly snake about to bite.

Then, as abruptly as he had started his tirade, the KGB official broke off. Turning the key in his desk drawer, he brought out an object which looked like a pistol, but unlike any model that Bogdan knew from his training in Kiev. It had a seven-and-a-half-inch barrel, the thickness of his thumb, which was made up of three separate parts. While Bogdan stared at it as if hypnotized, the official explained how this strange weapon, developed in the Secret Police labs, worked.

It was powered by a 1.5-volt battery. Hence it was noiseless. When the trigger was pulled, a small powder charge in the middle section went off and splintered a glass phial at its muzzle. This phial contained prussic acid which formed a gas the moment it was combined with air. Fired at a rage of a couple of feet, anyone who breathed it in would be dead within a matter of seconds and there would be no trace of poisoning left in the victim's body.

Bogdan opened his mouth to ask a question, but before he could pose it, it was answered for him. The murderer would be protected from the effects of the gas by taking a certain pill prior to the killing and quickly breathing in an antidote immediately it was over. As the official explained this, he looked straight at Bogdan. With a feeling of panic, the young agent realized the words were addressed to him, apparently in order to reassure him.

He was to be the murderer!

Bogdan Staschinski carried out his first murder on October 12, 1957. Using his fake identity documents, he flew into Munich and took up residence at a small hotel (a detail which had an important bearing on the fact that he was later disbelieved by Western intelligence officials until he could prove he had spent two days there). Then he posted himself near Rebets's office in Munich's Karls Square.

Punctually at ten o'clock, he spotted Rebets, a broad-shouldered, energetic man with a briefcase, alighting from a streetcar. His heart beating wildly, he ran to the entrance of the building which contained the exile's office and clambered up the stairs to the first floor. Within moments he heard Rebets open the door below, then begin to climb the creaking stairs. Hastily Bogdan swallowed the pill. The footsteps were getting closer. There was not a soul about. From somewhere behind one of the closed doors a typewriter was clacking slowly. The killer and his victim were alone. Bogdan took a deep breath and started to walk down the stairs to meet the man he had come such a long way to murder. Just as Rebets was within three or four steps from him, he aimed and fired.

There was a soft hiss; the same soft hiss he had remembered when Demon had made him murder the little dog tied to a tree in a wood outside Berlin as a demonstration of the weapon's efficiency. Rebets looked up startled. For a moment he did not realize what was happening to him. He half opened his mouth, but no words came from it. His hand clasped the stairrail hard. Bogdan could see how the knuckles whitened with the effort. But to no avail. He was already dying. Slowly his knees began to buckle and he slid downward. Bogdan did not wait to see him fall. Hurriedly he rushed by the dying man who had been born not many miles away from the same obscure village he came from in the Ukraine. He flung the door open. Crushing the little glass phial, he held it to his nose and gratefully breathed in the antidote. Then he walked swiftly away and disappeared into the crowds.

"Suddenly," he told the court later at his trial, "I became aware of the fact that the sun was shining and that my fellow human beings looked content and happy. I had the feeling that I was dreaming." But he wasn't. When he returned to Karls Square on his way to his hotel, a white-painted Mercedes ambulance was parked outside Rebets's building and two black-leather-coated policemen, standing next to a green Volkswagen with its revolving blue light, were trying to control an excited crowd of spectators. He walked on rapidly.

A few days later he was back in East Berlin. Demon was beside himself with joy. The mission had been a complete success. An autopsy had shown that Rebets had died of grave heart trouble (as the high KGB official had predicted would be the medical report). There was no trace of poison in the body. Demon called for vodka and set about getting Bogdan drunk.

But Bogdan could not get drunk—that night or for many nights afterward. He became moody, depressed, and could not sleep. When Inge questioned him about this sudden change in his spirits, all he could answer her was a helpless, "Perhaps I'll tell you everything about it one day." And with that he fell silent, sinking back again into the overwhelming horrifying awareness that he had become a professional, paid killer.

22

Although the Munich police attributed the deaths of Rebets and, two years later, Bandera to natural causes, the several thousand Ukrainian Nationalists in the Bavarian capital were not so sure. They knew well enough that the autopsy had proved the bodies free of poison, yet the two deaths had come too close to a whole series of kidnappings and similar sudden deaths to be accepted completely uncritically.

In the late fifties, Dr. Poremsky, chief of the NTS, had been murdered. His deputy in Berlin, Dr. Alexander Truschnovitch, had been kidnapped. In Austria, one of the organization's leading officials, Valeri Tremmel, had suffered the same fate. All in all, by the start of 1959, West Berlin's police had registered some 225 kidnappings and 340 attempted kidnappings, all carried out by Mielke's State Security agents working in close association with their colleagues of the KGB.

The Ukrainian Nationalist organizations which had supplied Gehlen with so many of his agents and saboteurs for work in the East began to break up. More and more of the leading officials started to turn traitor, winning their return to the "Motherland" by first betraying their comrades already working in Russia or behind the Iron Curtain as agents, and then fleeing to East Berlin to give one of the many celebrated "press conferences" of those years to the Western press.

Ossip Werhun, the OUNR official and ex-Gehlen

agent whose extensive press conference shortly after he arrived in East Berlin in 1962 has already been referred to in part, introduced himself to the assembled journalists with the initial statement that "I was born in the Ukraine when it still belonged to Austro-Hungary. During World War II I was a member of the Abwehr in Occupied Ukraine. For that reason I was recruited by a member of the Gehlen Organization, a Colonel Chamoutine who had been my boss in the Abwehr."

He then went on to give details of his work which had been mainly in Austria. "After the signing of the treaty with Austria in 1955,[1] I received orders to recruit Ukrainian Nationalists there and send them with faked papers to the U.S.S.R., Czechoslovakia, Poland and Hungary. I was also to arrange a crossing point near Linz (Austria). These V-men of mine were to send details of Soviet formations which I then transmitted to Pullach."

After explaining how the system worked, Werhun explained that Gehlen had agents in the ranks of the Austrian police, including some very high-ranking officers, who helped Gehlen find new agents among the refugees streaming across the border from Hungary.

But Werhun and others like him did not stop at simply explaining their activities behind the Iron Curtain; they also accused their former chief of trying to plant agents in allied countries: in a Belgian flying school, a British ministry, an Irish business—even in the United States. Indeed, Communist writer Julius Mader went so far as to accuse Gehlen, at that time, of having agents in eleven of the fifteen NATO countries (excluding his own West Germany); and French writer Sanche de Gramont could maintain that "they say that Gehlen had extended his tentacles throughout

---

[1] For the evacuation of the troops (British, American, French, and Russian) which had occupied the country since the end of the war.

the allied nations and that his agents work from Rome to Paris."

Even allowing for a certain measure of misrepresentation in some of the testimony, it was clear that the breakdown of the Ukrainian Nationalist organizations not only deprived Gehlen of one of his chief sources of agents, but also helped to blacken his reputation in general, and make him suspect among his allies in particular.[2] For those among them who had always disliked the ex-Wehrmacht general, the evidence of the turncoats in East Germany was fresh proof of what they had always believed; and even those who had worked closely with Gehlen for many years began to keep their distance, anxious not to be dragged down with him if it came to a crisis.

Some three hundred miles away from Pullach, Erich Mielke and his Soviet friends, who often enjoyed the luxury of his lakeside villa and his expensive boat that could hold twenty people comfortably, must have rubbed their hands with joy at their number one enemy's discomfiture. But they were not going to have it all their own way. Bogdan Staschinski was beginning to lose his nerve.

On April 23, 1960, Bogdan finally received permission to marry his Inge. That day, "Yoschi Lehmann" (as he was now called), married his blond bride at the East Berlin Golgotha Kirche. But there was little happiness about the ceremony in the bomb-damaged Protestant church on that fine spring day; Inge knew

---

[2] In 1963, the Foreign Affairs Committee of the U. S. Senate investigated, for instance, the business of a public relations firm, which was proved to be receiving secret funds from West Germany. One year later it also looked into another organization working on behalf of American citizens of German origin and discovered that it too received undercover money from West Germany. Whether this money came from Gehlen and for what purpose it was used has never really been disclosed.

by now that her new husband was a KGB agent, and Bogdan was only too well aware that soon he would have to return to Moscow for further orders.

A month later, the newly married couple began their training for the next assignment. Inge was to be given money to open a hairdressing salon in West Berlin, which would be an excellent cover (or so her husband's boss told her) for "Yoschi's" mission. Bogdan, for his part, was to undergo a special course of instruction in how to live, behave and react like a West Berliner.

Halfheartedly Inge agreed to go ahead, but she was already trying to encourage her morose, new husband to flee to the West. At first she had little success. Bodgan knew well enough that even if he did make it, there would be little security for him in West Germany. For all he knew, there were probably other licensed killers like himself at the disposal of the KGB. One evening, however, he saw that Inge was right; to some extent, at least.

In the dirty little apartment that the KGB had allotted them in Moscow, the couple were plagued by bugs —once they put the light out at night. For Bogdan it wasn't so bad; he had been used to them since his earliest youth. Inge was different. She had the typical German middle-class horror of vermin. One night she gave her husband an ultimatum. Either he got rid of the bugs—at least those in the bed—or she would move out. With a weary smile Bogdan gave in; he would find the bugs.

From years of experience, he knew that he'd find their source somewhere in the bed's iron framework, for no matter how often Inge changed the sheets, new bugs always appeared within a couple of hours. Stripping away all the bedding, he started to run a lighted match along the chipped, grubby, iron framework. This and the application of kerosene might do the trick, he told himself, especially if he then stood the bed on four saucers holding more of the liquid.

Then abruptly he forgot all about the bugs. For in the darkness under the bed, he had found another kind of bug—*an electrical one!*

Inge stared aghast, her hand held to her lips in the typical feminine gesture of fear, as he followed the wires which led to the tiny microphone hidden in the dirty drapes. His employers were watching him! Even though he had risked his life to murder two men for them, they still did not trust him. Every word he said to Inge was being registered somewhere. His face flushed hotly when it struck him that even their intimate moments would be recorded on tape to be laughed at by some fellow agent; perhaps the same men he worked with every day.

The start of Bogdan's defection dated from that day. But Inge knew he wasn't completely ready to defect, yet. Indeed, even if he were, how could they escape from Moscow? She knew that somehow or other they had to get back to Germany.

The months passed, and Inge found she was pregnant. The very next morning a happy Bogdan reported the news to his superiors, as was expected of him, to be told coldly that the time was not opportune for babies. Inge would have to undergo an abortion. Bogdan stood his ground, refusing to let the abortion be carried out. In the end his bosses gave in, but now they regarded Inge simply as a nuisance, who should be got rid of as soon as was convenient.

A few weeks later Inge was allowed to go to her parents in East Berlin so that the baby could be born there. But before she went, she agreed with her husband on a simple code, including the words "Have you been to your dressmaker?" which would mean, "Inge, get in touch with the Americans."

The months passed, and Inge's baby was born on January 31, 1961. Female agents of the KGB, who had the job of watching her, brought her presents and cooed over the new Russian as if they were simple housewives themselves instead of hardened spies. Then, at the beginning of May, Inge received a letter from her husband which contained the phrase she had been waiting for so long: *"Have you been to your dressmaker?"*

Inge took the next train to West Berlin. She knew where to find the offices which hid the activities of the CIA, but she met with disappointment after disappointment. Nobody seemed interested in her story until finally one sympathetic official told her, "Take the next train back to the East. Get there as quickly as possible. Tell no one you have been here. If they find out you've been here, your baby will be an orphan soon. You say your husband is in Moscow. How do you imagine we are going to get him out of there?" And that was that.

Sadly Inge returned home and began to make preparations to fly back to the Russian capital with their newborn son. From Bogdan came no new messages. It looked as if there was no hope for them.

Then tragedy struck. Almost overnight the little baby fell seriously ill. By the time the doctor had been called and diagnosed pneumonia, it was too late. Peter, the baby, was dead.

Almost hysterically, Inge called Bogdan in Moscow and ordered him to come to Berlin. Her father did the same, Bogdan answering him under the suspicious eyes of two agents, Sergei and Yuri, who were watching him at the other end. The next day Bogdan flew to Berlin with Yuri.

But he was not allowed to see his wife or dead baby at once. The ever-suspicious KGB and their German associates of the Ministry of State Security had first to be sure that Inge had no contacts with the West. In addition, they wanted an autopsy performed on the dead child to ascertain whether it had been poisoned or not by the Americans (their grossly perverted minds even went so far as to believe that such a monstrous deed was possible).

So Bogdan had to wait a day while they checked. Finally satisfied that Inge was free of suspicion and that the child had died a natural death, they allowed him to visit his wife. Inge broke down when she saw her husband, but even in the midst of her sobs, she sensed that he, too, was ready to defect if the opportunity presented itself.

But that day and the next, while they made the necessary preparations for the baby's funeral, they were never alone. Yuri went with them everywhere—to the florist to buy a wreath, to the local pastor to obtain his services for the funeral ceremony, to the tailor to buy Bogdan a dark suit—everywhere. Bogdan protested, but Yuri waved aside all his protests. At tragic moments like this, one needed a good friend at one's side, he said. Bogdan could have struck him in his greasy face. The agent was a thorough cynic and completely corrupted by his job with the KGB.

But in spite of Yuri's supervision, the two unhappy young people knew that if they did not take the chance offered by their family tragedy, they would both be on a plane to Moscow by the end of the week. It was now or never.

Just after the tiny oak coffin bearing the body of their beloved Peter had been lowered into the ground and the pastor had intoned his last prayer over it, the sad young couple walked down a narrow street to the home of Inge's parents. Behind them at a respectful distance came a handful of relatives—and Yuri.

Later, neither of them knew who had actually given the signal to run. Perhaps it was Yuri's distance from them—a matter of fifty yards or so. It was the first time he had been separated from them since the day Bogdan had arrived in Berlin. Perhaps it was the thick patch of bushes and rough undergrowth to their right which offered fair cover. But whatever it was, both of them knew that this was their last chance. Suddenly, to the astonishment of the rest of the little funeral group, and to Yuri's horror, Bogdan had grabbed Inge's hand and was running wildly with her through the undergrowth. For a moment the other Russian agent was paralyzed with surprise. He did not move. Then, with a surprised yell of rage, he was pelting after them.

But Bogdan and Inge were in luck. Arriving at the local Falkensee Railroad Station, they found themselves in the midst of a dense crowd. Yuri, sweat gleaming on his face, frantically tried to fight his way through it. Without luck. Before he could stop them, the black-clad young couple had stumbled into a taxi and yelled an order to the startled cabdriver.

The cabbie did not hesitate. He took off as if the devil were after them, forcing the utmost out of the ancient protesting Opel.

Sitting back in its cracked, smelly leather seats, the two of them took stock of their situation for a moment, gasping for breath as they did so. Yuri would obviously run now to the nearest telephone box. But as he did not speak German, he would have to call up his HQ at Karlshorst, the Russian headquarters in East Berlin. They would then transmit his message through the People's Police to the border stations: *"Stop Taxi Number So-and-So!"*

With luck they might be able to reach a crossing point before the message had been relayed to all their various border stations. Yuri's lack of German might just give them time enough!

Inge rapped out a few directions. The cabbie, who seemed to be enjoying the adventure, apparently oblivious to the danger he ran himself, drove up and down narrow, dingy surburban streets, avoiding the main avenues where People's Police cruisers might be encountered, generally heading in the direction of the frontier.

They were in luck. Again there was a group of people congregated at the frontier between the German Democratic Republic and East Berlin. In the confusion they managed to slip across unnoticed. A little while later they changed taxis, drove into the courtyard of the East Berlin Schönhäuser Allee Railroad Station, where they took a local train to West Berlin. Within a matter of minutes they were across the sector border and safely ensconced in West Berlin. They had escaped!

For several days no one would believe Bogdan Staschinski's amazing story. The fact that he admitted he had killed two men seemed to the American and German officials who questioned him to stamp him as a case for a lunatic asylum rather than a man who had had to flee for his life. But in the end the CIA officials believed him, and after they had interrogated the first-known "licensed killer," passed him on to the German authorities.

One year later, on October 8, 1962, Bogdan was put on trial in Karlsruhe in one of the most sensational legal hearings of the postwar period. Although the East German propaganda machine went into action, throwing in the full weight of its enormous resources to prove that Bogdan Staschinski had actually murdered on behalf of other Ukrainian exile groups and not on behalf of the two Eastern security agencies, no one believed them. Bodgan's evidence was too good to be shaken by their efforts.

In the second week of October, Bogdan was sentenced to eight years' imprisonment. The sentence was mild and there were several gasps of shock among the many Ukrainian exiles present, but Bogdan had made a good impression on the court. In addition, he had confessed to the two murders voluntarily. Besides, both the CIA and the BND were interested in rewarding the man whose confessions had contributed greatly to stamping the KGB and the East German Ministry for

State Security as "Murder Incs" in the best Mafia tradition.

The fifty-six-year-old, heavyset boss of the Ministry for State Security must have cursed roundly in that hearty Berlin manner which dated from the days when he was still known as "Brutal Eddie" when he read the newspaper reports of the trial. But then he probably shrugged and forgot the incident. It was just another move (which he'd lost) in a never-ending game. Besides which, he knew that fall that the next move would be his. In the next great West German espionage trial, scheduled for sometime in the coming year, the victory would be his and Gehlen would be shown to the world for what he was: a bungling, cold-blooded spymaster, who surrounded himself with ex-SS and SD men, whose aim it was to turn the clock to the glorious days of the Fascist "Great German Reich."

23

Some three months before Bogdan Staschinski made his daring dash for freedom, another East German agent had made his own somewhat less dramatic escape to West Berlin. His name was Günther Männel and he was the hundred and fiftieth German agent to defect to the West. Under normal circumstances his defection would not have caused any great stir in Western intelligence circles, because he was of little importance as such, but Männel was professional enough to have provided himself with an "insurance policy" before he fled westward; he brought with him hundreds of secret documents and tapes which he knew would heighten his value to the other side. He had also brought the names of fifteen of Mielke's spies operating in the West.

Understandably, Both the CIA and the BND welcomed the new defector with open arms, and Männel was hastily transferred by air to West Germany to one of the organization's special camps for intensive interrogation. In the isolated atmosphere of the camp, the "guest from the East" began to sing like a little bird. But part of his testimony did not sound too musical to Gehlen's oversized ears. According to Männel, *there was a key East German agent within Pullach itself!*

Angrily, the ex-Wehrmacht general immediatley denied Männel's claim as a defector's typical attempt to make himself more important than he really was. For the time being the matter was dropped. But not for long. From faraway Finland the CIA sent a report to its Frankfurt Headquarters in West Germany that another defector—a Russian named Klimov, who had just fled from his Soviet masters—was making the same accusation. Somewhere high up in the *Bundesnachrichtendienst*, there was a Gehlen employee who was working for the East Germans and through them for the Russians—or vice-versa, he didn't exactly know which. The man's code name was "the Frisian"; his agent's number, 25003.

This time Gehlen was forced to act. Five months after Männel had given himself up to the CIA on November 11, 1961, Heinz Paul Johann Felfe, Hans Clemens, and Erwin Tiebel were all arrested on the charge of spying, and lodged in the big prison at Karlsruhe which often housed political prisoners. The chief of the BND tried to keep the news of the arrests under control and limited to the back pages of the papers, but without success. The next day, most West German newspapers heralded the sensational news on their front pages with banner headlines:

FELFE, KEY MAN IN BND ARRESTED ON ESPIONAGE CHARGE!

A West German public woke up to realize as it read the papers over its morning cup of coffee that the Gehlen legend of infallibility looked as if it were about to be shattered; Heinz Paul had been chief of the vital counterespionage section (or at least part of it) within the Gehlen Organization for the last ten years. *This meant that the Russians and Mielke's men had known all about Gehlen's operations in this area for over a decade!*

That same day, Gehlen's subordinates "leaked" the story to the press that they had known all about Felfe for months. But they had been unable to arrest him immediately, because they had not possessed sufficient evidence to take "further steps" against him.

But the public was not taken in. They knew that one day soon, when Felfe and his two associates were put on trial in Karlsruhe (where most spy trials were held), the evidence that Felfe would reveal might rock the whole Gehlen Organization. The Gehlen myth appeared to be at an end.

Felfe's background was not prepossessing. Born into the authoritarian family of a Saxon police officer in Dresden, he had joined the SS as soon as he had been old enough, being posted to the SS Security Organization at the beginning of the war. The thirty-one-year-old SS man had volunteered for the *Waffen SS* (the Armed SS), but had been turned down for health reasons (as he was three times more in the later years of the war). Instead, he was posted to the SS's secret spy organization devoted to spying on Switzerland. Here he remained for most of the war until, in the immediate postwar months, he was arrested by the British.

In those days, members of his organization were subject to automatic arrest by the Allies, usually followed by long terms of imprisonment. But Felfe was lucky. He was only in the internment camp for a year before he was released. Nor was he penalized by the denazification court except for a relatively minor fine of seven hundred marks (in those days a matter of a couple of cartons of cigarettes). The reason was obvious: Heinz Felfe was already back in his old profession, working for the British, spying on students of left-wing persuasion at the University of Bonn.

Felfe was not satisfied with his new activity. He knew what the British "gentlemen" thought of him as a person and how they regarded the petty little reports he sent in on the "Communist activity" of the stupid, long-haired students at the University of Bonn. He was a man of nearly thirty years of age and he still had no firm career or even the chance of one.

In 1950, his fortune changed. He renewed his old

acquaintanceship with a friend from his Dresden youth, Hans Clemens.

Hans Clemens, like Felfe an ex-SS man, had not been as lucky. He had been in jail in Rome until 1949. On his release, he had made his way to Bonn to renew his friendship with the third man in the trio of ex-SS men, Erwin Tiebel, who had already built up a successful building contractor's business.

Tiebel had left his wife behind in Dresden, where she had formed an association with a Russian officer. The Russian was connected with the secret service, but neither the fact that he was a spymaster nor that he was probably his wife's boyfriend worried Tiebel. He had girl friends of his own, anyway. One day he had received a letter from his wife asking him to come and visit her in the Soviet Zone. He did not hesitate, and some time later he was celebrating the "reunion" with his wife and her Russian boyfriend. For nearly a week the strangely-assorted trio celebrated, until finally the Russian introduced the ex-SS man to "Colonel Max."

For the first time, he learned the real reason his wife had invited him to Dresden: the Russians wanted him to work for them, contacting potential agents in the West, his old pals from his SS days in particular, who would find it difficult to get a job in the new Germany anyway.

By 1950, Tiebel had recruited Felfe and Clemens into his new net. The "three musketeers from Dresden," as they sometimes called themselves in their more drunken moments, were ready to start. But where? That was the question.

Felfe and Clemens tried first to find employment with the *Bundes Verfassungsschutz* (the Federal Constitution Defense Force), the oddly-named German FBI. They managed to obtain an appointment with the Federal Minister of the Interior, Dr. Gustav Heinemann. The bespectacled, high-foreheaded minister listened politely enough to the two men's accounts of their pasts, but he soon realized that he was dealing with two unrepentant Nazis. The man who was one day to be West Germany's President was smarter than the country's master spy; he turned down their applications. Gehlen did not.

Clemens had an old pal from his SS days in the Gehlen Organization. He was former SS colonel Krichbaum, who now ran the Bad Reichenhall department of the "firm." Krichbaum welcomed his old buddy with open arms. That same evening, Clemens and Krichbaum went on a colossal drinking bout, filled with noisy reminiscences of the "good old days," and when the latter awoke with a terrible hangover the next morning, he found he had signed Clemens up for the "firm."

A little while later Clemens, the newest member of the Gehlen Organization, arranged for a meeting of Krichbaum with "an old friend who can be relied upon." Naturally, it was Felfe.

The ex-colonel and the ex-captain met near Bonn. Again the "cups were raised," as the SS phrase had it; the two men chatted about former friends in the SS; and soon relapsed into the familiar "thou" form of address used during the war among the Black Guards. When Felfe left that same night, he knew that he had a job assured within the secret organization. He was to be posted to a key position at Pullach to the vital Department IIIF—*counterespionage!*

The team had now established themselves: Clemens in Bad Reichenhall, Felfe in Pullach, and Tiebel, who had his offices in Rhöndorf, the little Rhenish town whose most famous inhabitant was the German Chancellor himself, Konrad Adenauer in nearby Bonn. The "three musketeers" were in a position to supply the East with the most vital information about the Gehlen Organization—and they lost no time in setting about their exciting new task, spurred on, in the case of the first two men, by the considerable sums of money supplied by their Soviet masters.[1]

Almost immediately after he joined the counterespionage section in Pullach, Felfe was appointed head of "Counterespionage Soviet Union." In other words, it was his job to run Gehlen agents in Russia. And, as if that were not enough, he also received information about the activities of other agents operating in the East, insofar as their missions affected the working of his own men. As Judge Weber was later to remark cynically, when he was told the full extent of Felfe's authority at the Karlsruhe trial: "Obviously the right man for the right job!"

But Felfe was not content with this. He outdid himself in his attempts to supply his Soviet masters with the information they needed, which was usually conveyed to them by Tiebel. With that typical German humorless thoroughness, he noted anything and everything: new building construction in Pullach; names of every BND man he knew, including relatively unimportant clerks and typists; routine conferences; even his own reports to the Soviet bosses were copied and carefully hidden away with the rest of his "files." Every month, eight to ten films of secret documents that Felfe had photographed with his Minox cameras were brought through the Iron Curtain by East German couriers. And if that did not suffice, he, Clemens or Tiebel would report virtually every month to Karlshorst, the

---

[1] It is hard to understand why the somewhat intellectual Tiebel, who received little money from the Russians and the East Germans, took such risks for the Communists whom he hated. After all, he was a prosperous businessman. Perhaps it was the thrill of knowing he was engaged in a forbidden activity. Perhaps it was because he had always admired Felfe and Clemens from their days together in Dresden as young SS men and could not refuse them a favor. We do not know. All we know is that he served his two friends loyally and selflessly.

Soviet Army HQ in Berlin, or to Frau Clemens in Dresden, with even more information. The prosecution at Karlsruhe calculated that Felfe had delivered some fifteen thousand photos and twenty tapes to the East in their decade of activity, so that there was hardly anything which took place in Pullach about which the East Germans and their Russian masters were unaware. In fact, there is still a security clamp on exactly what Felfe, and to a lesser extent Clemens, delivered to the East.

Thus the years passed. Felfe, the ex-SS man, became a highly respected figure in the strange, unreal world behind the high, whitewashed concrete walls of the Pullach spy headquarters. His reports were uncannily accurate. His agents in the East seemed to have access to excellent sources of information, which their chief was able to interpret and analyze with such amazing ability that his predictions were invariably one hundred percent correct.

Naturally, no one in Pullach realized that the Russians were supplying "their man in Pullach" with most of the details themselves, and that they were even prepared to sacrifice relatively important information in order that Felfe should retain his reputation for thoroughness and reliability. In addition, the Eastern spymasters were too conscious of Felfe's value to them to endanger his position by overeager use of the information with which he supplied them.

It was only when a Gehlen agent appeared on the verge of becoming too dangerous to them that they stepped in and arrested him. They preferred to let the Gehlen man believe they were obtaining vital information while at the same time ensuring that in fact, the German spies received no more than semiclassified information. And back at their Pullach HQ, the ex-Wehrmacht officers who were still running the various major sections were so convinced of their own infallibility and superiority to the half-educated "Reds" that they put down any failure to coincidence, or "bad luck." Inevitably at times, some of the men in the field complained that the Russians and the East Germans always seemed to know what the BND would do next. But Pullach, which over the years had become a typical bureaucratic organization, ignored their complaints and half-expressed suspicions that there must be a leak somewhere.

Obviously General Gehlen, whatever he was to state to the contrary later, had full confidence in Felfe. Ten years after the ex-SS man had entered the spy ring, Pullach gave a discreet little party for the head of the Russian section, its high point being the presentation of a plaque bearing a drawing of St. George slaying the dragon within the framework of a laurel wreath. It was the traditional symbol of loyalty and bravery. The man who presented it? *Reinhard Gehlen himself!*[2]

A few weeks later, Felfe was arrested on a charge of high treason, but the man who had been a double agent for so long was not finished yet. Not by a long shot.

----

[2]Somewhere about the same time, the Russians and the East Germans also expressed their appreciation of Felfe's ten years in their service. Their tribute was more practical. It was in the form of five hundred dollars.

24

The inquiries into Felfe's decade of spying for the East were going to take eighteen months. Perhaps Gehlen thought the lengthy period of investigation might suffice to quiet the public's discomfort at the realization that the East had had a spy in West Germany's top espionage service for so long. Or perhaps Felfe's amazing industry and Germanic thoroughness really did require so much time for investigation before a case could be made against him. We do not know. All we do know is that for some completely inexplicable reason, Felfe was allowed almost total freedom during most of the time he spent in the jail at Karlsruhe waiting for his trial to begin. And Heinz Felfe was too old a hand at the spying game not to take advantage of that freedom.

On orders that came right from the top, he was allowed to leave his cell on Saturdays and Sundays to play chess in the prison library with a former big businessman, Jürgen Ziebell, who had been jailed for alleged crooked manipulations and bankruptcy. The two men got on well enough together. They were both highly intelligent and used to exercising authority in a manner that impressed not only their fellow prisoners—petty thieves, pimps from Karlsruhe's eighteenth-century brothel district, perverts—but also the guards, especially those of them who had served during the war and knew the fearsome reputation of the SS.

The two crooks soon started to put their heads together to plan their escape from the Karlsruhe jail. First of all, Felfe wangled himself a job as trustee in charge of the prison library, despite protests on the part of the warden which were overruled for some reason by the top authority. Here it was part of his job to supervise the distribution of prison clothing as well as books. As a result, he was out of his cell for most of the prison's working hours, besides being allowed to move about the interior of the prison freely.

Felfe quickly used part of this privilege to contact a fellow convict named Kurrle, who was in charge of the packing of various popular periodicals for which the prison had a contract, and bribed him to start enclosing messages within them for certain selected addresses. Naturally these messages, written in a simple invisible ink of his own manufacture (alum and water) and in his own code, were addressed to members of the Eastern intelligence services in West Germany. In addition, Felfe was allowed to write a weekly letter to his aged mother in Dresden. Each letter was, of course, censored by one of the guards, but what the guard, unskilled in the tricks of the espionage service, neglected to do was to read between the lines. If he had done so, he would have been shocked. Felfe's mother was being used as a direct courier between her imprisoned son and his Soviet bosses in East Germany.

At first, Felfe's immediate thoughts were solely concerned with arranging an escape for himself and his new pal Ziebell. As he wrote to his "control" in the East, either they should attempt to free him, or they should smuggle in some form of poison, since what Clemens would have to tell the judges at the trial would ensure his having to spend the rest of his life behind prison bars—and that he couldn't stand.

His control smuggled back the answer that they would attempt to rescue him. They could do something if he could manage to be out of his cell at night. Felfe duly noted the point and set about obtaining a key to his cell.

His first attempt failed. The prisoner whom he had bribed to make him one in the prison workshop was caught in the act by a guard, but fortunately for the two would-be escapees, he did not reveal who had paid him to make it.

Felfe tried again. He smuggled a sketch of his lock out of the prison in a letter to his mother. She saw to it that it landed in the hands of the right people so that a key could be made and sent back by the same route. Meanwhile Felfe, realizing that time was passing, tried out an alternative scheme. Contacting a convict who was soon to be released, he bribed him to go to East Berlin and bring him back a sample of what the underworld called "angel's hair." This is decidely not as harmless as it sounds. It is a fluffy bundle of nylon threads into which diamond splinters have been sewn. With it a skilled crook can saw through iron bars as if they were made of matchwood.

For some time nothing came of either scheme. While they were being explored Heinz Felfe was transferred temporarily to another prison, though he was promised that he would be given his old post as librarian back when he returned. By this time, the prison authorities regarded him as a polite, intelligent, model prisoner. Fuming inwardly, Felfe said good-bye to Ziebell and allowed himself to be transferred.

Knowing he could not do anything more about the planned escape, he spent the next weeks relaying to his contacts and control on the other side of the Iron Curtain what he guessed the "old pals" in Pullach would have found out by now and suggested countermeasures, including a means of secreting the money his bosses had paid him for his services out of the Federal Republic.

In addition, he took careful note of the questions put to him by the various investigators and, on the basis of his twenty years' experience in the spy game, made educated guesses about what exactly they knew. These educated guesses followed the same tried route to the East via his gray-haired old mother, who by this time was developing a remarkable capacity for her new metier.

As the winter of 1962 gave way to a bright, green spring, Heinz Felfe, lying wide awake in his white-washed cell, hands under his head, staring at the low ceiling, listening to the crazy chatter of the sparrows and the hoarse cawing of the crows outside, felt a new burst of confidence. One day soon he would be a free man again. He knew that his bosses wouldn't let him down now. They would get him out. *They would!*

It is quite possible that the Russians had no intention of rescuing Heinz Felfe right from the start. He had served his original purpose. They had lost their top agent in the Gehlen Organization. Now that they knew —from his smuggled-out letters—just exactly how much Gehlen's men had learned of their activities in the West, Felfe would serve them better in a completely different role. Soon he would be brought to trial, and knowing the democratic procedures of the West German courts, they realized that even a man of Gehlen's enormous power would not be able to stop all the evidence of his organization's activities being revealed to the public at large. It would be a tremendous propaganda victory for the Russians, especially when it was made public that Felfe, Clemens and Tiebel had all been in the SS, confirming what they always maintained: the BND was run largely by former SS and SD men.

Naturally there was a catch. The propagandists in Gehlen's employ would speedily point out that *they* too had used the services of these selfsame SS men. But the Russians, with the aid of Mielke, soon found a way round that one. They decided that as soon as Felfe and his two fellow spies were brought to trial, they would stage a trial of their own: that of Dr. Globke, Adenauer's intimate and Gehlen's immediate boss, *in absentia*. Although the West might point out they used SS men, they would be able to reply that they employed these "Fascists" only of necessity and in subordinate positions. On the other hand, the man who actually gave Gehlen orders and was in a position of great power, with the ear of the German Federal Chancellor himself, was a convinced Nazi with a hundred percent Fascist past, as was proved by his infamous "commentaries" on the anti-Semitic Nuremburg Laws.

Thus it was that as Heinz Felfe, alone in his tiny cell, warmed himself with the fantasies of a new life in the East, respected for his services to the Communists and perhaps employed in a nice little espionage post somewhere in East Berlin, his masters had already decided to sacrifice him in order to achieve that stupendous propaganda victory and the consequent discrediting of the West's master spy Reinhard Gehlen...

One might have thought that a man of Gehlen's intelligence and experience would have realized what Mielke and his Russian associates were planning to do with Felfe. After all, Felfe's arrest meant that his whole organization would come under public scrutiny at the trial, which was to be the major one of its kind in postwar Germany, and knowing the efficiency of the Eastern intelligence and propaganda services, he surely could have guessed that they would make the most out of the trial.

But apparently Gehlen did not suspect what was in store for him. He let events take their course, without even ensuring that Felfe, imprisoned in Karlsruhe Prison, was under adequate supervision. Perhaps he was lulled into a false sense of security by the knowledge that Clemens was prepared to confess all and would prove to be of great aid to the prosecution at the trial.

Reinhard Gehlen, now white-haired and inclining a

little to portliness, was up to his eyes in work that summer of 1961 and the subsequent spring of 1962. In August, 1961, the East Germans had cut off their part of Berlin from the West by the surprisingly quick and completely unexpected construction of the infamous "Wall." At the time, his agents in the German Democratic Republic had warned him that the government was preparing to do something to stop the flow of refugees from the East who were using the West Berlin "escape route" to "vote with their feet." But he had ignored their warning, advising West German Chancellor Adenauer that there was nothing to fear in Berlin, basing his prognosis on the fact that his agents were unable to find any large-scale dumps of concrete, barbed wire, bricks and so on needed for building a wall on the scale of that which was later erected in the divided city.

Now, as 1961 gradually gave way to 1962, he was actively trying to repair his damaged reputation with the Federal Chancellor and at the same time to build up his organization, which had been hit both by Felfe's treachery and the fact that West Berlin was no longer of any use to him as a transit station for the smuggling of operatives in and out of East Germany. We have no statistics available of the number of agents who used this means of entrance into the German Democratic Republic. But we do know that Mielke invariably used West Berlin as the most satisfactory way of introducing his men into the West.

As the official publication of the West German Government on spying, which appeared in the mid-sixties, points out:

"The number of East German agents in the West has gone down since the 13th August 1961. . . . Both intelligence services of the Soviet Zone—the Ministry of State Security (civil) and the Administration for Co-Ordination (military)—had used the flood of refugees to the West to introduce spies into the Federal Republic. . . . After the building of the Wall the mass influence of agents came to an end."

Thus Gehlen, just like his rival Mielke in East Berlin, had to find new ways of slipping his men across the border into the East. However, all this said and done, one can also suspect that Reinhard Gehlen was getting old, and that the huge spy organization which he had built up since 1946 was too much for one man to manage successfully, though he was continually traveling from one branch to another to inspect his subordinates (often interviewing new V-men himself under a cover name, and making suggestions for new forms of technical appliances).

In addition, the BND was becoming too clumsy and awkward to control. Gehlen's insistence on the eight-step method of obtaining information and passing it on through the various subordinate organizations, each supplied by individual couriers, often meant that a vital piece of information took up to six weeks before it landed on his desk. Gehlen of course had secret radio operators established in the East, but they had strict orders to remain silent and not reveal their positions until they were quite sure that the "cold" war was about to turn into a "hot" one. Then—and only then —were they to be allowed to use their radios to inform Pullach.[1]

In brief, it may be stated that one of the reasons why Reinhard Gehlen, perhaps Europe's most experienced spymaster, failed to fully appreciate the dangers inherent in the coming Felfe trial was that he was getting old; and like most old men, he had become conservative and set in his ways, not easily persuaded to change his method of operating. In addition, he was jealous of any attempt on the part of his bright up-and-coming

---

[1]After the construction of the Wall and the resultant difficulties of communication between East and West, he allowed his radio operators to begin relaying coded information westward.

university graduates, whom he was now attracting into his organization, to seize some of his vast power for themselves. Possessively, with that one-track greed of an old man, he held on desperately to total power. Nothing and nobody had the right to attempt to infringe upon the Gehlen myth.

But that myth (already damaged by Felfe's arrest) was beginning to break down. Soon the "Spiegel Affair" and the 1963 Felfe-Clemens trial would crack it for good.

25

The operation began precisely at 2000 hours on the evening of Friday, October 26, 1962, and things went wrong right from the start. One of the little green police VW "beatles" watching the brightly lit offices of the magazine in Hamburg spotted two men walking hurriedly away from the building toward the nearest parking lot. The sergeant at the wheel in his dark-blue uniform and white cap nudged his neighbor. "Hey, look at that!" he said in his thick Hamburg dialect. "Do you think . . ."

He never completed his sentence; his companion was too quick for him. "Yes, I think so," he snapped.

The sergeant made up his mind. All of them hidden along every likely escape route from the red-brick magazine building had been waiting for the signal to go into action, and their nerves were on edge. He knew that he had strict orders not to make a move until the district attorney gave the word, but should he let the two suspicious characters escape? He decided he should not.

He twisted the key in the ignition. The high-powered motor sprang into life, despite the typical damp October weather and the wet fog stealing in from the sea. Ramming home the gear, he set off after the men. But they beat him to their car. Before he could stop them, they were off in a crunch of gravel and a squeal of protesting rubber. The sergeant pressed his foot down on the gas pedal.

"Shall we turn on the blue light?" his companion asked.

The sergeant, crouched intently over the wheel, shook his head. "No, we don't want them to know we're following." So the blue light on the car's roof was not switched on, but the sergeant did order his companion to report in to Hamburg Police HQ what they were doing. Moments later the alarming report went out: *"Augstein trying to escape!"*

The man they were referring to was undersized, slim, bespectacled Rudolf Augstein, the publisher of the Hamburg weekly *Der Spiegel,* something of a German *Time* with sharp teeth, so that in its fifteen years of publication it had become the most widely read and most widely feared (among politicians) of all German weeklies.[1]

But the two Hamburg policemen were not concerned with Augstein's record or position; they were too intent on preventing him from escaping. For several miles they followed the other car which kept up its high speed, despite the gleaming wet streets and the evening traffic, until finally it turned into a street of small houses situated in one of the port's garden suburbs.

The Police VW squealed to a halt. The two cops loosened their pistols in their black holsters. Swiftly they clambered out of the little car. Pelting across the dark damp pavement, they caught the fugitive just as he was about to enter one of the houses.

Even before the surprised man could open his mouth to ask what was happening, the two policemen realized they'd made a very bad mistake. The man

---

[1] It is confidently asserted that the *Spiegel,* which has often been called the "gadfly of the German establishment," is not only read in every civilized country in the world but is also required reading for any intelligence man concerned with Germany, ranging from the Moscow-located KGB to the Washington-located CIA.

facing them was obviously a workman. His clothes were shabby and he was carrying under his arm a battered imitation leather briefcase, probably used to hold his lunchtime bottle of beer and sandwiches.

"What's going on?" the man, a bricklayer named Dolata, wanted to know, more than a little alarmed by the sight of the two big policemen, their pistol holsters open and obviously ready for action.

The sergeant recovered just in time. "You were speeding," he snapped hoarsely. "Speeding all the way through town."

While a suddenly apologetic Dolata paid his five-mark-fine to the second policeman, who was writing out the ticket by the light of the nearest streetlamp, the sergeant stood to one side biting his lip and staring up the deserted street, its darkness broken only by the little yellow pools of light from the street lamps. "My God," he muttered to himself in typical police fashion. "What are they going to think at HQ! I got the wrong fella!"

But the damage had already been done. Police reporters had gotten word of the amazing news: Dr. Rudolf Augstein of the *Spiegel—Das Deutsche Nachrichtenmagazin* was on the run with the police after him. The "Spiegel Affair" had begun.

That same night, the Hamburg police arrested major figures on the magazine's staff, seized thousands of the *Spiegel*'s files, searched the private apartments of the editors, arrested Augstein, and even convinced Interpol to step in and arrest *Spiegel* editor Conrad Ahlers, the handsome, blond-haired ex-paratrooper who was the cause of the whole trouble (according to the authorities) and was now vacationing in southern Spain. The charge was simple but chilling in its implications: *high treason!*

The Spiegel Affair had really started some three weeks earlier during the Karlsruhe trial of Bogdan

Staschinski, when Federal Attorney Albin Kuhn was handed a *Spiegel* article which he interpreted as endangering national security by revealing military secrets.

The next morning Dr. Kuhn, who was too busy with the Staschinski case to carry out an investigation himself, handed the article and his instructions to a Dr. Wunder. Wunder was to consult with the military and try to ascertain whether the article entitled "Fallex 62 —Federal Army Conditionally Ready" really did reveal military secrets. Dr. Wunder read it through swiftly and came to the conclusion that there might be something in Kuhn's suspicions after all, even though they were based on no more than a summary reading of the article during a few minutes' break in the legal proceedings.

A few days later, Dr. Wunder, who apparently knew nothing of military matters, consulted Colonel von Hopffgarten of the German Ministry of Defense. The colonel, realizing more quickly than the legal "expert" where this might all lead, suggested that the article should also be submitted to the ministry's Press Department for its opinion.

On October 17, the Press Department dutifully submitted its report: a single typed sheet. But despite its brevity, the report was dynamite. With the aid of the military experts, the conclusion had been reached that the article "Fallex 62" had revealed twenty-eight military secrets, and was, from the security point of view, objectionable in fifty different places.

Dr. Wunder and Colonel von Hopffgarten decided they had a case against the *Spiegel*. Together they prepared an opinion, and one day later it lay on the desk of Dr. Franz Josef Strauss himself, West Germany's ambitious, dynamic Minister of Defense. Now there was no holding back. The "Bavarian Bull" was personally offended. He determined to press the case against the "impudent gadfly of the establishment" which had attacked him for so long and now had the temerity to criticize "his" army.

Franz Josef Strauss looks almost a caricature of the typical Bavarian. He is squat and immensely broad-shouldered without any visible sign of a neck. He likes his beer and never seems happier than when he is with his national-costumed *Spezis*—"special friends"—in some *gemütlich* Bavarian *Gasthaus,* sitting at the scrubbed bare tables, stuffing himself with the tiny white sausages of his native state and drinking its outstanding Munich beer. But there is a great difference between Franz Josef Strauss and his easygoing, if hot-tempered, fellow Bavarians. It is his great intelligence (his was the best high school diploma recorded in thirty years in Bavaria), allied to a demonstrably overriding ambition.

In 1945, Strauss who had served as a lieutenant in the artillery, went straightaway into politics and, despite his unprepossessing appearance, the "butcher boy," as many of his enemies called him contemptuously, both because of his looks and the fact he had been born the son of a butcher, swiftly rose in power within his own party, the Christian Social Union. Four years later he was elected to the first postwar West German parliament and, with the awareness of the true politician for public taste and opinion, he immediately added a "Josef" to his given name of "Franz." He knew that the name of Franz Josef, which had been borne by the last Austrian emperor prior to the debacle of 1914—1918, would win him unconscious support in the southern German Catholic states.

His guess was right. With his new "popular" name, his rhetorical ability, his intelligence and undeniable energy, Strauss soon made a name for himself in Bonn. He became a minister in 1953. Two years later he was appointed Minister for Atomic Questions. And then, in 1956, he captured the coveted office of Minister of Defense.

The armed forces would always be Franz Josef Strauss's major interest, but in those first years he developed a relationship to the new German Army (which had been officially incorporated into NATO in the same year that he took over the ministry) that was so highly personal and intimate that it sometimes went beyond the normal concern of a minister for his ministry. He guarded his new army, of all the services under his control, with the passionate, unreasoning concern of a mother hen for her newborn chicks. "When I took over the job," he would often declare proudly, "it was a number of men in uniform. I made the West's most modern and second-best army out of it [after the U.S. Army]."

He would brook no attack on it. With that earthy, rhetorical talent of his that made him stand head and shoulders above any other "orator" in the Bonn Parliament, he would tuck his head down, stick out his pugnacious chin, and in his thick Bavarian accent "go for" anyone who had the temerity to criticize the Bundeswehr.

It was during those mid-fifties that the *Spiegel* became his chief critic. The Hamburg news magazine uncovered scandal after scandal involving the young, bull-like minister, ranging from dubious building contracts to driving offenses.[2]

Strauss always gave back as good as he got, but nothing, apparently, could prevent the *Spiegel* from attacking him every Monday without fail. It was almost as if there was a personal feud involved in the continual criticism of the minister; as if the cool, cal-

---

[2]Even in these days, when Strauss has become something of an "elder statesman," his life is not without incident, as exemplified by his meeting with two streetwalkers, one white, one black, in early 1971 on the streets of New York City. That encounter ended with Strauss losing his wallet and fresh headlines in the more scandalous papers.

culating northerner, Augstein, was determined personally to force the hot-blooded, spontaneous southerner, Strauss, to withdraw from his high office.

By 1962, the long-standing feud was at its zenith, with Augstein not missing a trick and using every and any opportunity to snipe maliciously and cruelly at Strauss's conduct of the ministry. And as if that were not enough, Strauss realized that there were others who did not like the way he was leading the Army.

The Americans had once been his greatest admirers and supporters. That had been in the days of the cold war and the official NATO strategy of massive nuclear retaliation at the first sign of Soviet aggression across the West German border.

But in the late fifties, American thinking on massive retaliation had begun to change. As young President Kennedy was soon to make clear to the more hidebound of his military advisers, massive retaliation left a statesman no alternative save all-out atomic warfare; his hands were bound and there was no room for negotiation once the B-52s and their Russian equivalents had taken off with their deadly loads.

As the more progressive American military thinkers saw it, NATO needed a new strategy which would combine both nuclear and conventional potential, and allow the statesmen time to negotiate even after the first shots of a war had been fired. There must be some form of nuclear escalation, enough to show the enemy that America and NATO meant business, yet which at the same time would not force them immediately into all-out atomic warfare.

The construction of the Berlin Wall in 1961 proved to them that they were right. The Americans found themselves too weak in conventional manpower to force the Soviets' hand. All they had at their disposal was a massive nuclear arsenal. But to use it would have meant a total atomic war, and the question they asked themselves was: is the future of West Berlin important enough to risk a Soviet nuclear attack on the eighty prime targets in the United States, which would include cities such as Washington, New York, San Francisco? The answer they gave themselves was—no. So the American and other NATO planners began to rethink the whole of their European strategy, finally coming up with a totally new concept, that of the "flexible response," a combination of conventional and nuclear tactics which would allow the statesmen time to discuss and negotiate.

But of all the major leaders in NATO connected with defense, Franz Josef Strauss refused to accept the new concept. Conditioned by the cold war and supported by his chief, Adenauer, who was himself a convinced "cold war warrior," he resisted the new strategy with all his Bavarian stubbornness and histrionic ability.

The Americans were worried. Apart from West Germany's key position in the NATO "front line," Strauss's ministry controlled nearly twelve conventional divisions, more than twice the number of American divisions present in Europe. Conventionally the West Germans were the strongest force in West Europe; yet the bullheaded Bavarian still insisted on massive retaliation. Indeed, there were those among the American senior officers who believed that Strauss did not merely want the Americans to retain the full weight of their nuclear power in Europe. He wanted more; *he wanted nuclear weapons for the Bundeswehr!* And this was unthinkable in the light of Germany's more recent past, not to mention the reaction in the Russian, as well as in the West European camp, if Germany "got the bomb."

What were they going to do? How were they going to make the second most important man in West Germany, their most powerful and loyal ally in West Europe, change his mind?

In later years, an aging Franz Josef used to complain to his *Spezis* over their beer and sausages that the Spiegel Affair had been a put-up job all along, that the *Spiegel* and the CIA had "tricked him." The Bundesnachrichtendienst (BND) had been involved in the dirty trick too.

If this statement is true, then it seems to throw the whole absurd action of Friday, October 26, 1962, into some kind of realistic perspective which it otherwise lacks and makes it appear nothing more than a farcical Central European soap opera.

Let us assume that certain American authorities concerned with Strauss's lack of real interest in the new "flexible response" strategy decided to convince the German public that Herr Strauss's Bundeswehr was sadly lacking in conventional capability and that this should be the first concern of the Defense Minister.

That this view was already current at the time of the Spiegel Affair is revealed in an interview given by the liberal German congressman Wolfgang Döring to the Italian newspaper *Corriere de la Sera* in November of that year. The close friend of *Spiegel* publisher Augstein told the paper: "Strauss is an advocate of a European deterrent. That means the use of nuclear weapons from the first day of any conflict. The enemy as well as the Americans are inclined more to an increase in conventional forces. . . . In Ahlers's article ["Fallex 62"] he stated simply that Stauss's theory and his strategy would have deadly effects for us Germans in the case of war."

It is also reported that in that same month the Soviet Ambassador to Bonn, Smirnov, stated, in the course of a confidential discussion with Russian journalists accredited to Germany that it was not the Soviet Secret Service which had engineered the article that had now resulted in a major government crisis, but a "secret service organization of one of the countries allied to West Germany."[3]

What was that "secret service"? Today it is assumed that it was the CIA, in which case it is not unlikely that the CIA turned to its old associates in the BND for advice and aid. The CIA had maintained fairly good contacts with the BND since 1954, and it was probably through these contacts that they launched the idea of a major article which would reveal the conventional weakness of the German Army. With a bit of luck, the publication of such an article in an influential magazine like the *Spiegel* might effect a change in the burly Bavarian Minister of Defense's stubborn attitude.

Gehlen was all the more ready to do this, because he feared that one day Strauss might try to take over the BND as an organization that logically should come under the control of the Minister of Defense. He knew already that Strauss did not like him and was promoting the Military Intelligence Service (MAD), which Gehlen had once founded and staffed with his own people, as a major rival to the BND. In addition, the Bavarian minister had protested to Adenauer that it wasn't right that the BND should both obtain and interpret secret information from behind the Iron Curtain; the interpretation, at least, should be the responsibility of the Ministry of Defense.

So Reinhard Gehlen prepared to take the minister down a peg or two, but he and the mysterious gentlemen of the CIA had failed to take into account Strauss's explosive, pugnacious temperament and the extent of his terribly intense love affair with the army he had created.

The storm was about to burst!

---

[3]When Western journalists first obtained this tidbit of gossip they drew the wrong conclusion that the secret service in question was the British one working through a former secretary of Randolph Churchill, reportedly close to *Spiegel* owner Augstein.

26

When the report on the *Spiegel* reached Strauss on October 18, his temper flamed up. Despite the fact that the top lawyer of the U.S. forces in Europe, General Engel of the Seventh Army, advised that the article betrayed no secrets, since its conclusions that the German Army was only conditionally ready and that a buildup of German conventional forces was necessary reflected the American view, Strauss decided to go ahead with his massive action against the *Spiegel*.

On the 20th, a meeting was arranged between his legal experts and Dr. Wunder, at which various aspects of Dr. Augstein's high treason were discussed, including an alleged trip to France to obtain secret information from the French security service.

The innocent Dr. Wunder, who was now finding himself involved in something that he could not cope with, suggested naively that the Gehlen men in Pullach should be drawn into the case. Secretary of State Dr. Hopf turned down the suggestion at once. According to his view, there were very suspicious contacts between the BND and the *Spiegel*. Wunder suggested that they should be looked into immediately, and it was agreed that Hopf should supervise the whole operation against the *Spiegel*, using the Army's own security organization, MAD and *not* the BND to do the shadowing of the various *Spiegel* executives.

For the first time in over a half a decade of loyal

and successful work for the German Federal Government, which had gained Gehlen the respectful admiration of the German Chancellor Konrad Adenauer, the BND was to be excluded from the most important "espionage" case in the history of the young republic. The writing was on the wall: the days of Reinhard Gehlen's reign as the "gray eminence" in Bonn, with immediate private access to the Chancellor, were numbered. *The career of the "spy of the century" was now to start its irrevocable decline!*

As we have already seen, the hysterical and in many ways absurd action started on Friday, October 26. Thereafter things moved fast. Everywhere there were protests. Students marched through the German cities with their mouths stuck down with adhesive tape as a symbol that Strauss wanted the press muzzled. Professors organized petitions of protest. The press rallied one hundred percent behind their imprisoned colleagues in Hamburg, and outside Germany's frontiers the traditionally anti-German sections of the European press saw the *Spiegel* arrests as the beginning of a new Gestapo state.

In Parliament, the opposition Socialist Party and even the Liberal Party, which was allied in a coalition with Adenauer's Conservatives at that time, rose up in revolt; a revolt that grew to such a proportion as to cause wily old fox Adenauer to lose his temper and declare: "We have an abyss of treason in the country . . . when one thinks that a newspaper with a circulation of 500,000 copies appears to have committed treason systematically in order to earn money!"

Strauss lost his head. Before Parliament he stated that he had consulted Adenauer and the Minister of Justice before he had decided to raid the magazine, although he knew that this was not true and could easily be proved untrue. Frantically, he ordered his investigators, now working through the thousands of

Spiegel files, to find some proof that *Spiegel* had received its information on "Fallex 62" from the BND. They *had* to implicate Gehlen!

The investigators dug up the fact that there was some sort of a link between a director of the *Spiegel,* Hans Detlev Becker, and Gehlen, which had existed since the magazine had run a feature on Gehlen in 1954 which had been written by Becker. The police and the lawyers thought they had something now. They searched on. Then they had it! A list of thirteen questions from the *Spiegel,* asking whether certain aspects of their "Fallex 62" article might infringe security regulations. And the questions were addressed to a member of the BND—the Hamburg representative of the organization, middle-aged Colonel Wicht.

Strauss was triumphant when he heard the news. So there was a link after all! He had been right all along. One day later, both Hans Detlev Becker and Colonel Wicht were arrested. Now it was the turn of Reinhard Gehlen himself.

On November 12, 1962, the beige Mercedes 300 drove up to the official residence of the German Chancellor—Palais Schaumburg. As always, the smartly dressed rigid figures of the helmeted green-uniformed guards of the Federal Border Service did not move as the big automobile drove by. They already knew who was in the back seat of the car. They had been warned in advance by telephone, as was always the case. Woodenly, their rifles slung over their right shoulders, they stared straight ahead.

The car came to a stop at the gravel entrance. The chauffeur sprang out and opened the door. The elderly, medium-sized man with the dark glasses and hat pressed deep down over his bald forehead got out and mounted the steps, light-brown briefcase in hand.

He was expected, naturally. The same soft-voiced officials were there as usual, bowing and scraping, offering their soft hands solicitously to be shaken in the continental manner. Yet the elderly man, who had taken off his hat to reveal that what hair he had was pure white, was sure there was something different about the pompous, fat-bellied officials in their dark suits and light-gray ties with the mandatory pearl-tiepin. It was the look in their eyes. It was the way that they mouthed the usual meaningless clichés about the drive, his health, the weather. The eyes were wary and the clichés were without even that artificial warmth that the professional diplomat can give to the most pointless or nonsensical remark. Reinhard Gehlen, with his "nose" for such nuances of behavior, creased his high forehead in a thoughtful frown. *What was going on here?*

Had he known, he would have been shocked, although his years as German spymaster had accustomed him a long time ago to shocking situations. To understand fully what was going to take place on that gray November day we must put the situation into American terms. We must imagine that what has happened so far is that a secretary of state for Defense has ordered the arrest of the editorial staff of *Time* magazine and the placing behind bars of its owner. He has done this without the knowledge of the FBI, Justice Department or, more importantly, the President. As a result, the President is now involved in a major political crisis that might result in his own impeachment before Congress if he does not either support his secretary of state, of whom he thinks highly, or dissociate himself from the whole affair. Now his secretary of state has brought him somewhat vague evidence that the head of the Central Intelligence Agency has delivered military secrets to *Time* magazine and is pressing him to take the only logical action—*the arrest of the head of the Central Intelligence Agency!*

While Reinhard Gehlen waited impatiently in an anteroom, a heated conference was taking place in the office of the Federal German chancellor. Present on that fateful day were Adenauer and Dr. Kuhn, the Federal Public Prosecutor, who had been involved in the *Spiegel* business right from the beginning; and Dr. Stammberger, the Federal Minister of Justice, over whose head Strauss had gone when he had ordered the arrest of the *Spiegel* editorial staff and who was still angry that he had not been consulted. In addition, Stammberger was a member of the Liberal Party, which, grudging part though it might be of the government coalition, nonetheless did not want to be part of the expected collapse of the Adenauer Government.

Adenauer was angry. His ancient, wrinkled "Mongol" face (the result of a bad car smash in the twenties) was flushed with rage.

"Herr Doktor Stammberger," he ordered in that Rhenish dialect of his, which was so popular with the crowds, "you must arrest Herr Gehlen."

Stammberger stared back at the man who had controlled Germany's destiny since 1949 with an iron hand. He knew what it meant to cross the "Fox," as his ministers called him behind his back. He would soon lose his job or his reputation. But to arrest the chief of the secret service—that was something else again.

"But Herr Kanzler," he stammered, "it's not that simple. I need to have a warrant. And besides, what grounds have I got to arrest Herr Gehlen?"

Adenauer waved aside his objections with an irritable hand. "General Gehlen has communicated the measures to be taken against the *Spiegel* to Colonel Wicht, and he, in his turn, has passed them on to the *Spiegel*." It was a long speech for the Chancellor, who even in his major addresses to the nation was accustomed to the constant repetition of the words "Ladies and gentlemen," a few clichés, and then his main point expressed in phrases a five-year-old could understand.

Konrad Adenauer was an old man; he had no time to waste.

Again Stammberger objected. "But Herr Kanzler, we have no formal proof nor a judge to prepare the warrant for his arrest."

Irritated beyond measure, Adenauer swung his gaze from the Minister of Justice to Kuhn, who had been so keen to arrest Gehlen a few minutes before. "What do you think?" he asked.

Kuhn hesitated. "I think the Minister of Justice has said what I would have said to you."

Adenauer let his thin shoulders slump in defeat.

We do not know exactly what went on in the ensuing Gehlen interview with Dr. Kuhn. Apparently Kuhn asked Gehlen what he knew about the affair. Gehlen replied hesitantly. He seemed mixed up and his explanations came out in short, badly expressed phrases. He had seen the Minister of Defense in his office. Franz Josef Strauss had told him about the *Spiegel,* and what he intended to do. He had reported the details of the interview to two colleagues when he had arrived back at Pullach. One was Colonel Wicht. Otherwise he knew nothing of the whole business.

Kuhn persisted. There *was* some connection between Wicht and the *Spiegel!* Gehlen shrugged and gave in. It was not to be ruled out that a BND official might have acted off his own bat and contacted the news magazine. More he did not know.

When this was reported to another waiting BND man, Herr Winterstein, a leading official at Pullach, he retorted angrily, "If the president has said that, then he's making a great mistake."

Dr. Kuhn returned to Gehlen with Winterstein's remark, whereupon Gehlen withdrew his original statement. And so it went on.

Later, when Kuhn reported on the Gehlen interview

to Adenauer, the Chancellor fumed, "In my days as a public prosecutor, things would have been different!"

But by now, Adenauer's rage had run its course. Whatever his other failings might be, the Grand Old Man of postwar German politics was a realist; he realized that his favorite minister, Strauss, had got himself into a fix and that it was up to him alone to get himself out of it.

Strauss inevitably tried to persuade Adenauer to pursue the case against Gehlen. Two years before, on being asked jokingly at a German airport just prior to a flight to Washington whether he was going to buy a U-2 there (it was at the time of the great scandal caused by the shooting down of Lieutenant Powers's U-2 over Russia), he had replied good-humoredly, "Why? Our Gehlen can do it much better—and he never gets caught!"

Then Gehlen had been high in his esteem. Now everything had changed and Gehlen, whom he placed in the same category as those general staff officers who had always opposed him—Kielmansegg, Baudissin and Bermann (stiff aristocratic men like the masterspy himself)—became his favorite hate.

But Adenauer, well aware that the *Spiegel* crisis had rocked his whole government and that Franz Josef Strauss would soon have to be sacrificed to appease public opinion,[1] in spite of his great talents, did not listen to the pleas of his Minister of Defense.

Thus, as that long gray November afternoon with its bitter accusations and its even more bitter recriminations finally came to an end, Reinhard Gehlen could climb wearily into his Mercedes a free man. But as his big beige automobile crawled past the smartly saluting helmeted guards of the *Grenzschutz,* he must have

---

[1]Strauss lasted until December, when he was replaced by Herr Kai-Uwe von Hassel.

known that his power was finally and irrevocably broken.

The medium-sized figure slumped wearily in the deep cushions at the back of the car, who had once held the whole of Eastern Europe in fear and trembling, was now nothing more than an elderly, well-dressed gentleman soon to be pensioned off and put out to pasture.

27

But General Gehlen's cup was not yet full. On July 8, 1963, seven months after that disastrous scene in Adenauer's office, the Felfe trial began. Perhaps Gehlen hoped that the fact the trial was being held in July, the German vacation season, would mean it would be neglected by the press and public. But if so, his hopes were doomed to disappointment. The new court at Karlsruhe, where it was held, was packed to overflowing with curious private citizens and both German and foreign journalists eager for what promised to be a juicy scandal.

And they were not disappointed either!

Felfe made little impression as he was brought into court by two guards at shortly before nine in the morning. His nearly two years in jail and the knowledge that his former bosses had sacrificed him for the sake of a popular propaganda victory had taken their toll. He was pale, almost unnaturally so, and his dark hair was beginning to thin out noticeably.

Tiebel made no stronger impression. He was nervous and uncertain. He seated himself on the bench reserved for the accused, taking extra care to keep as far as possible from the others. He kept clasping and unclasping his hands repeatedly.

The star of the show was undoubtedly Clemens. The sixty-one-year-old ex-SS man, who had started his career as a party bully boy so long ago in Dresden and gained for himself the nickname of the "Terror of Pieschen" (a suburb of Dresden), still made quite an impression. For all that the prison diet had taken the pounds of postwar good living off his big bones, there was no denying the brutal strength of those heavy shoulders beneath the loosely fitting dark suit. The tallest and oldest of the "three musketeers" was still what he had always been; a tough, happy-go-lucky mercenary, who liked the good life.

While Felfe answered all the judges's questions with machinelike precision and in a completely humorless manner, and Tiebel tried to minimize his part in the whole affair (Clemens had told him: "The Russians know everything about you. They want you to work for them," and so on), Clemens seemed amused by the whole rigid formality of the trial.

Discussing Clemens's activities in the SD in Italy during the war, the chief judge, Dr. Weber, referred to his being responsible for the execution of three hundred Italian hostages.

Hans Clemens smiled. "It was three hundred *and thirty*, Mr. President," he said, and showed his teeth, amused at the judge's discomfiture. Asked later whether he had revealed the places where the "BND has its espionage schools," he answered (again with that irritating smile of his), "You mean where they *had* their espionage schools."

And so it went, with Clemens parrying point after point, seemingly only too eager to give away information in that good-humored manner of his. In fact, at times the prosecution had to stop him from revealing classified information. But if the prosecution was concerned with shutting his big mouth, the press and public were overjoyed at his relevations: the fact that he had wangled his first job with Gehlen through an old SS colonel pal (Krichbaum); that he been able to go over to report to the East every second month— and that for ten years without ever once being checked;

that, among other things, the Russians always had a can of choice Russian lobster waiting for him when he reported to them.

Asked by the prosecutor, who apparently was as petty bourgeois as Felfe, who had used his blood money to build a ten-room villa in Bavaria, "Didn't you build a house with the money?" Clemens replied, "No." And then with an impudent grin, "I'm no idiot."

"How much did you earn in this period?" the prosecutor persisted, "Let's say 100,000 marks?"

"Let's say *140,000*," Clemens corrected him.

The prosecutor in his black robe flushed angrily. "And what did you do with the money?"

The big ex-SD man grinned. "I lived well and saw the world." And with that, he looked down at the pale-faced lawyer as if he were something that had just crawled out of the woodwork and should speedily return there, if he knew what was best for him.

In the end, Felfe received fourteen years, Clemens twelve, and Tiebel five, and they disappeared from court to begin their sentences.[1] But the damage was done. Virtually every major German newspaper criticized the apparently lax policies of the BND and its chief, Gehlen.

On July 13, the Conservative *Frankfurter Allgemeine* wrote: "There is more and more criticism leveled at the personnel policies of the BND." The popular *Kölnische Rundschau* commented: "For ten long years a creature of the Soviets could work in the HQ of our intelligence service and reveal thousands of secrets to the East." The Liberal and Socialist papers, sensing a chance to injure the government by means of the scandal, were more direct: they wanted Gehlen's head. The Munich *Süddeutsche Zeitung* asked angrily:

---

[1] Felfe was exchanged in February, 1969 for three German students imprisoned in the Soviet Union.

"How come it was possible that old unrepentant Nazis and members of the SD could obtain leading positions in our official German intelligence service?" The Socialist *Frankfurter Rundschau,* owned by a journalist who himself once had had to flee from Hitler's Germany, was even more bitter. "It seems," its editorial commented, "that in Gehlen's HQ one SS man smoothes the way for another and that Hitler's elite celebrates happy reunions there!"

Desperately Reinhard Gehlen tried to save himself. He invited a writer for the German weekly illustrated magazine *Revue* to visit him in Pullach, one of the few journalists he had invited into his top-secret headquarters since the mid-fifties, when he had used them to convince the Socialists that he was harmless.

The journalist, Jochen Wilke, who wrote under the pen name of "Voluntas," described the boss of the BND at that time as "possessing the distinguished elegance of a London city gentleman. Spick-and-span. He wears a gray suit and a fashionable necktie. If one didn't know that he was a product of the German General Staff, one would take him for a retired Colonel of the British Colonial Army, a *Times* reader, who spends his leisure hours in his clubs."

Gehlen did his best to impress the Munich journalist, and he succeeded. Later Voluntas was to write: "Personally I found Reinhard Gehlen *sympathique.* He is very cultured. He is attentive and modern. He is an energetic person, who knows how to establish contact with other people. He replies clearly, and a discussion with him is lively. He could not hide the fact that he had been trained as a staff officer."

From that interview it is clear that although Gehlen was well aware of the danger of his position, he could not quite overcome that sense of responsibility of the man at the top for the actions of his subordinates which had been bred into him so long ago as a young staff officer. While he protested that he had "drawn the conclusions for his service of this affair [the Felfe case]," he still maintained that "I am completely responsible for the entry of this man into my headquarters."

Voluntas listened politely enough, while the aging ex-general talked with unaccustomed fluency. Later he reported fully on his exciting afternoon in the top-secret spy center at Pullach, yet his last comment on Gehlen (included in his description of the intelligence chief) reveals how his mind and those of other informed people was working at that time. It stated simply: "I am sure that if he changed his occupation, he would easily find another good job."

Still exerting every effort, Gehlen set about trying to reorganize his ruined outfit. The painstaking work of sixteen years was of no further use. His agents, his couriers, his V-men, the "dead letterboxes"—indeed, the whole complicated underground system he had built up so patiently behind the Iron Curtain since 1946 had to be dumped. In his Pullach headquarters all the main codes had to be changed, old and trusted employees who had been compromised by Felfe fired, and new men hired and initiated into their new tasks.

But new agents prepared to risk their lives in the East were no longer so easily found. The mass arrests of Gehlen's men in East Germany which had followed Felfe's arrest did not encourage even the boldest of potential spies to risk their necks for a paltry three to four hundred dollars' a month pay. As one of Gehlen's men reports, the feared spymaster was now forced to "make up" secret information. He records the following conversation with Gehlen:

"Herr Präsident, "I've noticed that one of our new sources of information from the East is marked from a member of the Communist Central Committee."

Gehlen nodded. "Yes—and . . .?" he queried.

"But we don't have a 'colleague' in the Central Committee," the man protested.

Gehlen smiled thinly. "Who can prove otherwise?"

"But we can't pretend to have a source in the Central Committee when we don't, especially in our reports to Bonn."

Gehlen held up a thin, deathly pale hand in protest. "Of course we can. I've told you already. Who can prove otherwise?"

The agent reddened and hesitated. "I don't think that's a very serious way to go about our job. Surely we don't have to descend to such levels!"

Gehlen ignored the man's protest. He rose to his feet and indicated that the interview was terminated. The source in the "Central Committee" remained in the reports.

But in his heart the spymaster knew it was all in vain. The myth of infallibility which he had built up so successfully since he had first joined intelligence in 1942 had been shattered. Public opinion had turned not only against his organization but against him personally. The newspapers, in particular, wanted his head and they had convinced a lot of German politicians too that it was time that the "aging man in Pullach" should be removed from office. An article in *The New York Times* of that year summed up the contemporary German mood: "In the last few days a legend and a reputation which have been painstakingly maintained for fifteen years have been destroyed. The legend is that of the extraordinary feats of a West German espionage organization, known under its official name as the *BND*. The reputation is that of its founder and sole chief, ex-Wehrmacht General Reinhard Gehlen."

In Bonn, too, things were changing. His old protector and admirer Konrad Adenauer was forced to go in the wake of the Spiegel Affair. The man who was sometimes known as "the Chancellor's favorite general" no longer had Adenauer's aged but powerful hand protectively over him.

The new chancellor, baby-faced, cigar-smoking Professor Erhard, who knew that Adenauer had had the BND spy upon him at times, disliked the spy organization intensely. One of his first acts in his new office was to order that the BND liaison team be removed from the building in which he had his office. "I don't even want to be under the same roof as those characters," he snorted to an aide. And Gehlen knew from sources close to the new chancellor that he did not even bother to read the daily top-secret intelligence digest prepared by the Pullach HQ. He simply tossed it to one side disgustedly when the aides presented him with it.

The visits of Gehlen's big Mercedes to Bonn became increasingly rarer as the cold war began to ease up and a new phase, "coexistence," started to dominate relations between East and West. The work of Gehlen's organization still went on, but the authorities in Bonn were no longer interested in his disclosures of the "machinations" of the Soviet Union and its satellites in East Germany.

In 1967, Gehlen succeeded in predicting to the day the outbreak of the Six Day War between Israel and its Arab neighbors, and scooped all other Western intelligence agencies. But his triumph did not help in any way.

The men of the Central Intelligence Agency still referred to his organization as the "Non-intelligence Service," and it is reported reliably that the British Intelligence Service referred to the BND contemptuously as "the Chancellor's News Service."

Driven, Gehlen spread his net even wider. His five-thousand-odd full-time employees, who in their turn employed perhaps twice that number of contacts, supplied the palace guards of the King of Saudi Arabia with machine pistols, smuggled a printing press for propaganda purposes to the enemies of Congo dictator Lumumba, and helped Indonesia's secret service to put down a left-wing revolt. By the mid-sixties, the BND had its tentacles spread out over the whole world, maintaining contacts in countries ranging from Korea in the East to Chile in the West, from Australia in the South to Sweden in the far North.

But none of this effected any change in the public and professional attitude toward the Gehlen Organization. It was generally known now that Gehlen still retained his old and trusted wartime colleagues at Pullach. There they were known among the younger employees as the *"Prothese und Prostata Bridgade,"* old men who wore false teeth and had prostate trouble. Safely ensconced at headquarters, their main concern was ensuring that their salaries were increased at regular intervals. The obtaining of intelligence seemed only of secondary import. There was a malicious rumor circulating through Pullach that one such ancient secret serviceman did not make a move before he had consulted an equally ancient female astrologer *who informed him of his future by means of the coffee grains at the bottom of a cracked cup!*

In its twenty-odd-year career, the Gehlen outfit had become a gigantic, bureaucratic, top-heavy organization, staffed by timeservers and toadies (one of its vice presidents was blessed with the nickname of "flamethrower" because of the haste with which he would offer a light from his cigarette lighter to any visiting dignitary). The inspector, who in the CIA, for instance, was a much-feared individual because of his merciless search for inefficiency and corruption within the organization, was a tame, elderly ex-officer whose primary concern was to ensure that the staff kitchens in Pullach were clean and serving "cheap but wholesome food." As one bitter ex-Gehlen man could comment cynically: "In the light of such checks on performance, the Federal Intelligence Service could go on sleeping peacefully—*permanently!*"

In the mid-sixties, the ruling West German Conservative Party was forced to accept the opposition Socialists into the government. It was a blow to Gehlen because he knew how the Socialists hated him. And with reason. In the good old days when crafty Chancellor Adenauer had ruled Germany with an iron hand, Gehlen had undoubtedly spied on all the main Socialist leaders for his political boss. Dutifully he had reported how many whiskies and soda the up-and-coming young Socialist leader Willy Brandt had consumed at official receptions, helping to contribute to that malicious Conservative pun of "Weinbrand Willy"[2] on the future chancellor's name. On Herbert Wehner, the chief ideologist of the Socialist party and ex-Communist, he had prepared a thick, extensive dossier. As BND Vice President Hans-Heinrich Worgitzky put it: "This man was and *is* a Communist. For us he is the most dangerous enemy of the state!"

Gehlen was astute enough to realize that the day of reckoning was close at hand. Once the Socialists had gained sufficient power in West Germany (and his internal researches told him that at the next election they would win and form a government of their own), they would make a point of getting rid of him. It was, at long last, time for him to bow out of the intelligence business. But there was still one problem to be solved. Who should succeed him in this vital office?

Finally, in 1967, it was decided to appoint Lieutenant General Gerhard Wessel, at that time serving with the NATO Military Commission in Brussels, to the important post. It was high time. The various Western ambassadors in Bonn were already bombard-

---

[2]*Weinbrand* is the German word for cognac or brandy.

ing the chancellor with questions about Gehlen's successor. According to French journalist Gerard Sandoz, writing in *Le Nouvel Observateur*: "Last week when it was announced that he [Gehlen] was to retire, the ambassadors of various countries, in particular the United States, had assailed the Bonn ministries with telephone calls, anxiously asking for news. So far they have not yet received an answer to their enquiries, but it is known here that Gehlen will be able to go and cultivate his garden peacefully without causing them grave inconvenience.[3]

Gerard Sandoz was confident, because he felt that the passing of Gehlen and the appointment of the new man would present few problems. The *new* man was not, after all, so new; Gerhard Wessel was that same staff officer whom Gehlen had retained at the Foreign Armies East headquarters all that time ago in 1942 when he had fired all the rest of the stick-in-the-mud officers he had found in his new command. The wheel, it seemed, had come full cycle.

On the last day of April, 1968, Reinhard Gehlen, Germany's master spy for so long, finally gave up his post, confident that a man of his own choice was going to continue to command his beloved organization. It had been an amazing career since that April day almost twenty-six years before when he had taken over Foreign Armies East with its few score middle-aged staff officers and built up an anti-Soviet intelligence organization which covered every country in the world and ran to thousands of agents.

But in the little farewell ceremony held at his Pullach headquarters, Reinhard Gehlen gave no hint of the emotion he must have felt at that moment, surrounded by those few intimates he had known right

---

[3]This is an allusion to the eternal optimist in Voltaire's novel *Candide*, who was able to retire after a series of hair-raising adventures and "cultivate his garden."

from the start, sipping slowly at a glass of champagne. As always, it was left to the new chief, Gerhard Wessel, to do the talking. Gehlen himself, as tongue-tied as he had ever been, limited himself to a few trite remarks, a mild joke, a word or two of appreciation, a passing reference to the "old days." Nothing more.

He smiled faintly when, at a larger, official ceremony held in the former officers' mess at Pullach, Secretary of State Karl Carstens announced in the pompous way common to politicians: "Your task [that of the Gehlen Organization] was unique. In all our history we have never been confronted with anything like it. No other country has ever faced up to anything of this kind before." Politicians would always have the last word, but in fact they knew nothing; *he* had been the man who had supplied the information on which they had based their speeches and pompous pronouncements.

With his customary reserve the "Grand Old Man of Espionage" (as *Der Spiegel* called him) said nothing. He contented himself with polite applause, clapping his thin hands, now mottled with the brown liver spots of age, hands which had pulled so many strings for so long, and kept his opinions to himself.

And then a little later he left: an old, amost completely bald man, dressed in a conservatively tailored suit which, if it admittedly stamped him, even to the uneducated eye, an ex-officer, still gave no clue to the fact that the benign-looking gentleman in his mid-sixties, who was now driving out of the gates of the Pullach HQ for the last time as head of the BND, was the spy of the century.[4]

Reinhard Gehlen, however, was not allowed to lay down his command of the Federal Intelligence Service so altogether unobtrusively. Just as pagan chiefs in an-

---

[4]Reinhard Gehlen continued to work for the BND on a part-time basis, using his house some eight miles away as his office.

cient days had been carried to their funeral mounds surrounded by their favorite possessions, animals, slaves, and women so that the latter could be slaughtered and thus join their once-powerful masters on their long, perilous journey to the dark reaches of the other world for which they were now destined, Gehlen too would in the end demand his own particular sacrifice in blood from his former colleagues and those who had been associated with him in one way or other. The day of reckoning was to come after all.

The last chapter had begun.

28

It was six months after Reinhard Gehlen resigned as president of the Bundesnachrichtendienst that the last chapter of his long and amazing career began: in October of 1968; the "October of the Suicides," as the West German press later called the month.

That October, not a day seemed to go by without some intelligence scandal or other, or—even worse— the suicide of a man or woman directly or indirectly connected with intelligence. A German Army pilot and a lawyer were discovered to have sent a sidewinder missile to Moscow *by normal air freight,* probably one of the most audacious pieces of espionage of the whole twentieth century. Four East German agents decamped to the East without discovery.

Forty-year-old Hans Heinrich Schenk, an important Bonn official connected with intelligence, committed suicide by hanging himself with his belt. Official Bonn explanation: he was newly married and greatly worried about having to perform the sexual act with his eager young bride.

German Bundeswehr Colonel Johannes Grimm went into his office, locked the door and blew his brains out with his service pistol. Official Bonn explanation: Lieutenant Colonel Grimm imagined he had cancer (without reason,) and had taken this way out.

Sixty-one-year-old senior official in the Federal Ministry of Defense Gerhard Böhn was found dead on the banks of the sluggish, oil-infested River Rhine near the capital. Official Bonn explanation: the elderly official had often threatened "to do away with himself."

Day after day the headlines of the more sensational newspapers were filled with the details of the strange deaths. It was almost like one of those inexplicable medieval outbreaks which sent people, all over Europe, dancing and dancing at an ever wilder tempo until finally they fell down—dead.

Even the more serious newspapers could not ignore the strange suicides of that bloody October in Bonn when, on the very same day, two of the most senior officials in government service and both intimately connected with that intelligence outfit once founded by ex-General Gehlen committed suicide under decidedly unusual circumstances.

The one was the acting vice president of the Bundesnachtrichtendienst, Major General Horst Wendland, a longtime associate of Gehlen; the other, Admiral of the Fleet Hermann Lüdke. The general had shot himself in Pullach, the Admiral far away in the lonely woods of the German Eifel not too distant from the Belgian border.

But despite the distance separating the two suicides, it didn't take the press too long to discover that there was some sort of curious, if vague connection between the two killings; and that the Federal Intelligence Service seemed to be undergoing an internal crisis.

As the serious French daily *Le Figaro* commented: "The mysterious 'suicides' could trigger off an espionage case of European dimensions." Even the then U.S. secretary of defense, Clark Clifford, in faraway Washington, could not conceal his dismay about the events taking place in West Germany. He told U.S. pressmen that the "suicides" (and by this time most newspapers were putting the word in quotes; it was a significant detail) "were a matter of grave concern."[1]

The wave of suicides seemed to have been started by that of Admiral Lüdke in the neighborhood of the Eifel Immerath, where he often went hunting, on October 8, 1968.

Two weeks before, on September 23, a lab assistant in a Bonn camera shop had been developing a roll of film taken by a Minox camera when to his surprise the usual holiday snaps that had become the boring daily routine of his life in the darkroom were followed by a series of pictures stamped NATO SECRET. He immediately informed his boss, who had called Bonn's political police. Quickly they discovered that the film belonged to Admiral Lüdke, who had just been transferred from his post at the Belgian NATO HQ at Casteau prior to his retirement.

Instead of informing the public prosecutor as they should have done, the Bonn police turned to the local office of Military Security for help. For four days the military counterespionage agents did not act; they did not even shadow the unsuspecting white-haired admiral. Instead, they decided to confront him with their evidence on the very day he officially retired from the service.

So, shortly after Admiral Lüdke had been wished all the best for his new life as a civilian by high officers and officials of the German defense ministry, he was ushered into a small office to be faced with a hard-faced major of military intelligence bearing in his big hand the photos that indicated he was a traitor.

The elderly admiral's weather-beaten face paled, but for a long time he denied that he had a Minox camera or that the film belonged to him. Then finally he admitted that he had bought a Minox camera from a

---

[1] By the end of the month, six prominent Bonn officials connected one way or another with intelligence, had committed suicide under strange circumstances.

chain store owned by a Herr Porst (two years later to be accused of spying and sentenced to five years' imprisonment himself), but still he denied knowing anything about the incriminating films.

Surprisingly, the military intelligence let him go. More surprising, they gave him five more days to get rid of any incriminating evidence before they finally decided to search his apartment. Naturally they found nothing. The admiral was allowed to leave for Immerath for a weekend's hunting.

He never came back.

At about three o'clock on the afternoon of October 8, the simple peasants of the poverty-stricken, white-painted village were startled by the sound of a single shot. A little later, the body of the dead admiral was found sprawled out on the ground near his white Ford. His rifle lay across the calf of his leg. There was a small wound in his left shoulder blade and a hole as a big as a fist in his chest. The blood was already beginning to cake hard and black around the wound and the big blue flies were settling on it in greedy expectation. It was obviously a case of suicide. Admiral Lüdke had shot himself "while the balance of his mind was disturbed" as the official formula had it.

Some three hundred miles away in Pullach, Vice President Wendland shot himself at just about the same time while "suffering from an acute state of depression" (again, the official formula).

Even three years later, at the time of this writing, it is still difficult to discover if there was any connection between the two suicides, and if so, to what purpose Admiral Lüdke was using his post in a top NATO command. Who was he spying for (if he was a spy)? And why had he been so careless about the film? And finally—was his death the spark that triggered off the "acute state of depression" which caused General

Wendland to put his service pistol to his graying temple and pull the trigger that blasted him out of this world?

One person who was not satisfied with the official explanation of suicide was the local doctor, who was the first to appear at the scene. A passionate hunter himself, he attempted to reconstruct the "suicide" after the public prosecutor had overruled his decision to describe Lüdke's death as "due to unknown causes."

He came to the conclusion that suicide was out of the question. At the angle at which the suicide victim would have had to fire his weapon, the bullet should have struck his chest at a vertical level. In addition, the point of the body where the bullet entered it would be smaller than the point of exit. This was not the case. Nor could the doctor find any explanation for the position of the admiral's gun across the calf of his leg. The country doctor also ruled out an accident, because Lüdke had been a hunter all his life and knew how to handle all types of weapons. "In my opinion," he told the pressmen sent to interview him, *"Admiral Lüdke did not commit suicide!"*

If suicide was ruled out, what, then, was the cause of death? And was the fact that Admiral Lüdke died on the very same day that Major General Wendland also committed suicide merely a coincidence?

Several possible theories have been advanced to explain the two deaths. One is that Admiral Lüdke was "helped" to commit "suicide" because he had been unwittingly caught by the lab assistant in Bonn spying on the organization for which he worked—NATO. But who were the men in the shadows who convinced him that he had better kill himself? Some say it was the Russians, who were eager to discredit the German officer corps in the eyes of their allies. Could this be the explanation for the carelessness with which the top secret NATO material was found on the undeveloped film in Bonn? In other words, was the film a deliberate

Russian plant to involve Lüdke in a scandal which had to reach the press and thus be splashed over all the papers of the West?

That is one theory. There is another which, if it is true, would indicate that the BND, while still under Gehlen's command, had been prepared to sink to almost unbelievable depths in its relentless search for classified information. It postulates that Admiral Lüdke had been a spy, but that he had spied on the secrets of his allies and not for the Russians, the East Germans or any other Eastern power. No, bluff Admiral Lüdke had busily photographed NATO material with his tricky little Minox camera *for no less a person than master spy Gehlen himself!*

This startling, if fascinating conjecture might explain why it took military intelligence so long to make any decisions about spy suspect Lüdke. Drawn into the affair by chance, they had unwittingly compromised the admiral and had to be warned off by a worried BND man somewhere in Pullach HQ (perhaps even by Wendland himself?).

So they marked time while high-level discussions took place in Bonn about what the official course of action should be in a case that no longer could be hushed up, since the camera shop, the police, and the military intelligence people knew many of its details.

When, for instance, Public Prosecutor Albin Kuhn, who had been so eager to prosecute in the Spiegel Affair some six years before, was informed of the Lüdke problem by a junior member of the Bonn police and was requested to draw up the warrant for the admiral's arrest, he hastily told the official he was on leave and that it was not his responsibility. He advised the man to contact another government lawyer and hung up. Thereafter he made no further appearance in the affair, although it was well known that he had an appetite for personal publicity.

Was his behavior a reflection of some top-level directive for him to "keep his nose" out of the Lüdke case?

We do not know—and we probably never shall know. But it seems very strange that a man who is suspected of top-level espionage against his country should be wined and dined by high-ranking officers and civilian officials on the day of his retirement, with military intelligence officers waiting in the immediate neighborhood to question him afterwards. Wouldn't these men, who conceivably would know of the investigations being carried out against Lüdke, run a mile rather than associate with someone whose name might soon make the headlines as the biggest spy ever discovered within NATO?

Could that retirement ceremony on the very day that Lüdke learned that he *really* was in trouble, and eleven days before that fatal instant when he committed "suicide," be the sugar to sweeten the bitter pill of death soon to come?

Could it be that Admiral Lüdke had been *ordered* either to kill himself, or if he didn't have the guts to do so, to let someone else do the job for him? And like the loyal old seadog he was, had he bowed his white head and accepted the decision of death for the "sake of the fatherland"; as did that other elderly officer who might have been responsible for his spying activities at Casteau—Major General Horst Wendland, vice president of the Bundesnachtrichtendienst and intimate of Reinhard Gehlen for many a long year?

It is a fantastic theory—one which Louis Hagen in his book on West German espionage[2] calls "the most dramatic of all"—yet the long history of spying is filled with such fantastic stories. One need only recall the case of the head of the Austrian Intelligence Service prior to World War I who, owing to his debts and homosexual activities, had become a Russian spy. He,

---

[2]*The Secret War for Europe*, New York: Stein & Day, 1970.

too, was forced to commit suicide in his hotel room to "save the honor of the Imperial Officer Corps."

That fall, when the then German chancellor was told on his return from a trip to Spain, what had just happened at Pullach and Bonn, he had groaned, *"It's monstrous."* Behind him a more cynical aide had grinned and commented, *"Über Spanien lacht der blaue Himmel, über Deutschland lacht die ganze Welt!*[3]

Asked by reporters to comment on the affair and the mysterious "suicides," a stony-faced, tight-lipped Gerhard Wessel, who had known Gehlen from those early days in Russia, refused to say a word. But his eyes were eloquent in their unspoken condemnation of what had happened that "red October," and of the man who perhaps was responsible; as was his bitter aside to an aide. "When I took up this job, the problem was already there."

Thus the elderly German spymaster passed into obscurity, after perhaps unwittingly demanding his last tribute in blood as a fitting token of his greatness. The work of the spy of the century was over at last.

---

[3]"Over Spain the blue sky laughs; over Germany the whole world."

EPILOGUE

A fool lies here who tried to hustle the East.

Rudyard Kipling

We do not know what Reinhard Gehlen thought of the strange deaths which accompanied his retirement in that "red October" of 1968; and we shall probably never know, even when one day his "official biography" appears, appropriately censored and cleansed of the dirt, degradation and death which had been part and parcel of his life for twenty-six long years.

Reinhard Gehlen, the ex-regular officer and scion of an aristocratic family, evidently believes in that old British upper-class motto that "the secret service is too dirty a game for anyone but a gentleman to play." Or, as he once expressed it himself in a rare moment of confidence, "This job is so dirty that only the cleanest of people should have the right to meddle in it."

In that October of the suicides, Gehlen obviously felt himself one of those "clean people": an honorable family man, a good husband, firm but loving father with no known vices. Yet for over two decades he had been instrumental in subverting, perverting, and prostituting thousands of men and women of a dozen different races for the purpose of espionage against their own countries or countries allied to their own.

Year in, year out, he had—directly or indirectly—sacrificed scores of these same agents to the moloch of Intelligence. Beaten, tortured, hanged and shot, they had disappeared into its bloody jaws while, in the safety of faraway Germany, the respected, if feared, president of the Bundesnachrichtendienst had grown gracefully older in that distinguished upper-class British manner which seemed to appeal to him increasingly in his later years.

The gray general wheeled and dealed for over two decades, pulling the threads which initiated the dance of death for so many men and women on the other side of the Iron Curtain, until, on April Fool's day, 1968, the whole grand game came to an end.

Or did it? Shortly before this writing, an anonymous letter to *Der Spiegel,* claimed that "the spy of the century" had still not retired after all. After warning the magazine to take great care that its sources of information were not revealed to the BND (the magazine was running a series on the former Gehlen Organization), the correspondent stated that "you have not yet mentioned the most prominent 'free-lancer' of all. President Gehlen was employed by the BND after he was pensioned off in 1968. In order to save him traveling the twenty-five kilometres to Pullach, an office was opened for him near his villa [at Berg] with his ex-WAC aide and later chief secretary in charge."[1]

Thus it would seem that ex-General Gehlen is still possibly unable to drag himself away from the heady, all-pervading magic of the second oldest profession.

SIC TRANSIT GLORIA INTELLIGENTSIA.

---

[1]It was clear from internal evidence in the letter that the anonymous correspondent was a disgruntled BND employee, who took this way of getting back at his former boss.

VITAL DATA OF
REINHARD GEHLEN

April 3, 1902   Born: Erfurt, Germany

April 20, 1920   Entered into the German Army

December 1, 1923 to March 1, 1939   Various military stations, promotion from lieutenant to major

August 26, 1939 to March 31, 1942   General Staff Officer

April 1, 1942 to April 10, 1945   Head of Foreign Armies East

June 1945 to July 1946   American prisoner of war

July 1946 to March 1956   Head of "Gehlen Organization"

April 1956 to April 1968   Head of West German Intelligence Service

May 1968   Retired?

BIBLIOGRAPHY

Guderian, Heinz. *Panzer Leader*. New York: Ballantine Books, 1957.

Guèrin, Alain. *Le Gènèral Gris*. Paris: Julliard, 1969.

Hagen, Louis. *The Secret War for Europe*. New York: Stein & Day, 1970.

Joesten, Joachim. *They Call It Intelligence*. New York: Abelard-Schuman, 1963.

John, Otto. *Zweimal Kam Ich Heim*. Dusseldorf: Econ Verlag, 1965.

Mader, Julius. *Die Graue Hand*. East Berlin: Kongress Verlag, 1961.

Roth, K. *Invasionsziel: DDR*. Hamburg: Konkret, 1971.

Scharnhorst, Gerd. *Spione in der Bundeswehr*. Stuttgart: Hesta Verlag, 1965.

Strong, Kenneth. *Intelligence at the Top*. London: Cassell, 1961.

Strong, Kenneth. *Men of Intelligence*. London: Cassell, 1970.

Von Hornstein, E. *Staatsfeinde*. Munich: Kiepenheuer & Witsch, 1962.

Whiting, Charles. *Werwolf*. New York: Stein & Day, 1972.